The Temple Experience

PASSAGE *to* HEALING *and* HOLINESS

Wendy Ulrich

This is not an official publication of The Church of Jesus Christ of Latter-day Saints. The opinions and views expressed herein belong solely to the author and do not necessarily represent the opinions or views of Cedar Fort, Inc. Permission for the use of sources, graphics, and photos is also solely the responsibility of the author.

ISBN 13: 978-1-4621-2237-0

Published by CFI, an imprint of Cedar Fort, Inc.
2373 W. 700 S., Springville, UT 84663
Distributed by Cedar Fort, Inc., www.cedarfort.com

The Library of Congress has cataloged the hardback 2012 edition as follows:

Ulrich, Wendy, author.
The temple experience / Wendy Ulrich.
    pages cm
Includes bibliographical references and index.
ISBN 978-1-4621-1085-8 (alk. paper)
    1. Temple work (Mormon Church) 2. Mormon temples. 3. Christian life--Mormon authors.
4. Church of Jesus Christ of Latter-day Saints--Doctrines. I. Title.

BX8643.T4U47 2012
246'.95893--dc23
                                    2012016152

Cover design by Brian Halley
Cover design © 2012, 2017 Cedar Fort, Inc.
Edited and typeset by Whitney A. Lindsley

Printed in the United States of America

10 9 8 7 6 5 4 3 2 1

Printed on acid-free paper

The Temple Experience

PASSAGE *to* HEALING *and* HOLINESS

Wendy Ulrich

CFI
An Imprint of Cedar Fort, Inc.
Springville, Utah

FOR CARRIE, MONIKA, AND MICHAEL

ACKNOWLEDGMENTS

———— ⤬ ————

The journey of healing and holiness is never taken alone. I am indebted to many people for insights and relationships that have blessed this work and my life. When it comes to my understanding of the temple, I am deeply indebted to Kathleen Flake, Chris Packard, and Karen Blake, whose friendship and insight have profoundly influenced both my thinking and my experience of the journey, and who each read and contributed to this manuscript. My understanding of the temple has also been shaped by such dear friends as Lucile Anderson, Helen Bauss, Donna Benson, Nancy and Wayne Brockbank, John Costello, Monika Gerszewski, Scott Gordon, Lynn and Rand Johnson, Conrad LaPlante, Jan Larsen, Ty Mansfield, Pierre Paul Morin, Sylvia Mupepi, Marci Nickell, Thom Nielson, Byron Thomas, Karin and Richard Ulrich, and Paul Williams. I'm also grateful for the companionship of Eric, Carla, and Belinda and their beautiful families; the Fine Nine; several hundred missionaries from the Canada Montreal Mission (je me souviens!); and ward members in Los Altos, Santa Monica, Ann Arbor, Montreal, and Alpine. Among the mentors and colleagues who have both trained and sustained me, I must mention Allen Bergin (whose detailed comments on an early draft of this manuscript were invaluable), Richard Ferre (my warmest cheerleader), David Klimek and Theresa Kestly (who taught me how to be a therapist), and Scott Richards (who believed I had something to say). Special thanks go to Lyle Mortimer, Whitney Lindsley, and the gracious folks at Cedar Fort, Inc., for their confidence in me and for their hard work and constant cheer. I am ever grateful to colleagues in the Association of Mormon Counselors and Psychotherapists for providing a receptive forum in which to begin developing these ideas.

I owe a particular debt to all the clients with whom I have walked for days or years the holy paths of self-discovery—theirs and mine. I am thankful to my wonderful parents, Barbara and Les Woolsey, whose reactions to the temple, each in a different way, undoubtedly shaped my enthusiasm for this subject.

Special thanks to my children, Carrie, Monika, and Mike, to whom this book is dedicated, and to their dear families. They have provided the greatest incentives to both my writing and the efforts at personal change it reflects. Finally I thank my life's mate, David Ulrich, for bounteous intellectual and spiritual infusions, technical assistance, emotional support, multiple mercies, and the irreplaceable foundation of committed love. He is the best earthly thing that has ever happened to me, *plus qu'hier, moins que demain.*

CONTENTS

PREFACE XI

SECTION ONE: PREPARING FOR THE TEMPLE EXPERIENCE

ONE: THE SEARCH 3
TWO: LEARNING THE LANGUAGE 17

SECTION TWO: EXPERIENCES WITH DESCENT

THREE: NEW BIRTHS 35
FOUR: CLAIMING THIS BODY 55
FIVE: THE CREATOR'S CHILD 79
SIX: NOT ASHAMED 99
SEVEN: THE DESERT OF DISCERNMENT 119

SECTION THREE: EXPERIENCES CLIMBING THE MOUNTAIN

EIGHT: LEARNING TO LOVE 143
NINE: THE PRESENCE OF AN ABSENCE 167
TEN: IN HIS PRESENCE 183
ELEVEN: TO RECEIVE AND BE RECEIVED 199
TWELVE: HOLINESS TO THE LORD 219

APPENDIX: HEALING FROM ABUSE 231

NOTES 243

SUGGESTED READING 249

ABOUT THE AUTHOR 253

PREFACE

The scriptures and history of The Church of Jesus Christ of Latter-day Saints are replete with examples of the gifts of healing. I love these stories that whisper hope to my soul. They stir my imagination with questions and possibilities: How can Christ heal us not only physically but also emotionally and spiritually? Does all healing ultimately flow from him? Why was healing the most common of his miracles? What place do such gifts have in our lives today? Is something about healing important to not only our health but also our salvation?

As a psychologist, I spend much of my professional life trying to help people heal. As an ordinary woman, I spend much of my personal life trying to heal, which is like saying I spend much of my life trying to get free— free from old templates that no longer serve me, free to seek God with an unfettered heart. The temple is both road map and hospital, ambulance and vision-lodge for the wounded pilgrim.† It teaches us to search not only for healing but also for The Healer. When we find him, we find all.

The many names of Christ remind us that each of us relates to the Savior differently, however, and he in turn relates to us through our unique needs, gifts, and experiences. Part of the temple's genius is its reliance on symbols and stories that can be applied by different people in different ways

---

† Obviously no book can replace the skills of a competent therapist or doctor, the inspiration of a spiritual leader, or the compassion of a loving friend. When the pain of self-discovery becomes too intense, when repenting from serious sin, when dealing with past or present abuse, or when confronted with mental illness, we may need and certainly deserve all of these. Readers facing these challenges should seek such help.

to serve different needs. I can see the temple as a hospital, and you see it as a school, an artist's studio, a market, or a judicial court, and we can both find help. I would be dismayed if anyone thought this or any book were more than one set of possibilities among many about how to approach the temple journey, a journey through which we create the house of our soul.

The usefulness of this book will be limited to those unfamiliar with the temple from personal experience, but even to those who have attended the temple, the scenery from your window as you travel along will not necessarily look like what I describe from mine. Each traveler's perspective and interests will be different. One person may search out local cuisine, while another delights in native birds, and another, political history. As with any lovely home, one guest may be especially drawn to the stonework, while another notices the room layout, and another is fascinated by the innovative plumbing. My purpose is not to be comprehensive about this house-journey of the temple but to offer a glimpse of one viewpoint in the hope that my observations may trigger curiosity about what you need or love or seek as you contemplate this journey and build this house for yourself.

Many types of people have written books about the temple's purpose and meaning: General Authorities, historians, scholars, teachers, and scripturians. I write from my perspective as a Latter-day Saint psychologist, one with deep respect for the healing power of symbols and stories to help us make sense of our lives. Learning through symbols and stories—temple learning—does not lend itself to linear, one-size-fits-all explanations, however. How each of us understands the temple's lessons is highly personal. What I find meaningful may not work well for you, so what you read here should be taken as only one person's perspective, one approach among many. For each of us, much of the temple's deepest meaning, like healing itself, unfolds privately, somewhere under the dressings that block it from view. We approach such healing in whispers. It does not draw attention to itself. It distills on our soul as dews from heaven as we wonder, seek, and grow still.

In order to profit from the temple's lessons, we must learn its language, lay its templates on our lives, and follow the path it illuminates for us, room by room. The first two chapters of this book explore the purpose of the temple and the language of ordinances—these profound teaching tools that point us toward the face of God. Calling us away from our busy, task-oriented world, the temple invites us into unfamiliar realms of poetry and dreams. In the temple, we move through an external stillness that fosters internal movement. Through ordinances we dance our prayers and dress in promises and tune our hearts to voices from other realms.

Using the Salt Lake Temple as a template and drawing on scriptures about the Creation, the Fall, the ministry of Jesus Christ, and the Restoration, the remaining chapters consider each room of the temple. In section one, we explore five of these rooms, all of which focus on our experience with descent. The baptistry reminds us some part of us may have to die before we can claim new birth. False identities we have clung to, false traditions of our families or cultures, and false patterns we have copied must be dismantled and buried before new life can take hold. Baptism for the dead reestablishes the living as well on the path toward the essential passage of being born again. The baptistry suggests vital lessons in responsibility, agency, and forgiveness.

The ordinances of washing and anointing both acknowledge our inevitable mortal injuries and prepare us for new identities and powers. Witnessing, experiencing, and sometimes perpetuating the sin and violence in this fallen world all leave us emotionally and spiritually bloodied. These ordinances call us to take seriously our need to have our spiritual wounds cleansed, anointed, and dressed. In our initial steps toward holiness, we remember that our body, with all its frailties, appetites, and passions, is not a curse we must transcend, but a precious gift we must fully embrace here if we are to claim it in eternity.

Beautiful murals on the walls of a creation room remind us of the wonders of the physical world, which God has prepared so lovingly as our home away from home. When our spiritual life grinds to a halt among the overwhelming responsibilities of daily living, when business and busyness preoccupy us and peace seems elusive, when we simply lose sight of the meaning and purpose of our being here, the creation story depicts chaos yielding to order under the Creator's hand. We recall the eons we spent observing the unfolding of that creation and preparing for our time here. We anticipate the visions and powers we might yet gain if temple promises come to fruition in our lives. As a palliative against our tendency to get too absorbed in this world, we are invited to invest in our own creative gifts. We are tutored in descending and ascending, planning and evaluating, being active and resting. We are reminded of who we are and who we may become.

The garden room evokes the Genesis story of Adam and Eve. Rather than looking at this story as history, we will explore it as a metaphor for our personal fall. When our self-confidence is undermined by failure and sin, or when betrayal rocks our confidence in others, the story of Adam and Eve welcomes us to our humanity. It strengthens our hold on forgiveness and forgiving. It invites us to learn, try again, and access at the most personal level Christ's healing grace and Atonement. It tells us how to find anew the path toward Life.

To our surprise, or perhaps our dismay, that path does not lead us back to Eden but through a one-way passage out into the wilderness. In this desert place, we struggle to distinguish our own voice from the voice of the adversary or the voice of God. We must learn the difference between a mirage and an oasis. It is hard to hold on to truth amid all the uncertainties of life. Addictive patterns, power struggles, deep hungers, and anxious fears obscure our discernment. Christ's wilderness experience with God, angels, and Satan teaches us how to navigate our own wildernesses of uncertainty and competing voices. In this unlikeliest of places, we also glimpse spiritual high roads of patience, charity, and trust as we learn to follow the voice of the Spirit and obey, obey, obey.

With section three we conclude our experiences with descent and begin the climb toward God. Within the terrestrial commission to build Zion, we are privileged to work in God's kingdom and to work on ourselves in the process. On the unlikely bedrock of our failures and wounds, our life callings finally emerge. However, work is not our primary goal. Love is. On what principles can loving communities be built despite our fears about getting close? When we feel love-hungry and love-impaired, how can we heal our hearts, bless other people without exhausting our own resources, and grow toward life-giving power? Can the messy complications of relationships really foster spirituality instead of detracting from it? How can we access the faith necessary to pray down light and power from heaven to bless and heal those we love? Terrestrial principles instruct us in personal commissions, interpersonal communities, and spiritual communions.

As we near the end of the journey, awareness of death helps us both value this life and hope for something more, but death is not the only way to approach the world beyond the veil. God is near at hand. The temple helps us imagine how to find the passage to our share of veil-piercing intimacies with deity. We can prepare to claim the healing gifts of resurrection, holiness, and eternal life even before we die.

The peaceful beauty of the celestial room characterizes God's abode, a place we long to internalize as a fountain of living water within. Is it possible to live in an inner state of celestial glory even while walking in a telestial world? What are the characteristics of celestial living we can aspire to here? How do we make healing and holiness truly our own?

We are familiar with pictures of sealing rooms with their mutually reflective mirrors, symbols of eternity. The sealing ordinances offer hope of lasting relief from our mortal isolation and loneliness. Sealing rooms further remind us that a relationship worth perpetuating for eternity comes at the culmination, not the inauguration, of the marriage journey. At these altars we become rightful recipients of the blessings of Abraham, Isaac, and Jacob. Then we become conduits through which others become legal heirs to these blessings.

Even when we gain access to the heights of spiritual bliss, we have to get up for work on Monday, face the laundry and the yard work, and deal with the evening news and the children's report cards. How do we retain the deep peace of the temple experience? How do we use temple insights to bring more consciousness and intentionality to our daily living? How do we maintain perspective when earthly realities impose on the joy of spiritual communion? Is it possible for us to become a living temple, a place where deity can dwell? The concept of a Holy of Holies suggests some final lessons for preserving us in the healing and holiness of temple life.

In the temple, the Savior comes to each of us with both healing in his wings and the offer of holiness in his outstretched hands. He is Life, and life is his consummate gift. It is my hope this book can help us receive his offers and come to fit our jagged and blemished lives into the artful stonework of his holy house.

Christ is the Master Carpenter. We are the temples he builds. He has walked this road. He will walk with us.[‡]

---

‡ When presenting the true experiences of clients, names and identifying information will be changed unless specific permission has been obtained.

Preparing for the Temple Experience

CHAPTER ONE

The Search

❦

As the hart panteth after the water brooks, so panteth my soul for thee, O God. My soul thirsteth for God, for the living God: when shall I come and appear before God?

—Psalm 42:1–2

This is a book about the temple's role in helping us find the passageway to holiness—the Holiness that is God and the holiness we may become. That passage is clearly marked, but it is indeed strait and narrow. Christ is the only river pilot experienced enough to guide us to it and through it. The temple provides the chart, the compass, and a kind of 3-D virtual tour of what we can expect and how we can succeed on this crucial journey. If we learn its lessons well, then we will find God and obtain all the Father has. "And he that receiveth my Father receiveth my Father's kingdom; therefore all that my Father hath shall be given unto him" (Doctrine and Covenants 84:38).

Temple ordinances depict simultaneously a journey and a destination. The temple is God's map for this journey of healing, his blueprint for a house of personal holiness. The journey involves birthing, bandaging, creating, covenanting, discerning, loving, and receiving. The house requires healing and sanctifying principles and tools for turning the raw materials of our daily experience into a House of the Lord. Along that journey and within that house is a strait and narrow passageway that leads us to the pearl of greatest price. The temple shows us where.

Thanks to recent building efforts, over 90 percent of Church members today can travel to a temple within four hours. Some members still make great sacrifices or surmount enormous obstacles to get to the temple, but the sacrifices and obstacles many of us encounter are more internal than external. These obstacles include feelings of unworthiness, competing priorities, and confusion about the temple's real value in our lives. Too often we see temple attendance as one more demand on our busy schedules rather than as a resource, a glowing white stone to give us light as we travel in the dark. We strain to understand temple teachings. We struggle to access its promised endowment of power. We can get to the temple, but we don't always get the temple. And when we don't, the temple may not satisfy the deepest longings of our souls. We want more than to get to the temple, more even than to get the temple. We want to get home. Home to the God who gives us life. Home to the truest light within us.

Obviously, getting to this home is not about renting a moving van or buying a plane ticket. This "getting home" is a process of becoming, of being shaped into the home we seek. The temple not only takes us home but also makes us home, creating in each of us a living place for God to dwell. This is a home that, as Deity's full heirs, we will inhabit throughout eternity. As Paul states, "Know ye not that *ye are the temple of God*, and that the spirit of God dwelleth in you?" (1 Corinthians 3:16; italics mine). The Church is busy building temples so God can use them to build temples of us. In that cause we are not building hundreds of temples, but millions. With the reverence the temple requires, the purpose of this book is to explore this healing house and journey.

The Destination

Before taking a journey, we like to have some idea of what we should be looking for when we arrive. When it comes to the temple journey, the answer is simple: We should be looking for God. God himself has encouraged us in that expectation:

> And inasmuch as my people build a house unto me in the name of the Lord, and do not suffer any unclean thing to come into it, that it be not defiled, my glory shall rest upon it;
>
> Yea, and my presence shall be there, for I will come into it, and all the pure in heart that shall come into it shall see God. (Doctrine and Covenants 97:15–16)

I feel as if I have been looking for God my whole life with varying degrees of success. At times I want to give up in frustration, unable to maintain the closeness I seek. At other times I get distracted and forget to look at all. Occasionally I find a hidden portal to eternity in the most unlikely of places. My search for God is the bright, enduring warp through which the multicolored threads of my living are woven. Still, sometimes I wonder why the portal to God seems so hard to find.

My husband and I love to hide Easter eggs for our children in the most obscure places we can think of. Sometimes we are so successful they don't find all our handiwork for years. But we don't hide Easter eggs to keep them away from our children. We hide them to enrich the experience of finding. I think maybe God is a little like this. He does not make us search for him because he wants to stay hidden, but because the very process of seeking helps prepare us to discover him. In the end, God wants to be found. He says, "And ye shall seek me, and find me, when ye shall search for me with all your heart" (Jeremiah 29:13).

Too often we blame God for the distance between us when we are the ones who hold the door shut. Sometimes we keep our distance through disobedience or neglect. Often I think we keep him away out of fear of the very intimacy we seek. It can make us feel vulnerable to get too close.[1] We feel exposed and afraid when we have to stand too near the light. We may seek, but not with all our self-protecting hearts.

Throughout the world, people seek God in many ways. They build cathedrals and mosques, read holy books, walk on burning coals, retreat to monasteries, fast, pray, take hallucinogenic drugs, and trek to mountain retreats, all in attempts to connect with a power beyond them that will give meaning to life and death. A chosen few somehow find the hidden portal, pierce the veil, and perceive the infinite. The places where they find God become holy sites others seek. Through visiting such places we try to make the otherworldly more real and imaginable. We try to feel something that transcends the daily humdrum and gives us courage and hope as we live in the dark. When Muslims travel to Mecca, Catholics to the Church of the Holy Sepulchre, Jews to Sinai, or Latter-day Saints to the Sacred Grove, they all go to find some vestige of the sacred that might light up the hidden passage to God.

When someone makes a trip to a sacred place with a sacred purpose, we call it a pilgrimage. A pilgrim differs from a tourist, even though they may visit identical locations. A tourist goes to see a place; a pilgrim goes to demonstrate holy desires, engage in a process of personal transformation, and seek out the divine.

I once made a pilgrimage to Bethlehem Square on Christmas Eve, seeking the Prince of Peace while soldiers with machine guns patrolled from rooftops overhead. I guess it was personally transforming, but not in the way I hoped. Perhaps you have made a pilgrimage to the Sacred Grove and wondered which trees shared the witness of the young boy whose name God spoke there. Pilgrims travel to now-empty pyramids built by ancient Egyptians trying to ensure the survival of their souls or visit Muslim mosques in

Istanbul or Muscat and marvel at the devotion of those who heed a call to prayer five times each day. Pilgrims join the reverent Jews who pray at the Western Wall that once flanked Jerusalem's temple or climb the legendary mount where Moses saw God face-to-face. Pilgrims weep in the Garden Tomb, accepting the inscription on its door, "He is not here. He is risen."

While I have felt the Spirit in such places, I have also learned searching for someone else's old Easter eggs is not the solution to my current hungers. Historical sites of pilgrimage might help me imagine God revealing himself to others, but exotic places and mysterious traditions are not the objects of my search. Fortunately, I don't need to book a flight to a distant city to find the gateway to heaven. The "house of *my* pilgrimage" (Psalm 119:54; italics mine), the living door to the living God, is the temple. Within these sacred walls, God promises he can be found, today, by "all the pure in heart." A hefty qualifier to be sure, but is there a more astounding, radical, consummate promise?

So the temple is much more than a place to commemorate sacred history. It is a place of living fountains of eternal life. Elder Boyd K. Packer states, "All roads lead to the temple, for it is there that we are prepared in all things to qualify us to enter the presence of the Lord."[2] "Without [temple] ordinances," the Lord reminds us, "no man can see the face of God, even the Father, and live" (Doctrine and Covenants 88:21–22). Well then, with such ordinances, what might we see? God invites us to the temple today so we might seek his face and so we might find him.

People seek the face of God for many reasons, of course, some good and others not so good. Sometimes I am still tempted to think seeing his face would end the rigors and uncertainties of my mortal journey and put my doubts, struggles, or feelings of unworthiness to rest. Church history suggests I am wrong about that, however. More purely perhaps, I seek him for forgiveness. I seek him to worship at his feet. I seek him to learn about his ways. I seek him because I love him because he first loved me (1 John 4:19). I want to acquire his identities, his attributes, and desires, for when it comes to holiness, I know I can see only what I have at least in part become. I seek him because I want to be his, both by lineage and by nature, engraving his image upon my countenance and shaping my life to the pattern of the Son. I seek him because I want him to find me.

Given such a destination, it goes without saying this will be a journey like no other. It is a personal journey. Although we may enjoy the company of fellow travelers from time to time, much of this journey is taken alone, without earthly purse or scrip to rely on. The Savior alluded to this journey when he said to his Apostles near the end of his life:

In my Father's house are many mansions: if it were not so, I would have told you. I go to prepare a place for you. And if I go and prepare a place for you, I will come again, and receive you unto myself; that where I am, there ye may be also. (John 14:2–3)

What is "my Father's house"? While it is certainly heaven, is it not also the temple? Brigham Young University religion professor John Welch pointed out to a class of his I attended that at the time of the King James translation of the Bible, the word *mansion* did not refer to an elaborate, expensive home but to a stopping place on a journey, a way station for a traveler. The Greek word translated as "mansion," *monai*, can also have this meaning of a resting place or way station. Welch also taught us the word translated here as "receive" connotes escorting a person or taking someone with you. So this passage of scripture might be understood to communicate, "In my Father's temple are many way stations along a journey. I go to get everything ready for you, and I will return and be your escort, taking you with me to where I am, that where I am, ye may be also." These words reiterate the idea of the temple as a series of way stations on the road through mortality that leads to the face of God.

The Journey of Healing

On this mortal journey, even our perfect Savior experienced great injury and was left with many scars. This journey entails danger to the body and the spirit, and no one gets through it alive. Christ blazes this trail, making everything ready. He assures us his power is sufficient to heal and redeem every wound we might sustain in our travels.

And wounded we are! Just as most of us eventually break a bone, run a fever, strain a muscle, or skin a knee, we also experience broken dreams, feverish emotions, strains on our most important relationships, and abrasions of regret we cannot will away. Our personal journey may not entail a heart attack, cancer, a snakebite, or starvation, but we can hardly escape heart blockages to our creativity, malignant struggles with power or powerlessness, or some poisonous or hungry parenting practice we pass on to yet another generation. Imprisoning addictions, soul-shaking failures, heart-wrenching betrayals, and personal tragic flaws unravel the spirit as well as the body. Mortal experiences that leave us physically wounded and emotionally disabled can also lead to "secondary infections" of spiritual doubt, disillusionment, or despair.

Among many things that drew early converts to The Church of Jesus Christ of Latter-day Saints was the promise of spiritual gifts of tongues, prophecy, visions, healings—gifts they eagerly claimed and explored. I am especially moved by their attempts at spiritual healing. I don't pretend to understand how healing occurs, whether through gifts of the spirit or medical interventions, but as I read those early accounts of laying on of hands and pouring on of oil, I touch my sores and remember wistfully where I hurt. I need those healing gifts.

Surely I am not alone. The road of life we all set off on with such high hopes is quickly revealed to be the legendary road that descends from the Holy City toward the city of Jericho on the banks of the Dead Sea, the lowest place on earth. This is the path we take as we leave our holy home and descend to earth, and indeed this path is trod by murderous thieves who leave us beaten and bleeding by the wayside. "All that ever came before me are thieves and robbers," Jesus says, "[who] cometh not, but for to steal, and to kill, and to destroy" (John 10:8, 10). In the story, the Samaritan finds the wounded traveler and brings him to an inn to heal. Christ is our good Samaritan, the outcast and despised one who joins us on every step of our long descent. As he journeys, he comes where we are, sees us, and has compassion on us (Luke 10:33). He brings us to the healing inn of the temple and pays in full for our care.

When Christ finds us, he does not merely offer to nurse us back to what we were, however. He says, "I am come that they may have life, and that they may have it more abundantly" (John 10:10). He offers us abundance—enough and to spare of the things that matter most. The temple teaches us what matters most and how we might obtain it, generously measured, pressed down, and running over. Temple ordinances point us to the Abundant God and to Jesus Christ, whom the Father has sent. Our Rescuer and Healer is also our Daily Bread, our Living Water, our Tree of Life laden with the fruit of God's incomparable love.

Healing versus Cure

As I have noted before, each of us must find the temple's meaning through the lens of our own understanding. Because I see the temple as a hospital does not mean that is the "right answer" or that it is not also a ship, a switchboard, an umbilical cord, a tree, a fountain, a kitchen, or a stone.

Since I am exploring the metaphor of healing, let me first distinguish healing from cure. Cure returns us to our previous state of wellness, which is usually what we long for. But the scriptures never speak of the gift of cure. They speak of the gift of healing. Healing is a different process from cure. Healing involves a spiritual and emotional reweaving of our life story to incorporate, not merely remove, our injuries. It involves growth and personal change, maturation into a new state of deeper trust in God despite, not in the absence of, suffering. It includes acceptance of our lost innocence, while reaching toward greater wisdom. Healing does not mean going back to Eden, but going forward through the wounding world of mortality to a wholeness that transcends rather than excludes evil. While we cannot expect the temple to *cure* all our mortal ills, returning us to what we were before, it can help us *heal* from all our ills as God comforts, redeems, and changes us into something new. The temple helps us regain momentum and direction when we become paralyzed. It offers relief and calm when our hearts race amid life's challenges. It teaches us of God's most powerful healing promises: forgiveness, sanctification, resurrection, and redemption. We can begin to access these healing promises today, even if a cure must wait for tomorrow.

A colleague once told me he appreciated my holding out for healing in a discipline (psychology) that speaks mostly of coping. Actually I hold out for both. God's promise to those who want only cure is that we can get along in a leper colony if that is our lot, and we can find even in such a place the ways we are *not* poor or broken as well as the ways we are. In contrast, he tells those who settle for coping out of fear of the surgeon's hand that we can also truly, deeply, permanently heal, although such healing will not just return us to what we were before. In fact, his healing is an act so radical it partakes of dying and of being born again.

Within that new birth, the temple journey cannot only turn our holes into wholeness but our wholeness into holiness. The words *healing*, *health*, *wholeness*, and *holiness* have much in common, in fact. *Oxford English Dictionary* definitions of *healing* include both restoring to wholeness and saving spiritually. Salvation *salves* the wounded soul. Christ teaches:

> [If] they will return and repent, and come unto me with full purpose of heart . . . I shall **heal** them; and ye shall be the means of bringing *salvation* unto them. (3 Nephi 18:32; italics mine)

Christ saves and heals us through the instrument of his own wounds:

> He shall go forth, suffering pains and afflictions and temptations of every kind; and . . . will take upon him the pains and the sicknesses of his people . . . that he may know according to the flesh how to succor his people according to their infirmities. (Alma 7:11–12)

> He was wounded for our transgressions, he was bruised for our iniquities . . . and with his stripes, we are healed. (Isaiah 53:5)

Among the Savior's miracles, the most common, sought after, and freely offered was healing. He is compassionate for our wounds because he joins us in them all.

The Journey of Holiness

Healing is only a beginning, however. As we make the journey of healing, the temple walks us toward a holiness that transcends our wounds and our losses. Christ wants to do more than heal us; he wants to sanctify us—to touch our eyes that we might truly see; to purify our hearts; to foster our creativity, power, and compassion; and to bring us toward glory. He wants to help us become fully alive and fully ourselves and then capacitate us to engender that spiritual life in others. Yet even among those he taught, fed, healed, and loved so personally, relatively few stuck around for holiness. Will we?

The principles of holiness include purity of heart, charity and compassion, humility, sacrifice, repentance, and forgiveness. Even as our physical health fails, these spiritual capacities can increase. The *LDS Bible Dictionary* includes this definition of *holiness*:

> According to the [Old Testament], things or places were holy that were set apart for a sacred purpose. . . . The Israelites were a holy people because they stood in a special relationship to Jehovah. Under the guidance of the Prophets it was seen that what distinguished Jehovah from the gods of the heathen was his personal character. The word *holy* therefore came to refer to moral character. (pp. 703–4)

Holiness entails (1) being set apart for a sacred purpose in a special relationship to God and (2) a refined moral character. Holiness is essential to our journey toward the face of God. Paul enjoins the Hebrews to "Follow . . . holiness, without which no man shall see the Lord" (Hebrews 12:14). Paul also tells us we can increase in holiness by submitting to God's corrective chastening "for our profit, that we might be partakers of his holiness" (v. 10). Paul doesn't promise this will always be fun: "Now no chastening for the present moment seemeth to be joyous, but grievous: nevertheless afterward it yieldeth the peaceable fruit of righteousness" (v. 11). The sting of being chastened is more than worth the blessings we can receive as God coaches us toward the righteousness or holiness we need if we are to find the passage that will allow us to see his face and live.

We can gratefully seek God's correction or avoid it out of shame or fear. To avoid chastening is to leave the path that leads us to him. No unclean thing can enter his presence—end of story. Unless we see our rebelliousness for what it is, we cannot change our minds and repent, and we cannot get home.

Thankfully, the story is a little different when we are dealing with mortal weakness, which does not have to hold us back from him and which does not in itself make us unclean.[3] Weakness includes being subject to emotion, temptation, physical and emotional illness; predispositions we are born with; the fallout of trauma; or any limitation on our energy or capacity. God gives us *weakness* as part of our mortal experience (Ether 12:27), but we can be clean from *sin* only if we repent and exercise faith in the Atonement of Jesus Christ. Jacob teaches that even when we have qualified through repentance and effort for great spiritual power, far beyond what most of us would claim, we will continue to have weakness to remind us of our dependence on the Lord:

> Wherefore, we search the prophecies, and we have many revelations and the spirit of prophecy; and having all these witnesses we obtain a hope, and our faith becometh unshaken, insomuch that we truly can command in the name of Jesus and the very trees obey us, or the mountains, or the waves of the sea.
>
> Nevertheless, the Lord God *showeth us our weakness* that we may know that it is by his grace, and his great condescensions unto the children of men, that we have power to do these things. (Jacob 4:6–7; italics mine)

If we are willing, there is perhaps no quicker route to spiritual growth than to humbly and sincerely ask the Lord to show us our sins. In my experience, this is a prayer he always answers. We can also ask him to show us our weakness and help us grow into the strengths weakness can engender—strengths of compassion, humility, patience, trust, wisdom, hope, and charity. These are the very characteristics that make us more like our Father. They are the gifts mortal weakness can lead us toward as we rely humbly on Christ's Atonement. In contrast, when we are unwilling to see ourselves clearly, our spirituality stagnates. We wander off. We lose sight of the path. If we want to see the Lord, then we must first accurately see ourselves.

Rules of the Road

Having clarified both our destination and something of the nature of the trip, we realize how much we stand to gain from the temple journey. However, a few caveats are in order before we proceed.

First: Expect the Unexpected

Pilgrimages are not always orderly affairs. In the temple, as in life, we may feel as though we are being thrust onto a road to an unknown destination before we have even had time to pack. This is not how we imagined it would be when we set out for our endowment, a mission, marriage, parenting, therapy, a calling, aging . . . or just our morning walk. But here we are, trudging nervously along as the smooth, paved road of personal transformation turns to gravel, then a dirt trail, then a faint row of footsteps in the sand, visible only in retrospect. Enemies appear from nowhere. Familiarity drops out from under us. At times, everything we thought we knew about life, ourselves, or God seems suspect. *Is all this uncertainty really necessary?* we wonder.

Life unnerves us and stretches us in many ways. Sometimes the path of growth is gently watered with a soft, accumulating recognition that we are not yet who we want to be. Other times a sudden storm floods and unbalances us, threatening all we own. Introduction to the inner rooms of the temple can feel like such a flood, sweeping us without warning onto unfamiliar ground. Shaking us up a bit may be part of the temple's purpose. Enoch, Samuel, and Joseph Smith remind us that a prophetic call disturbs the initiate's comfortable world, and the endowment is in many ways such a call. The temple announces our priestly and prophetic mission. It calls to us from our personal burning bush. We begin this journey not by putting our shoes on but by taking them off.

Second: Safeguard the Sacred

Once inside the temple, we quickly recognize we are in a new country with a different language and culture from our ordinary life. This place has more in common with our dreams than with offices or kitchens or even chapels. Remember though: our most intimate human relationships unfold in privacy. So must our most intimate encounters with God. Just as healing unfolds somewhere under the dressings that block it from view, the temple unfolds its mysteries in privacy. Holiness is not bought in the marketplace. We approach these deep alchemies in whispers. They distill on our soul as dews from heaven as we wonder, seek, and grow still.[§]

Latter-day Saints are not the only ones to expect reverence and a certain silence to surround the sacred. As Malidoma Patrice Somé, an African

---

[§] That the temple is kept private does not mean what happens there is seemly or improper in any way. Nothing occurs in the temple that is salacious, demeaning, or outside of conventional morality.

of the Dagara tribe, says of his native rites of initiation,

> Every initiation has its esoteric and exoteric parts. As years have passed, I have realized that some things can be told and others not. Telling diminishes what is told. Only what has been integrated by the human aspect of ourselves can be shared with others. I have also come to believe that things stay alive proportionally to how much silence there is around them. Meaning does not need words to exist.[4]

Temple ordinances also have their esoteric and exoteric parts—things that can be told and things that cannot be told outside of their sacred context without diminishing them, or rather, us. For this reason, one-dimensional explanations of temple meaning will not help us much. Words and ideas without soul-level understanding are not only inadequate but also potentially dangerous, since people do not keep searching for something they think they have already found. Nor can words alone communicate the meanings of temple ordinances to those unprepared by desire, experience, and righteousness to receive them. Temple ceremonies ultimately claim their meaning within the sacred confines of the spiritually prepared human heart.

Simplistic explanations of temple meaning will also fail because temple wisdom is simply too large a pearl for anyone to circumscribe. Elder John A. Widtsoe explains:

> The endowment is so richly symbolic that only a fool would attempt to describe it; it is so packed full of revelations to those who exercise their strength to seek and see, that no human words can explain or make clear the possibilities that reside in the temple service.[5]

Like the parables of Jesus, temple ordinances house both broad, universal truths and the potential for private discovery. We rightly search for both. While the temple's "meaning" resides in a private relationship between us and the Lord, that meaning must be engaged and cultivated if it is to bear fruit in our lives, and others' perspectives can be useful as we clarify our own. There is no need for concern if the sweetest fruits are on branches "way over our head." As we continue to grow, our reach will be extended. Meanwhile, patience is called for, along with gratitude for blessings and understanding we already grasp.

Third: Stay with the Journey

I have gone for years without resolving some temple questions only to have an answer *pop!* into my awareness with sudden clarity. Many answers come only after completing the prerequisites: specific experiences, problems, relationships, repentance, study, or prayer. We rightly expect temple lessons to be accompanied by intellectual insight, feelings of comfort, increased perspective. But sometimes these gifts come only after long stretches of intellectual confusion, tremendous discomfort, and groping in the dark. The temple may not immediately illuminate the yellow-brick road to our future. More often it confirms we are on a good path only after we have headed out into the dark, no flashlight in hand.

A friend recently told me, "Everything will be all right in the end. If everything is not all right, it is not the end." *Pop!* This is also true in the temple: if everything does not yet feel all right, then remember we are not yet at the end. We may need to go more often to become more immersed in temple language and images. We may need to ask different questions or look in more diverse places for answers. We may need to wait patiently and enjoy the view already before us. And sometimes we may just need to get back to living for a while, trusting God will help us figure it out as we go.

The House of the Soul

As noted earlier, the temple experience implies both taking a journey, which requires leaving home, and building a house, which implies staying home. In ancient myths, journey-taking was primarily a man's task that took him out into the world to find himself. An oft-repeated phrase in the Doctrine and Covenants is the call to someone to "take his journey."

In contrast, psychotherapist Maureen Murdock writes, "Women find their way back to themselves not by moving up and out into the light like men, but by moving down into the depths. . . . The spiritual experience for women is one of moving more deeply into self rather than out of self."[6] The temple takes us deeply into ourselves, rebuilding our foundation stones and reorganizing our inner identities. Perhaps this is one reason God refers to the temple, this place of deep self-reflection, as *"the house of the daughters of Zion"* (Doctrine and Covenants 124:11).[7] Both men and women build this inner temple, though perhaps in different layouts or with different furnishings. Both men and women take the journey of the soul, but perhaps at different times or in different vehicles.

Our temple destination is God, our Home. The journey of healing and holiness we will explore here, tentatively and from one person's vantage point, is designed to take us to him by making us like him. Taking this journey is itself a way of building and rebuilding the house of the soul. The tools and the blueprints are found on the journey, enabling us to make of the raw material of our lives a fitting home for the spirit—both God's and ours. The temple path leads us away from the sleepy comforts of home and civilization and wanders through an inhospitable wilderness so vast and dry it can suck the life out of us. And then, mysteriously, the path brings us to a fulness of life and a sweetness of connection, opens our eyes, and makes us whole.

Don't be put off by surprises. Reverence the sacred. Be prepared to change and change. Keep walking. Stay alert for a man in camel's hair or a woman by a well—faithful witnesses who know the Lord and can point us toward Living Water, the Carpenter's Son. Then trust. Even when your feet are dirty, your knees buckle, or your heart fails—trust. Though we cannot imagine how, God can heal our hearts and hallow our eyes to see his face and live. His promises are sure.

HEALING PRACTICE FOR CHAPTER ONE: THE SEARCH

At the end of each chapter are a few questions and exercises to invite you to experiment with the ideas you've read. I try to provide a variety from which to choose. Those exercises that seem the most interesting or the most threatening may give the most useful information. In most cases, you will gain more if you write things down rather than just think about them, so consider getting a notebook or opening a computer file for the written exercises.

- *Observing prayer.* Think of yourself getting ready to pray. Where are you? What posture do you assume? Where do you look (even if your eyes are closed)? Where do you imagine God? What do you imagine him doing? If you have any interest in pursuing this exercise, don't read further until you do this part.

- *Observing more.* Again, think of yourself getting ready to pray. Imagine inviting the Father to sit very close to you. Imagine him listening to you with full attention. Listen for what he says to you. Notice what feelings this evokes in you. Write down what you learn.

  - What are three specific areas of your life that need healing, fixing, or adjusting right now? (Consider your physical and emotional well-being, relationships, self-image, and relationship with God.)

CHAPTER TWO

LEARNING THE LANGUAGE

—⚬⚬⚬—

Symbolism is the very language of scripture. To be unversed in symbolism is to be scripturally illiterate.

—ALONZO L. GASKILL[1]

We go to the temple to listen for God's voice, but our world does not prepare us well for the symbolic language he uses. We feel illiterate and thick-tongued with this unfamiliar dialect. But really, wouldn't we be a little disappointed to come all this way only to have everything look and sound like our hometown? We've gone looking for "a city which hath foundations, whose builder and maker is God" (Hebrews 11:10), and things are rightly a little different here.

Still, we may wonder about the temple: What is it saying? Is it talking to me? Why this language of symbols and signs and ordinances? Do we really need ordinances to be saved when they are just symbols? Isn't it what the symbols represent that really counts? Are ordinances just convoluted ways of getting a point across, or do they really *do* something that cannot be done in any other way? How can I know what they mean? In this chapter, we will consider the value of ordinances in creating the healing and sanctifying changes we seek. We will then discuss ways to approach temple ordinances to increase their meaning and usefulness to us.

Symbols as Instruments of Change

The use of complex symbols is a uniquely human capacity. Language itself is a set of symbols—sounds and ink spots with no inherent meaning. Yet even our customary words do something that cannot be done in any other way. They are more like hammers or hands than we might guess.

For starters, if French is the language of the country we live in, then French *will* get things done for us there and in ways Bulgarian or Chinese would not. French word-symbols, spoken or written, communicate information that influences real people to take real action in the real world. In this way, French symbols not only describe but also help create the way traffic flows, buildings take shape, or relationships form. So if ordinances and symbols are the language of the country we call Eternity, we can rightly expect them to set things in motion and initiate change in the eternal worlds.

In addition, symbols change us—literally and physically. Words and symbols change the very chemistry and structure of our brain. The neurons in our brain grow and connect in response to the words we speak, the stories we tell, the symbols we use, and the activities we observe. Symbols, stories, and observations, then, have at least the power to change the actual physical development of the human brain and body. They not only represent our experience of the world, ourselves, and the relationships we have with others, but they also change us at both a personal/cellular and an interpersonal/societal level.

Ordinances do not rely on only spoken words (which are useful to only a small part of the brain) to embody meaning. Ordinances also tap into the symbolic power of gestures, thoughts, movements, clothing, music, color, and touch, which resonate through our brain and body more deeply and broadly than words alone.

If ordinances, stories, rituals, and other symbols can change human brains, bodies, and relationships, perhaps it is not too much of a stretch to imagine they can also change the order of heaven. Ordinances make real things happen in this new country. They communicate not only with words but also at a level deeper than words, and perhaps to beings we cannot see. They mark important events and express important truths on many levels at once in the multifaceted language of the city of God. Ordinances call us away from our busy, task-oriented world into the territory of poetry and dreams. Through ordinances, we dance our prayers, dress in promises, and tune our hearts to voices from other realms.

Christian theologian Tom Driver advances in *The Magic of Ritual*:

Rituals are primarily instruments designed to change a situation: They are more like washing machines than books. A book may be about washing, but the machine takes in dirty clothes and if all goes well, transforms them into cleaner ones. . . . Rites of passage are performed not simply to *mark* transitions but to *effect* them.[2]

Ordinances are rites of passage that do "not simply . . . *mark* transitions but . . . *effect* [produce, cause] them." For example, the purpose of baptism and confirmation is not only to *symbolize* a change in our hearts but also to actually *produce* a change. "If all goes well," I am a different person after baptism and confirmation than before. At minimum, my status with other people changes as I become, through these ordinances, a member of The Church of Jesus Christ of Latter-day Saints. The missionaries prepare me to desire and internalize this change, the baptismal interview attests to my eligibility, my repentance qualifies me for its blessings, and an official certificate acknowledges my new status, but neither the discussions, nor the interview, nor the repentance, nor the paper make me a member of the Church. Participating in these rituals—enacting them willingly with my body—makes me a member of the Church. Whether or not I fully understand the symbolism, whether or not I complete the inner change thus initiated, I am changed from a nonmember to a member of the Church with these acts, expanding my identity and giving me new responsibilities and rights within a new church community. The symbolic ordinance further teaches me to work toward an actual spiritual reality of being born again, leaving behind the person of sin I have been and becoming a child of Christ. In this way, I become more than a member of record; I become a faithful witness, a true disciple—a Saint. All gospel ordinances are designed to teach us about spiritual realities we are invited to attain.

An ordinance might also be compared to a peace treaty signed between two sovereigns. Does the signing of a treaty really *do* anything? Yes and no. It does not mean the sought-for peace will immediately follow. It does not disarm the warriors and return them to their families, rebuild the infrastructure, or renew trade. Yet without the treaty, these actions will not follow at all. The signing of the treaty signals the intent of both parties to enact a change in their relationship, and it specifies the parameters of those intentions. This symbol sets in motion a series of real changes to physical, emotional, political, and social structures.

In addition to words, ordinances use clothing, gestures, stories, and movements to convey important information about our new status and connections. We sign the "treaty" of an ordinance with our whole body in gestures and movements. God's authorized representatives place his name upon the treaty as well through similar symbolic forms. We alone determine if the treaty really *does* anything, or if it becomes a meaningless gesture. We may violate the treaty and return to war if we choose, or we may continue to invest in peace and "at-one-ment" with God until God sends his ambassadors to minister to us personally or until we are visited by his Head of State. On his part, God always takes these "treaties" seriously.

Do the dead really need the living to sign a treaty for them with God? Apparently they do—but why? What might either the living or the dead stand to gain from using such a symbolic language? Several possibilities come to mind:

First, temple work for the dead is a poignant reminder that the dead are not dead in any ultimate sense. God deals with us all as his living children but in different stages of life.

Second, ordinances remind the dead, the living, and perhaps the yet unborn of the crucial importance of the body. Ordinances underscore the importance of the mortal experience, which God privileges as a favored and powerful state.

Third, we are all reminded God knows us and saves us one by one, and each individual chooses to sign the treaty of salvation by name.

Finally, because the sins of each generation are connected to the sins of past and future generations, the need for repentance and new life must also cross multigenerational boundaries. My birth into mortality unwittingly connects me to a wounding chain that may wind through multiple generations of the mortal experience. As I participate in ordinances for the dead, I help forge a healing chain that also crosses generations. Perhaps the ordinances of the gospel are the designated treaties for making peace with one another as well as with God, both here and in the eternal worlds.

If thoughts and symbols can change the actual structure of the brain, then certainly they can also change the structure of the even more adaptable spirit. Ordinances help engrave our deepest meanings on the very tissue of our souls. We can rightfully expect ordinances to change us, but we are not always sure going in what that change will entail. After being baptized at age eight, I remember feeling *different*. After receiving my endowment, I felt many things—peaceful, bewildered, overwhelmed, touched—but I also felt irrevocably *changed*. The best way to describe that change was that I felt for the first time in my twenty-one years I was a woman and no longer a girl. That perception continues to inform my perspective of the endowment as a rite of passage into the spiritual adulthood I am still attempting to mature within.

We spend more ritual time enacting the endowment than any other ordinance. What reality is produced by participation in this ordinance? Into what new life does it initiate us? What changes as we mold our bodies into its forms, hear its words with our ears, and commit to its covenants with our mouths? What happens to our identity when we are named with its names? How is our spiritual authority augmented when we are anointed and clothed with its powers? How is our place in the community of Saints altered when we join in its prayers? Whom do we find when we pass through its veils? God? Other people? Ourselves?

Ordinances as Vehicles of Revelation

Understanding the temple is ultimately a revelatory process. While I accept ordinances can change us unconsciously, I also fully subscribe to Elder John A. Widtsoe's assertion, "No man or woman can come out of the temple endowed as he [or she] should be, unless he [or she] has seen, beyond the symbol, the mighty realities for which the symbols stand."[3] To reiterate, we may be endowed without attempting to grasp the symbolism of the temple, but we will not be endowed as we might be—as we should be. By tackling the meaning and symbolism of the ordinances, we increase their power to *do* something in us: to help purify our hearts, transform our lives, and prepare us to meet the Lord. Our questions, prayers, scripture study, and life experiences, as well as the books we read, the people we talk to, and our worthiness and receptivity to the Spirit, all affect the meanings we can grasp and prepare to realize.

Church leaders tend not to explain much, leaving us the privilege of coming to our own conclusions. We are not always happy about this "privilege." How often do we say to our leaders, as Israel said to Moses at Mt. Sinai, "You go talk to God and find out what he says, then teach us and we will listen. But don't ask us to go up to that smoking mountain, lest we die" (paraphrasing Exodus 20:18–19; see Doctrine and Covenants 84:20–24). God invites each of us to the mountain of his house to claim for ourselves its healing and transforming potential and to find him for ourselves at its summit. He gives us the right to learn from him what the temple "means," how its language works, and how we might embody its teachings. But we must climb the mountain.

As we make this private pilgrimage, God expects us to ask questions and search for answers in order to find our way. Consider four types of questions as a start, questions relevant to (1) body, (2) mind, (3) application, and (4) relationship. First, we can embody the ordinance, participating physically and emotionally in the experience, allowing it to register powerfully on our body and heart, and then wondering deliberately about this process. Second, we can think about the intellectual components of the temple experience as we analyze, compare, ponder, and organize information with our mind. Third, we can apply the temple to our personal concerns and problems to find answers relevant to us. Fourth, we can use the temple to build relationships that connect us to ourselves, to others, and to God. Together, these four vantage points encourage us in the spiritual process of making the temple a revelatory experience. They can inform our search for God.

(1) Body—Physical and Emotional Approaches to the Temple

Significantly, ordinances require us to do, not to merely consider. An ordinance is performed. We learn with our flesh as we mold it into temple forms. We learn with our heart as we respond with emotion to our temple experience. We learn such lessons somewhere in our bones. Meaningful temple moments come as we simply remember to be present, entering into the temple drama fully. Engaging the world differently, not just under- standing it differently, is key. We came to mortality precisely for the pur- pose of learning by our experience, the experience of our body. When we come to the temple, our body serves a greater purpose than carrying our head around. It becomes a powerful teacher in its own right.

Being alert, present, and engaged during the presentation of temple ordinances is easy to *do*—we just have to pay attention. It is just not easy to keep remembering to do. We drift off, come back, coast awhile, come back again, start thinking about the dog or the news, and come back again. When we come to the temple fresh from the hectic pace most of us think is normal, our brains hit the rhythmic, almost hypnotic cadence of the temple, and we may find ourselves "getting sleepy." In contrast, revelation is facilitated by a state of focused attention and concentration.

I do not wish to imply that striving and struggling are the only ways to learn. Sometimes temple learning comes most powerfully through peace- ful experiences of being held and nurtured, surrounded by love, provided for, watched over, reached after. But whether we are quietly receptive or actively reaching, focus and intentionality help us transform ordinary acts into sacred experiences.

When I went to the temple for the first time, I experienced this state of attentive, focused presence—the kind of presence that notices and won- ders and feels—but the newness of it all was also a little overwhelming. I started to feel a little numb in the face of all the unfamiliar stimuli. After going back to the temple many times, I sometimes get to a different level of numbness, and my attention drowns in a sea of repeated familiarities. But if I can be alert, attentive, and reverent, allowing myself to rejoice in or wonder about things I would otherwise numbly ignore, a creative process begins. To this end, I resonate with the words of the character Patricia in the Warner Brothers 1990 film *Joe Versus the Volcano*: "My father says that almost the whole world is asleep. Everybody you know. Everybody you see.

Everybody you talk to. He says that only a few people are awake and they live in a state of constant total amazement."

If we want to receive, God invites us to wake up and to ask, holding out our hands to be filled. Asking questions is fundamental to the process of revelation and personal discovery. I find I can only really hold on to about one question at a time in the temple, so the questions listed in this chapter have kept me engaged for a long time. However, this list of questions is certainly not exhaustive. I hope it can spark your curiosity and lead you to your own questions, which will be much more relevant to you.

Questions that have helped me learn at this physical level include

- How does each ordinance feel to perform? What does it remind me of?

- As I participate with my whole body, what emotions are evoked?

- What does it feel like or look like *physically* to be open, receptive, and inviting to the Spirit?

- How can I calm my worries about performing or understanding and simply experience the temple's soothing, nurturing atmosphere?

- What is the physical experience of joy, gratitude, awe, or hope? How can I allow these emotions to be expressed as I consider the beauties of God's plan?

- What preparations help me be awake and be amazed in the temple?

(2) Mind—Intellectual Approaches to the Temple

Performing an ordinance is enriched by thoughtfulness. We might begin by simply comparing the ordinance to similar experiences in ordinary life. As we think about temple clothing, gestures, or phrases, we can ask ourselves how each is familiar, what it is like, where we have observed or done something like it before, or where in the scriptures we find something similar. What do these similarities teach us about the meaning of the symbol? The more we know about scriptures, service, prayer, repentance, and relationships, the broader the variety of contexts we can bring to bear on answering the question, "*What is this like?*"

For practice, what is the sacrament like? We can compare the ritual act of partaking of the sacrament to the ordinary act of eating or drinking. Waiting our turn, we remember what it feels like to hunger for nourishment and then to receive it. Are we hungry today for God's presence? We consider the ways we feed our bodies well and poorly, in company or alone, often or sparingly, with pleasure or disgust, and we compare this sacramental experience to those common ones. We remember that we become what we eat and that eating is essential to life. How does this inform our understanding of the sacrament?

We can bring all these experiences and understandings to the symbolic act of nourishing our spirit and satiating hungers bread alone does not fill. As the elements of the bread and water will literally become part of the fabric of our body, so too we want to internalize the nature of Christ into the fabric of our soul. His mercy becomes the sustenance of our spiritual life. We eat in remembrance of other meals we have learned about in scripture, where Christ himself was the breaker of the bread. We imagine what it might have been like for his apostles to eat with him at the Passover table or on the shores of Galilee. We eat in anticipation of his promised return, when he will eat and drink with us again to inaugurate his millennial reign. Partaking now is a symbol for a reality we one day hope to experience of eating and drinking with the Savior when he comes again (Doctrine and Covenants 17:5–14).

Asking, "*What is it like?*" provides an initial context for unpacking the meaning of elements of the sacrament or other ordinances.

We can also consider the question, "*How is this different?*" This distinction helps us learn more about how God's ways are different from our own, inviting us to stretch beyond obvious similarities to see new lessons. That the bread and water are prepared in a special way by certain people at only a particular time and place helps focus our attention past ordinary bread and water to the body and blood of the Lord. The emblems, passed without the normal abundance and chatter of the dinner table, are eaten to fill the spirit, not the stomach and not social ends. They are not served by a waiter but by one who acts in the Savior's name, and we are the guests at his table. We eat to acknowledge him as the Bread of Life, the Living Water. The morsel of bread and shared drink are tiny, humble forms, reminding us he is meek and lowly of heart and that even the smallest morsel of his Spirit can truly nourish us. Christ serves and joins the weakest disciple who comes to his table in his name.

As we participate in the ordinances of the gospel, then, we do so at the juxtaposition of the ordinary and the extraordinary. We look to both how the ordinance action is familiar and how its particularly chosen "disfamiliarities" might contribute to its meaning. In those differences we learn something of how God's ways differ from our ways, suggesting how we may become more like him.

Another useful question at this intellectual level is, "*What is the story?*"

Some gospel ordinances use stories to help us imagine the life course those ordinances set us upon. The scriptures are replete with stories of spiritual journeys of healing, seeking, and transformation. These stories parallel our own pilgrimages and can be reflected in temple ordinances. As we look beyond the historicity of these stories, we can contemplate their relevance to us today. Truth lies not in facts alone, but in the meaning we give the facts. Temple stories do more than tell us how the earth was formed or how humanity came to be. They also help us find meaning and purpose in *our* creation, *our* fall, and *our* redemption. As we consider these stories, we see not only our first parents but also ourselves. We gain courage and imagination for the journey ahead. Every room within the temple's walls, every person, and every act can represent some aspect of ourselves and of our journey.

Adam and Eve, Nephi, Hagar, the brother of Jared, Rachel, Abraham, and others are not unlike the heroes of epic tales. They leave home and innocence behind. They wander in the wilderness in search of a new birthright. They are wounded by enemies and sustained by friends. They must orient their lives within new orders and vows. They learn to discern true teachers and reject false ones. They participate in sustaining families and communities. They traverse stony deserts and climb smoking mountains of vision and discovery to see the face of God. At last, they return home with new powers and wisdom to take their place upon the thrones of God's kingdom. Their stories echo through the temple experience. Their stories are our stories.

We can enter the temple, participate in the ordinances, intuit their significance, feel the Spirit, and come out changed, even if we can never put in words what we learn. Nevertheless, the meaning we create can be enhanced exponentially as we engage the ritual's stories, startle at its paradoxes, struggle with its oddities, and lay its templates upon our lives. In that process, an observation by C. S. Lewis from *The Weight of Glory* seems apt:

> If our religion is something objective, then we must never avert our eyes from those elements in it which seem puzzling or repellant; for it will be precisely the puzzling or the repellant which conceals what we do not yet know and need to know . . . the truth we need most is hidden precisely in the doctrines you least like and least understand. Scientists make progress because scientists, instead of running away from such troublesome phenomena or hushing them up, are constantly seeking them out. In the same way, there will be progress in Christian knowledge only as long as we accept the challenge of the difficult or repellant

doctrines. A "liberal" Christianity which considers itself free to alter the Faith whenever the Faith looks perplexing or repellent MUST be completely stagnant. Progress is made only into a *resisting* material.[4]

Some questions that assist an intellectual exploration of the temple include

- What questions are asked in the temple, and who asks them?

- What surprises me? What can I conclude from these surprising elements?

- What do I learn about God's character and attributes?

- What words are repeated most often, and by whom?

- What are Satan's lies, and how do they affect me now?

- What happens the same number of times? How might those things relate to and inform one another?

- What promises and blessings are offered? If I really believed God's promises to me, what would change?

(3) Application—Bringing Our Lives to the Temple

A third approach to temple wisdom involves bringing our personal thirst to the temple well: "*What does it have to do with my life now?*" Sometimes we will find fresh answers within the ceremony itself. Sometimes we will come to see how we might be asking the wrong question or trying to change the wrong person. And sometimes when we need nothing so much as a break from the rigors of our journey, the temple simply offers precious moments of stillness and hope.

The temple is a house of healing. We can bring every aspect of ourselves to God's house: the injured child, the insecure adolescent, the fearful parent, the resentful employee, the shameful sinner, the grieving mourner, the lonely spouse, the cynical intellectual, and the trusting disciple. We should not necessarily feel free to inflict all of these aspects on other patrons or workers, but we can allow them to speak to us and to God. Every part of us that needs healing can come to the temple to be cleansed, anointed, and bound up. Every part that is sick or afflicted can find a place on the rolls of those for whom faith and prayer is requested. Every part and passion that is subject to death in this world can find resurrection and redemption in our final benedictions.

The temple is a house of learning. When we need practical answers to practical problems, the temple is our tutor. Its soothing cadences can take the mind to a different level where more creativity can be brought to bear on our concerns. When we struggle with real-life questions about how to discern God's voice, repent, resist temptation, or overcome despair, we learn in the temple that such questions are both universal and answerable.

The temple is a house of hope. When relationships founder, the temple drama helps us see and change our tendency to act more like Satan than Christ. When we long for meaningful work, the temple models many positive roles to play in other people's lives. When we wonder who we really are, when we ask what good it does to have a relationship with God when he doesn't solve our problems, when we struggle with shameful feelings of unworthiness, when we are afraid and alone, the temple quietly reminds us that struggle, error, fear, and loneliness are the common lot of humankind. God, though not always seen, is always seeing—always making preparations for us, always sending messengers to show us a better way, always reaching a hand out toward us, bidding us homeward.

As we bring our questions and problems to the temple, and as we bring the temple into our lives, we learn the subtle art of stillness when life has become frantic with doing. Upon its paths we find the keys to movement when life has ground to a halt.

(4) Relationships—Connecting to Self, Others, and God

In recent years, psychology has discovered anew the importance of relationships for healthy human development. Current technologies let us actually see how a child's brain develops differently when the child is solidly and warmly attached to parents versus a child whose bonds are insecure. Our attachments to other human beings continue to affect our sense of identity and well-being throughout our lives. On average, securely attached children are more resilient, healthier, less fearful, more even-tempered, more self-disciplined, and eventually better parents than the insecurely attached.

Of particular interest to me, however, are those adults who, despite poor attachments in childhood, break this cycle and parent their own children differently. How do they learn to provide secure attachments to their children when they did not experience them? The means of change apparently lies in the power of stories. Parents who come to understand their own story, the place of their story in the larger stories of their families, the characters, plots, and alternative endings that could have been—these pioneering parents not only begin to reshape their lives, but they also attach more securely with their children, fundamentally changing the children's stories as well.[5] Instead of being disabled by old traumas, they find a plot line of growth.

In the temple, God tells us a story—our story. Telling stories is not just about imparting information. Stories are how we both understand and build relationships. God tells us the story of his love and care, his personal awareness of us even when the deceiver has come between us, and his plan to bring us close to him again if we so desire. Through stories, symbols, and actions, the Lord whispers in our ears of his love and purposes.

In a touching Old Testament story, we become privy to the relational ups and downs of Jacob, son of Isaac, son of Abraham. Jacob's early relationship with his brother is marred by mutual competition and even apparent deceit. Jacob flees for his life to his mother's distant family, where he takes four wives, sires many children, and acquires great wealth. But eventually God directs an older, wiser, more humble Jacob to return to his homeland after his long absence. En route, he learns that his estranged brother Esau is headed his way with a virtual army of four hundred in tow. Jacob fears. He sends gifts to appease his brother. He places his wives and children on the far side of an obstructing brook. His problems are not esoteric spiritual dilemmas. He has enemies to face, a family to protect, and a trial to his faith to surmount, for was it not God who sent him on this dangerous journey home? He pleads with God for help, saying,

> O God of my father Abraham, and God of my father Isaac, the Lord which saidst unto me, Return unto thy country, and to thy kindred, and I will deal well with thee:
>
> I am not worthy of the least of all the mercies, and of all the truth, which thou hast shewed unto thy servant; for with my staff I passed over this Jordan; and now I am become two bands.
>
> Deliver me, I pray thee, from the hand of my brother. (Genesis 32:9–11)

Jacob is desperate yet grounded in gratitude, faith, and humility. The rift created all those years ago no longer feels like all was his brother's fault. Will his apology and amends be too little too late to save his imperiled family from his brother's wrath? Will God come to his rescue or feed him up to the man whose blessing and birthright he took? Jacob, no longer interested in wrestling with his brother, now must wrestle with God instead for the desires of his heart. The scripture records:

> And Jacob was left alone; and there wrestled a man with him until the breaking of the day. . . . And [Jacob] said, I will not let thee go, except thou bless me. . . . And he said, Thy name shall be called no more Jacob, but Israel: for as a prince hast thou power with God and with men, and hast prevailed. . . . And Jacob called the name of the place Peniel [the

face of God]: for I have seen God face to face, and my life is preserved. (Genesis 32:24, 26, 28, 30)

We, like Jacob of old, must wrestle with the Lord in the deserts and swamplands of our lives for the blessings we need to keep our current enemies at bay, protect our current children, and preserve our current faith. The temple is not just about how to live in a palace in eternity; it is also about how to live in a tent here and now, camped among both friends and enemies. It is about our moments of personal encounter with God as we struggle to acquire the identity God gave to Jacob: the name of Israel. Israel is not a haphazard choice of a name for God's covenant people. According to the Bible Dictionary, the name suggests "one who prevails with God" or "Let God prevail." To be Israel is to wrestle with God through the dark night until we gain faith and power to claim his promises. It is to prevail upon God to name us anew, not symbolically, but by his own voice.

Questions relevant to relational aspects of the temple include

- With whom does this ordinance put me into a relationship?

  Aspects of myself, whether currently, in my past, or in my future?

  Family members?

  Other covenant people?

  People I've never met?

  People who have influenced my life, either for good or for evil?

  Men? Women?

  People in the future?

  People in the past?

  The adversary?

  The Father, Jesus Christ, or the Holy Ghost?

- What is the nature of each relationship and my role in it?

- What does the temple teach me about who I am, and how does it confer these identities?

- What might I learn in this part of the ordinance about how to strengthen my good relationships?

- What does the ordinance teach about what I might gain from a particular relationship?

- What does it teach about what I might contribute to or through this relationship?

- How might temple teachings help me heal relational difficulties I've had in the past?

- What positive attributes might I develop through relationships such as those the temple depicts?

- How does the Atonement of Jesus Christ affect my relationships?

- What might it feel like to be each person in the temple dramas—to assume their postures, gestures, and expressions? What part of me does each one represent?

Fluent

Christ is called both the Cornerstone and the Way—the foundation upon which we build and the path on which we walk. He escorts us on the journey to God. As we learn the language of the Lord's house, we feel more at home there. It can become more the house of healing God intends it to be, and we can become more the holy people God intends us to be. We can hear his voice more clearly. We reacquire our native tongue. We are "no more strangers and foreigners, but *fellowcitizens* with the saints, and of the household of God" (Ephesians 2:19; emphasis mine).

We can come to the temple's doors with more than our temple recommend; we can come with our body, our mind, our relationships, and our whole life of personal challenges and opportunities. We can come with our personal histories, our ancestries, our cultures, and our inherited proclivities toward righteousness or sin. Indeed, God invites us as a people to come to the temple with every name of every person who has helped shape the world and the families that in turn shape us.

The first way station on the temple journey is the baptistry, where we present ourselves before the Lord on behalf of our ancestors and humanity. There, God gives every person the opportunity to join the chosen lineage of the House of Israel. What new births can we too find in a font that rests on the backs of twelve oxen, representing the twelve sons of Israel, or Jacob, the man who wrestled with God?

There is in each of our lives right now something that calls us to the temple—to a journey of personal transformation, healing, or discovery. There is some enemy we fear, some wrong that needs righting, some question that puzzles us, some wound to be healed, some goal that needs clarifying, some obstacle to surmount, some attribute we long for, or some relationship to build. In the language of temple ritual and symbol, God can speak to all of us at once and still address individual hungers or needs. He expects us to learn enough of his language to formulate and ask our private questions to guide this tutoring process.

So consider: What promised homeland are you trying to reach? What covenant children are you trying to protect? In what promised blessing are you trying to preserve your faith? Who are you trying to become? What is the nature here, today, of your personal wrestle with God?

Healing Practice for Chapter Two: Learning the Language

- *Morning pages.* As described by Julia Cameron in her delightful book *The Artist's Way* (1992), morning pages involve simply filling up three handwritten pages (or the typed equivalent) every morning with whatever is floating around in one's head. This may include trivial worries, plans for the day's projects, personal feelings, or struggles . . . anything. They are not a journal and should not be shown to anyone or even reread unless there is a reason to. They are simply to keep the mind and the heart clear and integrated. They have become one of the most valuable tools in my spiritual and emotional life (although I don't always write them in the morning).

- *Dreams.* The temple has more in common with dreams than with textbooks. Coming to appreciate the language of dreams can help us become more conversant with both the temple's language and with our own inner worlds. Tony Crisp's *Dream Dictionary* (1990) is a good beginning place for entering the world of dreams. Unlike many such books, his is research based, not just imaginative. If not recorded when you first wake up, dreams will fade quickly, so if you don't regularly remember your dreams, put a pencil and paper by your bed and "program" yourself the night before to recall one. Set your alarm ten minutes earlier than you usually awaken, and your chances of being in the middle of a dream when you wake up improve.

  To work with a dream, draw a line down the middle of a page and record a dream on the left side. Then in the right column record impressions, memories, and associations you have to the various dream images. Look them up in the dictionary or talk to friends for further insights. Your dreams will often represent symbolically the unfinished business or unresolved issues you are struggling with. Asking yourself what problem a dream portrays and how you might solve it will help you benefit from the dream.

- **Prayer.** The kind of prayer I refer to has two characteristics. First, it is vocal. Second, it is gut-level honest. This type of prayer is most likely to move beyond the rote and open up a path to personal insight and change. I believe that God will tutor us in prayer if we ask and listen with a patient heart. It is our most important spiritual practice.

Additional questions to consider:

- God invites us to ask that we might receive. What are some specific questions you have about any of the gospel ordinances? If you don't have any questions, how might you come up with some?

- What three lessons have you learned about yourself lately that you don't want to lose? How might the ordinances of the gospel help you remember?

- What are five small changes you would like to make in your life? The desire for change is often the first step in personal transformation. Just write them down and let them register on your heart.

- What would need to happen for you to go to the temple—again, more often, or for the first time?

SECTION TWO

EXPERIENCES
WITH DESCENT

CHAPTER THREE

New Births

—————— ⬯⬯⬯ ——————

You and I, we live as part of an invisible web, a web we also help to weave. . . . If we learn to hear what is difficult to hear and see what is difficult to see—then we can grasp, better understand, hear and see the repetitions and coincidences in our family history, and our individual lives can become clearer.

—Anne Ancelin Schutzenberger[1]

The presence of the baptistry in the temple serves as a reminder that our own baptism is the first step of the spiritual journey, the first room of each new temple of the soul. The temple baptistry is rightfully located at a foundational level. It reminds us of the foundation upon which the temple of our soul rests: the foundation of a covenant relationship with God. In some ways this relationship both replaces and cements our previously foundational relationships of family, ancestry, and culture. Exploring those previous foundations can help us understand the influences that shape our worldview and sometime limit the choices we can imagine.

Joseph Smith described baptism for the dead as the "most glorious of all subjects belonging to the everlasting gospel" (Doctrine and Covenants 128:17). This is a superlative that arouses my curiosity. Of all the glorious subjects belonging to the gospel, why would this one command his attention? I can think of three reasons. First, baptism for the dead extends God's covenant promises back in time to reach those who are *dead*. It testifies of the infinite extent and eternal nature of his love and power to save—power not limited by earthly notions of "what's done is done." Second, baptism for the dead reminds the currently *living* of God's mercy to us. It reminds us that the spiritual rebirth symbolized in this ordinance must literally occur in our lives if we are to progress toward God. We must die and be born again as children of Christ. Finally, baptism for the dead brings the *yet unborn* within the scope of the covenant promises because those we are baptized for acquire godly promises for themselves and their *posterity*. Baptism for the dead thus secures to all who will claim it (the dead, the living, and the unborn) a rightful inheritance within God's covenant promises. It gives every person the opportunity to enter the family of Jesus Christ and the gateway to the temple, where he or she may become a rightful heir of all covenant blessings.

As we contemplate the baptismal font resting on the backs of twelve oxen, the room seems replete with the spirits of our kindred dead, on whose backs our lives also rest. In this room we participate in bringing new birth to ourselves, to our ancestors, and to all ancestors. That new life unfolds as we recognize and respond in new ways to sinful predispositions we have inherited (biologically or by learning) from our families and cultures. Exploring propensities to sin we learned from the unrighteous traditions of our fathers may help us interrupt the transmission of those propensities to future generations. A glorious subject indeed!

Every spiritual step we must take to find the passage to God is represented in ordinances: being born again, being nourished spiritually, having our sins remitted, being sanctified by the Holy Ghost, and many others. Baptism is an essential ordinance, just as being spiritually born again is an essential passage into the path of Life. For those already baptized, however, the temple baptistry is an optional room, so to speak. One could conceivably qualify for exaltation without ever performing baptisms vicariously for others. Some lessons of the temple baptistry may also be optional, but most embarking pilgrims can afford to consider some questions implied by the baptistry: What part of my genetic code, what learned predisposition to sin, what spiritually limiting cultural practice can die in me when I am immersed with the dead in a watery grave? What new birth can come to me as I offer new birth—one person at a time—to the families and cultures that bred me? In what ways does the officiator's claim of a commission from Jesus Christ reach out to find and claim me as well as the person I represent?

When I note that even young adolescents are welcome in the temple baptistry, I recall my own adolescent years. One of the first new cognitive abilities to mark the transition from childhood to adolescence is the development of a keen hypocrisy detector. Teens are quick to note and become incensed by the faults of their parents and other adults. As they begin to realize these former icons are really ordinary folks with the same weaknesses they have, it must strike a silent terror to the heart: How safe can I be if those I have so depended on in fact have feet of clay? But this is also the beginning of a new hope: If these great ones are fallible and flawed, then perhaps there is room in the kingdom for flawed and fallible me.

A burgeoning awareness of the weaknesses of our elders and progenitors is a disconcerting but valuable step in growing up. But it is also a wounding experience that robs us of a bit of our innocence and security. This growing-up process may continue for decades as we gradually diminish our parents' and forebears' emotional power to rule our lives, and we assert our own truths and agency. The baptistry can become a place of healing, where we grow into our more equal adult status of saviors on Mount Zion, even for those we have viewed as our saviors in the past.

Watery Graves

When it takes us months and years to accept and make peace with the death of a loved one, it is startling to realize how quickly death occurs. We move in only seconds from this world to the next and from one state of awareness to another. Baptism, a symbol of our death and rebirth, also takes only seconds—a few seconds for the old man or woman of sin to be laid in a watery grave and for the new creature in Christ to be brought forth. In this way, baptism is like the deaths we fear and fight. But such similarities only get us part of the way to understanding what this ordinance might mean. We must also look at the dissimilarities that teach us how God's ways are different from our ways. Baptism is a benevolent death, one that holds us safely in the arms of Jesus as he both lays us down and brings us forth in a new birth. It is neither violent nor unexpected, but chosen and sought after.

Nevertheless, it is a crucial death, and the truths it represents can include painful and frightening aspects. We easily forget deep change is not just about what we are trying to acquire but also what we must let go of. Perhaps the hardest part of change is not to specify what the change will entail, make a plan to enact it, weigh the costs and benefits of the change, or even maintain it. Perhaps the hardest part is to figure out what has to die. What will we *stop* doing as we *start* doing this something else? Who will we no longer be as we acquire this new identity? What will we need to give up permanently as our understanding of what is real changes? Will it be our identity as a child or a victim? Certain ways of fleeing our emotions or our responsibilities? Connections with people who sustain our old life? Old desires for vengeance, control, or status? Avoidance of real work or real closeness? What part of us will have to submit to the dissolution of a watery grave or a consuming fire in order to be reborn under a new parentage, with a new identity, new desires, and new bonds? Baptism—death and rebirth— helps us visualize and prepare for a radical reorientation of our life.

There is a saying, "Everybody wants to see Jesus, but nobody wants to die." While our goal is to see the face of God and live, it is still true on many levels that death is the first step of this journey home. When we speak to an eight-year-old or a new convert about baptism, we emphasize cleansing, washing away sins, and new beginnings. But the temple reminds the emerging spiritual adult that in one sense baptism is *always* for the dead—the dead in us as well as the dead who precede us. It is always about letting go of one life that we might lay claim to another. Mercifully, God promises the righteous death will be sweet (Doctrine and Covenants 42:46) and resurrection will be close at hand.

The Traditions of Fathers and Mothers

Beyond reminding us of our personal baptismal covenant, baptism for the dead is also its own experience. Every time we attend the temple, we attend it for a new person, and we are also a new person each time. In the baptistry, some of the people we represent may be parents or relatives, people we have known and who have directly influenced our lives. Others may be strangers whose names we have never heard but who have helped to shape the cultures that constrain our options and contour our desires. In one sense, each person's choices, victories, and sins reside in us. Ralph Waldo Emerson writes, "A man finds room in the few square inches of his face for the traits of all his ancestors; for the expression of all his history, and his wants."

Family and culture are both contexts for our self-definition. Often we don't see how much these contexts define or constrain us until we move to an unfamiliar place (whether a different country or just a new dorm room), marry into someone else's family (and begin to see the subtle and not-so-subtle differences in what they expect from a spouse, children, work, or the Church), or try to do something our family traditions don't model or encourage (such as undertake a new type of work, befriend a new type of person, or pursue a new type of risk). Many of our relationship challenges boil down to this disconnect between what we have come to expect of others based on our life experience and what they have come to expect based on theirs. The challenge of growing up includes changing untruthful or unhelpful familial and cultural patterns while still making room for appropriate, loving connections with our roots. The baptistry speaks to this challenge.

Nephi states, "For [God] gave commandment that all men must repent; for he showed unto *all* men that they were lost, because of the transgression of their parents" (2 Nephi 2: 21, italics mine). Even when we have been born in the covenant of gospel promise, redemption of some aspect of our ancestral lines may be called for. Nephi's upbringing in a promised land does not spare him the necessity of seeking a new one. Each of us is "taught somewhat in *all* the learning" of our families—both the faith-promoting and the false (1 Nephi 1:1; italics mine). In fact, throughout the Book of Mormon the traditions of the fathers can lead to either spiritual growth or spiritual destruction. Sometimes, like Nephi, we can afford to follow parental visions, patterning our lives in large measure after them. At other times, a tradition of father or mother must be left behind for our spiritual life to flourish.

We can learn from both constructive and unfortunate familial patterns as we shape our lives. We can also take comfort in knowing "the sins of the parents cannot be answered upon the heads of the children" (Moses 6:54); that is, neither we nor our children nor our parents will be held eternally responsible for anyone else's choices. When we become bound up with others' sins as either innocent victims or as unwitting recyclers of similar transgressions, the promise of salvation for the dead becomes our promise as well.

As we attempt to recognize and forsake these outworn patterns, our purpose is not to vilify or to blame.[2] Both our life choices and our parents' choices are complexly determined. Agency and premortal choices are certainly major factors in how we all behave, as are upbringing and genetics. Science currently estimates about half of our traits derive from our genes, and the other half are indelibly influenced by all the experiences of early life. There may be only a small percentage of our behavior we consciously and freely choose, as important as those choices are. What we learned as children is not necessarily what our parents intended to teach us, or even what we would learn as adults in the same situations. Yet these primitive lessons can permeate our lives, compromising our vision and options.

Only God can sort out issues of ultimate responsibility. Our task is to learn by our own experience good from evil so we may change, forgive, and come to Jesus to be healed and set free. Being baptized for the dead can powerfully remind us of these possibilities for new birth for us, for those who raised us, and for those we do our best to raise.

From Prison to Freedom

Spirit prison is the abode of the dead who are yet to be healed and freed by obedience to the laws and ordinances of the gospel. I suspect being in spirit prison literally limits where such people can go or with whom they can associate. But I wonder if spirit prison is not also symbolic of other kinds of spiritual bondage.

For example, what of the spirit prison of our ancestors' guilt and pain when viewing with eternal perspective the negative consequences of their behavior in our lives?

Or the spirit prison of being unable to fix what one has broken, unable to gather back all the repercussions of sins one has unleashed upon future generations and the world? Perhaps we help the dead to complete their repentance by our repentance: our acknowledgment of the ways their shortcomings reemerge in our choices, our resolve not to pass these on to yet another generation, and our commitment to restitution and renewal.

What of the prison to which we confine people, even dead people, by our judgments or blame over having suffered at their hands? This is a spirit prison from which we too may need freeing.

As we undertake the challenge of change and peacemaking to which the gospel invites us, we may find keys to "spirit prisons" of many kinds. The baptistry immerses us in this healing work.

Freedom has a double edge, of course. We don't want people running around free who would use their freedom to do harm. To those who may have suffered deeply as a result of the poor choices of others, the idea of setting such people free can feel dangerous. Importantly, God's plan ensures the eternal fate of the innocent is not determined by sinful tendencies inherited from others but by their own consciously chosen desires, intentions, and behavior (Alma 41:5–6; Doctrine and Covenants 88:109; Moses 6:54; Second Article of Faith). His plan further ensures that those who have injured others will not be set free until sincere repentance is completed or justice served.

Repentance and forgiveness help us override multigenerational predispositions to sin. People who succeed at such deep change seem to follow a path that acknowledges both justice and mercy. We can fall off the path on either side, which is what makes it a "strait" path (that is, a narrow path between two obstacles as opposed to a path in a straight line). We might move too quickly to mercy. We do this by ignoring our wounds or by over-blaming ourselves so we don't have to acknowledge the limitations or sins of people we still look to for safety or approval. Or we might insist on justice when mercy is called for. We do this by angrily insisting history be undone so we can somehow have the past we longed for—a past we imagine would have left us less afraid or more prepared than we ended up. Overreliance on either justice or mercy can keep us from finding the baptistry's promised new birth. The strait passage between them balances the demands of justice and the rights of mercy to help us claim our birthright as free and righteous children of God. How do we find this passage?

Establishing Truth: The Demands of Justice

Justice can feel harsh when we are the ones pleading for mercy, but justice is the truth-teller that exposes evil for what it is. Justice demands the innocent be fairly recompensed for their suffering. When we are the innocent who have been wronged, we can trust God to acknowledge all his children's losses and insist they be taken seriously. Justice calls for an accounting of what really happened, what debt is really due. Justice further requires we not assume responsibility for sins we have not committed, not pretend we could control decisions we could not control, and not ignore or excuse others' actions when they were deliberately hurtful or wrong-headed. It also expects us to take responsibility for *our* behavior and not rationalize our own moral failings and abdications of agency. Justice helps us to find a fair balance between our own contributions to problems and the contributions of others.

Allowing ourselves to acknowledge and feel the painful consequences of others' mistakes reinforces our efforts to avoid those mistakes. At the same time, restraining our tendency to anger and blame—although it requires giving up false hopes for perfect parents or a different past—keeps us focused on our personal responsibility for our own lives. Justice is simply about getting as close as we can to truth. It is about learning good from evil by our own experience.

Alma reminds us that within God's great plan, "mercy cannot rob justice" (Alma 42:25). This is also true in our personal lives. To forgive others in a merciful fashion is not to condone their sins or approve that which causes pain and dysfunction. Neither is it to imply they were right and we were wrong if that is not the case. The baptistry insists that some things do have to die (sin and evil).

Broadening Truth: The Privilege of Mercy

When we have acknowledged the demands of justice, we are also commanded to forgive. Like a creditor holding a bad note, we may not see how we have anything to gain if we forgive the debt. How will we get back what we lost if we simply forgive? How can this be fair?

In most cases, and certainly in the case of serious wrongdoing, those who have injured or robbed us are not in a position to restore what they have taken. They cannot make full restitution for our lost peace of mind, self-esteem, or sense of well-being. They cannot give us back lost trust, hope, or safety. They cannot restore our lost options or heal our worldview. So if the people who hurt us cannot restore these things to us, how can we ever get back what we lost?

This is where mercy comes in. I have come to believe mercy is primarily for our benefit, not just the benefit of the wrongdoer. In fact, the more we have been wronged, the more we deserve to forgive, for forgiving others is what gives us access to the storehouse of the Redeemer, from which all debts can be finally and fully repaid. As we grant mercy, we gain the right to reclaim our lost blessings from Jesus Christ himself. We can further allow him to reassure us of our infinite worth, our capacity (with his help) to heal, and our opportunity to also sin and repent without being eternally cast off. When we forgive others, Christ assumes their debt to us, and we can then look to him for the healing, peace, security, hope, trust, well-being, and self-image he alone can restore. He is willing to take this debt if we are willing to release the original debtor to him to deal with on his terms and with his infinite wisdom and perspective on all the factors involved in their choices. We allow Jesus to deal as he sees fit with those who owed us, for now the debt is between him and them alone. We get out of the middle.

Seen in this light, forgiving others their debts is not simply pretending nobody owes us, which would not be just. It is rather a process of turning to Christ for the things we have lost, rather than turning to those who cannot restore our losses anyway. It is a willingness to acknowledge that if Christ is willing to pay us back, then no one else owes anything. To be sure, we must be willing to see, receive, and accept as full payment the blessings God is willing to give us, and trust they will ultimately be as good as or better than what we had before. Sometimes we must extend credit to God that will not come due until after this life, but given the bounty of his offerings, we need not worry about being paid in full. In fact, under the law of Moses, things taken from another illegally were to be restored not only in full but also with a surplus before the offender's relationship with God could be restored (Leviticus 6:5). Surely God holds himself to at least as high a standard in his payment of debts to us on behalf of those who sin against us.

Mercy is easier to extend when our overall relationship with the offender has been good, when the offense is acknowledged and apologies rendered, or when we realize we have offended and yearn for forgiveness ourselves. But whether or not these conditions prevail, we can make our way to the peace of forgiving as we acknowledge our losses, turn the debt to the Redeemer, attend to our own repentance, and grow up in God. The baptistry reminds us new birth is the birthright of all God's children as they repent and exercise faith in Christ's Atonement.

Forgive and Remember

As we seek to forgive others, we might note that the notion of "forgive and forget" is not scripturally founded. In fact, doing baptisms for the dead is a way to help us *remember* our heritage, the influence of others on our lives, and the need we all have for new birth. True, God promises *he* will not remember sins we have repented of, but given his omniscience, I assume this does not mean he will literally forget them, but rather that he will cancel our debt for them. He does not require us to forget either, as if we could magically erase our history from our memory. He requires only that we stop dealing with those we've forgiven as if they still owed us, and that we respond to them with kindness and compassion.

God offers the repentance we need to not feel harrowed up with pain when we remember our sins or other people's sins against us, because we can also remember Christ's cleansing Atonement and healing gifts (Alma 36:19). The painful past is reworked into the story of our lives in new ways. God no longer relates to us as "sinners" whose sins define us, and he asks us to do the same. We can acknowledge what went wrong, see our choices for change, and move into the future with hope. It makes sense that we will always regret our sins and feel remorse for them, and that we will feel compassion for the suffering of the innocent victim, but we can also rejoice in God's incredible skill at turning bad choices and even horrible injuries into life-giving lessons and eventual blessings as we turn to him. Forgiving others or ourselves does not mean we forget a debt was ever incurred, but that we release the person from the debt, both literally and in our hearts, without continuing to act as if they owe it to us.

Forgiveness also requires acknowledgment of the good things in our relationships and in ourselves. Our goal is not simply to revisit all the pain in our lives, but to see the past more accurately and honestly. It requires, in essence, that we grow up. To forgive may also require us to stop letting other people continue to incur debts we know they cannot repay. We don't permit transgressions we are in a position to stop. We keep others from violating our boundaries, stealing our well-being, or forcing their viewpoints upon us unrighteously. Doing this in a respectful yet firm way takes confidence in the validity of our point of view. It requires humility, curiosity, and compassion. This can take a lifetime. We may need to forgive others seventy times seven not only because they offend us again and again, but also because we may need to make the choice to forgive repeatedly even when we think it is over and done. Being on this forgiving path is more important than how far we are down it.

Except in extreme cases of ongoing threat, it is not generally helpful to cut off contact with family members who have offended us. We grow most as we firmly but humbly claim our own viewpoints and choices even while acknowledging that others see things differently. However, in some cases we may need to limit contact at least for a time, take a break when we are flooded with disquieting feelings, or get outside support as we try to change our relationships. We can do these and still remember new birth can come to *us* when we cast off the past regardless of the choices of others who share that past. When I can accept my own capacity to truly change and be healed, I am no longer dependent on others to approve, agree, or change as well in order to validate me or set me free.

As previously stated, leading researchers who study attachments between children and parents propose that little influences a child's future more than the quality of early relationships with caregivers. Fortunately, they also find it is never too late to acquire at least many of the benefits of secure, healthy attachments even if those early relationships were difficult, we are adults, and our parents are gone.[3] This is a truth baptism for the dead affirms. Much healing can take place as we learn to *retell our life story* with both truthful justice and forgiving mercy, integrating our painful experiences into a more coherent, whole picture of who we are and may become. When we change our understanding of our story, old brain structures begin to die and new ones are born. We can help the brains and minds of our children develop differently as well, with new possibilities for security, strength, and peace. We are no longer constrained by the past in ways that keep us from seeing the present accurately. We can see what really is and respond to it from our highest values. New birth comes to us as well as to the dead.

Self-Forgiveness

Each of us is not only wounded by the choices of others, but we also wound others in our turn. As challenging as it can be to forgive others, sometimes we have more trouble forgiving ourselves.[4] When we deeply regret our past choices and want to take full responsibility for them, we may fear self-forgiveness is merely self-indulgence.

Self-forgiveness may require abandoning our illusions of self-sufficiency and instead finding true humility. Forgiving ourselves also requires giving up the illusions that (1) we can be perfect, (2) being perfect would protect us or others from all harm, (3) we cannot tolerate our weakness or past sin and still be happy, or (4) we cannot tolerate legitimately painful emotions and still feel safe or trusting. Forgiving ourselves means being willing to *receive*, not just believe in, the Atonement of Christ. It means accepting Christ's Atonement as sufficient, even when part of us would prefer he somehow turn back the clock and make us innocent and whole again.

We all take strengths as well as weaknesses from our history, however. It is easy to assume we would be far better people if we had only been raised by far better parents in far better cultures, but this may only be partially true. We might have an easier time with obedience but a harder time with compassion, an easier time with work but a harder time with humility, or an easier time with relationships but a harder time with courage. And compassion, humility, and courage may be exactly what we personally came here to learn.

Sometimes it helps our self-compassion to consider what the world would be like if everyone in it were exactly like us. When one woman considered this question, she realized there would be no murders, no kidnapping, no violence, no war, and no drug abuse or alcoholism because she was not prone to any of these problems. There would be no need for locks on doors or police or criminal courts, for she had never stolen or been arrested. Children would be nurtured, bills would be paid, and the homeless would be fed, for these were her chosen lifestyles. There would still be problems, but overall, people would be considerate and friendly, devoted, and fair. Although we tend to minimize such moral accomplishments, they are amazing in the perspective of the larger world in which we live. Many of us are better than we know.

Letting Go

Forgiving self or others can require giving up old beliefs about the world that have made us feel safe in the past but that limit us now.

Examples of such beliefs are

- I have to get mad or no one will take me seriously.
- She's trying to embarrass me—she must know I'll make a fool of myself if I try that.
- I'm so tired—other people should see they ask too much of me.

Giving up such beliefs can be a scary prospect, for we put these beliefs together precisely to help us cope with or avoid pain and uncertainty. If we change our beliefs, won't we be endangered again?

When I feel unforgiving or resentful, a good friend reminds me to ask myself what I am still hoping for that I am not ready to give up. For example, to forgive I must let go of my innocent belief that the world is fair. I must release the illusory hope of changing the past so as to get the perfect love or protection I did not get. I must give up the false hope that others will give me what I need without my having to risk asking for it and being turned down. I must give up the childhood desire of being provided for without work or risk of failure on my part. I must accept that in this life I will not be perfectly understood or unconditionally accepted. And I must face and acknowledge I too am flawed.

Rationally we know these things, but some childlike part of us may still cling to them as one clings to a life raft on a stormy sea, even while the Savior is extending his hand to pull us to a more enduring safety. Our tightly held beliefs that we cannot face that fear, we can only be that kind of person, or we cannot tolerate that kind of disappointment may be doomed if we are to receive new life. More dying and rebirth.

Other examples of such self-limiting beliefs include

- I need someone to take care of me to be happy.
- I cannot afford to be dependent on others.
- I must not disappoint people I care about.
- I cannot tolerate being disappointed.
- I have to have a decision right now or I'm wasting time.
- I cannot make a decision before I know all the facts.
- People won't like me unless I impress them, so I had better keep talking.
- People won't like me if they get to know me, so I had better keep quiet.
- If people won't do what you want, getting angry will change them.
- If people won't do what you want, making them feel guilty will change them.
- I have to be better than others to be respected.
- I have to be unthreatening or I'll be attacked.
- I have to obey perfectly, or it doesn't count.

- Obedience is too difficult so I shouldn't even try.
- Pain will cause me too much suffering, so I must find a way to avoid getting hurt.
- Pain will cause me too much suffering, so I must find a way not to feel.

Repentance is defined by the Bible Dictionary as "a fresh view about God, about oneself, and about the world." Participating in baptisms for the dead can reinforce this fresh view and strengthen our determination to die to limiting beliefs and behaviors learned from others. We can come up out of the waters in which we are baptized for another with one less of our own dysfunctional beliefs in tow and grasp Christ's saving hand.

Raising the Dead

The Doctrine and Covenants description of baptism for the dead specifies, "the baptismal font was instituted as a similitude of the grave, and was commanded to be in a place underneath where the living are wont to assemble." It further states that all who are baptized are "immersed in the water *and come forth out of the water* . . . in the likeness of the resurrection of the dead in coming forth out of their graves" (Doctrine and Covenants 128:12–13; italics mine). Baptism is not just about dying but also about resurrection. That resurrection promise is extended through Christ to all of Adam's posterity. Through it we are both re-begotten (re-fathered) and reborn (re-mothered) in Christ:

> And now, because of the covenant which ye have made ye shall be called the children of Christ, his sons, and his daughters; for behold, this day he hath spiritually *begotten* you; for ye say that your hearts are changed through faith on his name; therefore, ye are *born* of him and have become his sons and his daughters. (Mosiah 5:7; italics mine)

With this new birth, our old familial lines are no longer all-defining. We are reborn as children of Christ. Only as our ancestors accept a similar process will they and we be reconnected in eternal families with new cultures and new patterns of living. When we relinquish our need for our caregivers to be bigger than life and accept Jesus as the only parent worthy of our worship, our relationships can begin to heal.

Baptism for the dead is a powerful reminder of the combined power of human repentance and Christ's Atonement to break intergenerational cycles of sin, potentially changing both our kindred dead and ourselves into new creatures, new creations, in the process. We do not have to remain as we have lived thus far. Our ancestors do not have to remain as they have lived. Even death cannot stop Christ's power to redeem and to change us. We can all find new birth within the parentage of Jesus Christ.

Seeing new options does not mean following them will be easy. Sometimes we will fail, and that can hurt. Then others will get to offer us the forgiveness we seek to extend. They will get to learn from our mistakes and try to avoid them and use our lives as the context of their own bittersweet experience with good and evil. Some of those people will be our children, grandchildren, students, ward members, clients, or friends. Our failings will be part of our legacy and gift to them, which God will work together for their good if they will let him—just as he can do for us. Their failings will be part of their gift to us as well, helping us to be humble and softhearted. We need not be unduly ashamed of any of these weaknesses, even if we must struggle with some of them as long as we live, if we try with a true, honest heart to keep our covenants.

Born to See

I especially like the moment when I come up out of the baptismal water and open my eyes. The darkness of my watery grave is broken. New light breaks upon my soul. I rub the blurriness away, and the miracle of sight is mine as if for the first time. The light God offers me feels tangible, new, and good.

Jesus once encountered a man born blind. Other people standing around posed the interesting question, "Who sinned, this man or his parents, that he was born blind?" "Neither," the Savior answered, and he simply anointed the man's eyes and healed him. The blind man greatly rejoiced in his new sight and in his healer (John 9:1–7).

Modern medicine has occasionally been able to restore sight to someone born blind, only to discover the new sight does him or her little good. The person continues to depend on touch and sound to navigate in a world of disorganized visual stimuli that only confuses. It is not easy to figure out how to let our old ways of getting around die, even when new light is available. Learning to see in new ways is not as easy as it sounds.

The story of the blind man also makes clear that casting blame is a tricky matter and largely irrelevant to our purposes of gaining new sight, new freedom, new faith. Is it our parents' fault we seem to have certain moral handicaps or personal weaknesses? Is it our fault, due to some unremembered sin from a past existence, some deep and irredeemable flaw? Or is the assignment of blame simply less important than acknowledging our blindness and bringing it to the Lord, however we acquired it? As we take in the light of his laws and love, rejoicing in our Healer and in his healing power, we begin to let our blind ways of operating in the world die. We learn to live instead as one who sees. This story captures some of these essential lessons of the baptistry while foreshadowing the healing work of the next temple rooms encountered on the journey of the soul.

HEALING PRACTICE FOR CHAPTER THREE: NEW BIRTHS

- *Writing your story.* Writing a personal history, especially of your early years, is a valuable but daunting project. If you are willing to take the time to write out your personal history, begin by writing it for yourself so you will feel free to tell it as you see it without trying to sanitize it for others. You will learn more. Later, you can decide what you want to keep in your official history and what is for your eyes only.

  Or begin by putting down the left column of one or two sheets of paper the major periods into which you would divide your life, and the most influential events under each period. In a middle column, note what you concluded or learned about yourself, God, and relationships in each period. In the right column, make note of situations in which these early templates may color your interpretations or restrict your choices today.

- *Healing splits.* Although sometimes necessary to our sanity or safety, family splits (where some family members do not see or speak to each other or simply have little contact) almost always put a stop to constructive processing of family dynamics and their effect on our lives. Where possible, begin working to heal family splits in whatever way feels manageable to you. This may involve contacting a family member you are distanced from. You might start with a letter, a phone call, or a personal visit. Where feasible, repairing family splits can often help all to heal.

  If the split is long-standing or results from any kind of abuse or trauma to you, proceed cautiously. Plan any contact carefully with a trusted friend or a therapist, take small steps at a time, and safeguard your physical and emotional well-being. There is usually little to be gained by confronting abusers with the abuse unless it is ongoing and escapable.[5]

- *Family gatherings.* If feasible, plan a family reunion or other positive, enjoyable family event that brings extended families together. These build both bonds and positive experiences and help us see more clearly the patterns in our family dynamics. Even if you think you've had enough of such things, children will benefit from opportunities to watch the extended "family dance" and to see how they fit into the larger family patterns.

- *Interviews.* Make a list of questions you would like more information about from various family members. Formally or informally interview them, asking any questions you don't know the answers to about their early years, their perceptions, their struggles, their strengths, and their beliefs. If you notice that you feel uncomfortable bringing up certain topics, consider the possibility that family secrets are operating or that this is a topic that has not been processed well in your family. Proceed carefully, but see if you can find a way to air these issues. If not, you may still be able to learn a lot about family patterns with simple, straightforward questions or by approaching family members who are more distant from you and perhaps more objective. Here are some questions to get you thinking:

  - What was it like where you lived as a child?
  - What do you remember about school? Church? Friends? Siblings?
  - When were you the happiest as a child?
  - What do you regret as you look back on your life?
  - What has brought you the most satisfaction in your life?
  - What are the values that are most important to you?
  - How did they become so important?
  - What do you think are your strengths as a person?
  - How did you get along with (y)our father?
  - What was (y)our mother like with you?
  - What was hard about growing up in (y)our family?
  - What events in your childhood had the biggest impact on you?
  - What did you conclude from those events?

- *Genealogy with a twist.* Family therapists use genograms to help identify patterns within families, and genograms can help us see patterns that cross generations in our own family history.[6] This looks like a big project, but it can usually be done quite quickly. The genogram starts with a basic two- to four-generation family tree, drawn on a large piece of paper, with the oldest generation across the top and the younger generations branching off of it (see diagram on p. 53). Boxes represent men and circles represent women. A horizontal line represents a marriage, and slashes are drawn through it to represent divorce. Multiple horizontal lines can represent multiple spouses. Children are drawn off the line representing their parents. Crossing out a box or circle represents a death.

Indicate where family members cut each other off socially or where other major separations within the family occurred by drawing a line separating those family members. Indicate tension between certain family members with a squiggly line drawn between them. Show strong bonds between family members with a dark or double line. Other indications of identity, connection, or difficulty can also be created according to the details of your family.

Add details to capture the essence of various relationships and challenges within the family. Note the ages of children when deaths, divorces, or major traumas occurred. Note the birth order of siblings and the kind of expectations the family seemed to have for children of your same sex or birth order. Look for the family patterns that may influence you and your family by asking questions such as

- What was it like for you when you were the same age as either parent at a particularly stressful time in his or her life?

- What is it like for you when your children are at the same age you were at a particularly stressful time in your life?

- Who gets cut off in your family and who is typically close? Is there any pattern to these relationships?

- Are there patterns in how, for example, youngest boys or middle girls or oldest children are expected to behave, or in how they actually choose to live?

- What happens to marriages in this family, and why?

- What are the lessons here about abuse, addiction, economic hardships, or other failures?

- What are the lessons here about how women can be, how men can be, how single people can be, how old people can be, how sick people can be, or how rebellious people can be?

- What family secrets may be influencing the way the family interacts? Are particular family secrets showing up across generations?

- What issues seem to come up repeatedly, either down a generational line or across several families of the same generation? How are these especially loaded issues influencing your relationships today?

- What cultural influences and beliefs can you imagine having influenced each of the oldest ancestors on your genogram? Are they still operating in the family today? How do you imagine those cultural influences originating? How would you choose to modify or continue them?

- What unfinished business from past generations has been passed on to new generations (such as, how to deal with conflict, how to cope with loss, how to accept differences, how to manage shame, or how to be separate or independent without being cut off)?

- How do you feel as you look at each of these issues?

- What does this exercise teach you about yourself, your family, your children, and your future?

- How would you "abridge" or summarize this record of your ancestors, and what do you take out of it for your own life?

- *If the entire world were your mirror.* Reflect on what the world would be like if everyone in it were like you. List both the problems the world would have and the advantages it would have over the world we actually live in. Ask the Lord specifically in prayer to help you see your own good qualities and to receive the love that is available to you, just as you ask him to help you see your sins and repent. If you have trouble seeing yourself accurately, ask people you trust and who know you well to help you with this task, and consider their ideas carefully.

- *Ancestral waters.* When you are ready to do so, arrange to do baptisms for the dead for your ancestors or others who might symbolize them to you. As you participate in this ordinance, consciously release your ancestors and your culture from your anger or judgments, and consciously extend forgiveness to yourself and to them. Pray for spiritual insight into the meaning of this ordinance for you.

- *Dying and new birth.* As you renew the covenants of baptism when you partake of the sacrament, contemplate releasing your ancestors and yourself from the spiritual bondage of old patterns and behaviors, allowing these to die that new life may be born in you, in them, and in your children through the Atonement of Christ. Consciously nurture yourself with the spiritual food of the teachings and mercy of the Savior.

Diagram: Sample Genogram

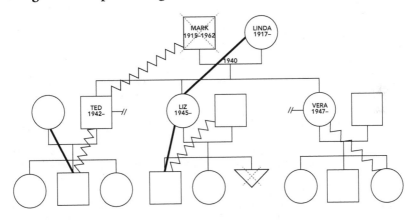

This genogram summarizes a lot of information about this family. We see that Mark and Linda were married in 1940. They have three children, Ted, born in 1942, Liz, born in 1945, and Vera, born in 1947. The heavy solid lines suggest strong ties, and the zigzag lines suggest conflict. In this family, conflict is common between fathers and sons; strong ties are common between mothers and sons. There is a cutoff between siblings Ted and Vera.

A more complex genogram would show additional details of the family story. For example, Vera and Liz are both alcoholics, and both began serious drinking after a serious loss. For Vera, that loss was the cutoff with her brother, which occurred when she was seventeen, the same age her mother was when she lost her father. Liz began drinking heavily after a miscarriage.

Mark's death had serious repercussions for each of his children. Ted's marriage hit serious problems when Ted's son was the age Ted was when his father died. Liz's daughter and son cut off their relationship when the daughter was the age Liz was when her father died, which is also when Liz cut off her relationship with her brother, Ted. Vera's conflict with her youngest daughter, in the same sibling position as herself, began when that daughter was almost the same age as Vera when her father died.

To summarize: When repetitive patterns emerge across generations, there is a higher probability of those patterns repeating in some way in current generations. Recognizing those patterns increases our chances of understanding and changing them.

CHAPTER FOUR

CLAIMING
THIS BODY

———— ⌘ ————

Their sleeping dust was to be restored unto its perfect frame, bone to his bone, and the sinews and the flesh upon them, the spirit and the body to be united never again to be divided, that they might receive a fulness of joy. . . . For the dead had looked upon the long absence of their spirits from their bodies as a bondage.

—DOCTRINE AND COVENANTS 138:17, 50

As we continue the journey of new life beyond the new birth of baptism, we grow under the watchful parenting of Jesus Christ. In this world of challenge and struggle, we also learn quickly that the sins of past generations are not the only ones that affect us. We are also bloodied by our own sins and by the sins of the generation we live in. While these emotional and physical injuries are an unavoidable aspect of gaining experience in this world of good and evil, they leave us, like the traveler in Jesus's tale of the good Samaritan, naked and bleeding by the side of the road. Let's visit this story once more:

> A certain man went down from Jerusalem to Jericho, and fell among thieves, which stripped him of his raiment, and wounded him, and departed, leaving him half dead. . . .
>
> But a certain Samaritan, as he journeyed, came where he was: and when he saw him, he had compassion on him,
>
> And went to him, and bound up his wounds, pouring in oil and wine, and set him on his own beast, and brought him to an inn, and took care of him. (Luke 10:30, 33–34)

Many of us come to the temple as to the traveler's inn: stripped and wounded by our encounters with the spiritual thieves of this fallen world. Our wounds too call for washing, anointing, and binding up. We need a place to rest, to regain perspective, and to rebuild trust in God's restorative

55

power. The initiatory rooms introduce us to a healing refuge, inviting us back into our skin again. Here, we gain promises about turning wounds into sacred scars—marks that attest we have met the enemy and been wounded, but that God's power to heal is greater than the power of the devil to destroy. We are reminded of who we are when our injuries have left us amnesic to our true identity. We are initiated into spiritual adulthood, and we prepare for adult spiritual powers for parenting, leadership, warfare, and work. Whereas we have been as one who is half dead, we are restored to the sacred gift of living embodiment.

Ordinances in general and the ordinances of the initiatory rooms in particular remind us of the great blessing of having a body, even a wounded body. We will consider here some of the ways our wounds may prompt us to ignore or distance ourselves from our flesh, the consequences of which include inability to receive a fulness of joy. We will explore then our need for healing and reintegration of mind and body, including the symbolism of various parts of the body as they relate to our psychological well-being. Finally we will briefly visit other uses of the symbolism of washing and anointing in scriptures, and how they take us toward the passage to God.

Ordinances of Embodiment

Gaining a body is crucial to our mortal experience. The story of the wounded man and the good Samaritan reminds us that life happens to our body, not just to our personalities or ideas. Likewise, gospel ordinances can bring healing to us at a level below words, somewhere in our cells. As an example, think about all the ways your body is engaged in taking the sacrament. Your eyes open as the faint smell of bread announces your turn to receive. In the stillness, your hand reaches out to take the handle of the metal tray. Movements flow effortlessly, your body responding to unverbalized intentions: choose, eat, pass. Your mouth perceives the subtleties of taste and texture. Your chest registers movement on some inner lining. Your mind creates images and ideas to ponder. Your stomach mobilizes to digest the food and send its nourishment into your cells.

When I was a child, I never understood why the sacrament bread tasted so much better than any other. I got my mother to search out the exact brand of bread the priests laid out. I broke it into pieces to see if that act released some culinary secret. I wondered if the priestly prayer produced a certain magic. Only as an adult have I discovered the abundance I experience rests neither in the quantity I consume nor in the excellence of the loaf, but in my whole-soul *presence* at the Lord's table, where I eat in loving remembrance of the body of Christ. Presence, this full-bodied awareness of the present moment's experience, epitomizes what it means to fully claim the body. Many of us spend relatively little time in this mindful state.

One would be hard-pressed to find a religion that pays more theological homage to the body than ours. We often fail to grasp how unusual our position is among world religions that almost universally eschew the body as something to be transcended—a remnant of our fallen condition that will be ultimately, gratefully escaped. Many spiritual seekers deliberately try to flee the body through altered states of consciousness or to subdue its "downward" pull through self-flagellating discipline. In contrast, ask any Latter-day Saint why we are on earth, and the answer will likely include, "to get a body"—a body we believe God intends us to keep through eternity.

Of course, in our day-to-day living, Latter-day Saints are as prone as others to act as if the body were more of a nuisance than a holy blessing. We often ignore the body's needs, distrust its appetites and passions, feel ashamed of its appearance, and disregard its teachings. We may blame the body for our sinful dispositions, feel imprisoned by its desires, or imagine that if we could only rid ourselves of our fleshly inclinations our spirits could truly soar. The healing journey invites us to claim joyfully the sacred gift of embodiment and to learn to trust the plan in which our highest aspiration is that *in our flesh* we shall both see and emulate the body of God (Job 19:26). A brief review of LDS teachings about the body reminds us

- "The Father has a body of flesh and bones as tangible as man's; the Son also" (Doctrine and Covenants 130:22).

- We are literally created in the image of the body of God (Moses 6:9).

- The embodiment of Jesus was essential to his saving mission (Alma 7:10–13).

- He commands his disciples to remember his living body, his physical presence in their midst, by partaking of the sacrament (JST Mark 14:21).

- We believe in the literal, physical resurrection of not only Jesus Christ but also every human being (Alma 40:23).

- Ordinances must be enacted in the body for salvation, and the bodiless dead depend on the embodied living to vicariously perform them (Doctrine and Covenants 128:8).

- Spirit and body inseparably connected constitute the soul, the true temple of God, of which our glorious temple buildings are but paltry representations (Doctrine and Covenants 93:33, 1 Corinthians 6:19–20).

- Rather than seeking to escape the body, we view embodiment as essential to spiritual progression (Doctrine and Covenants 88:28–33; 67–8).

- So important is the body that virtually every one of us will be better off for having come to earth, no matter what our course or choices in life, simply because we will forever after be embodied (Abraham 3:26; Doctrine and Covenants 76:42–3).

The greatest of all gifts, the gift of eternal life, is to live embodied forever, in the holy presence of the body of our Maker.

The body, then, is our nature, our gift, our freedom, our tutor, our holy edifice, and our eternal home. Embodying gospel ordinances helps us experience these sweet perspectives.

Absence of Body

In contrast, according to the prophetic vision of President Joseph F. Smith, even the righteous dead look upon the absence of the body as a type of bondage. Only the reuniting of spirit and body, never again to be divided, permits a fulness of joy (see Doctrine and Covenants 138:17, 50, quoted at the start of this chapter). But the dead are not the only ones who suffer from being cut off from their bodies. The trials and abuses of mortality incline us, the living, as well to cut off awareness of our body, which is to cut us off from ourselves, leaving us in that joyless state of bondage President Smith envisioned among the dead. We do this in many ways:

- Bodies that are diseased or in pain can feel more like a burden than a blessing, and a common response is anger or resistance.

- Trauma or shock may cause us to emotionally distance or dissociate from our body in an effort to escape pain, fear, or shame.

- The mirror of public opinion can rob us of the joy of experiencing who we are as we instead attend to the burden of how we appear. When we yield to society's treatment of the body as simply an object for approval or disapproval, we may attend more to what we look like to others than what we feel like to ourselves.

- We may further objectify and distance the body in preparation for work or war, which seem to require ignoring the body's natural states of fatigue, boredom, revulsion, or fear.

- In infancy, parents coax us into embodiment with safe, loving touch, helping us begin the task of organizing the body's complex sensations and abilities. Inadequately touched babies have difficulty staying "in" their bodies, and sometimes they simply die. Even as adults, a consistent lack of comforting contact with others can lead us to tune out our bodies.

- The numbing overstimulation of media bombardment or a frenetic world can distract us from the simple pleasures of nature, the subtleties of gentle feelings, and the love in still, small voices experienced when body and spirit are in tune with life.

- When we don't trust the appetites or passions of our body, we may assume the body is our enemy, making us an enemy to ourselves.

- When numbing and dissociation become chronic, they cut us off from joy, creativity, wholeness, and other people.[1] Perhaps even more tragic, defenses that cut us off from our body also interfere with the emotional growth and spiritual lessons we became embodied to learn. The repeated laying on of loving hands in our infancy invites us to receive our spirit into each part of our earthly tabernacle. Gospel ordinances draw on that imagery again to invite us into our body, dedicating it to rightful purposes and setting us on a path of living resurrection.

Indicators of Disembodying

Of course, if we are accustomed to acting as if our body's real purpose were merely to carry our head around, we may not even realize how thoroughly we ignore and distrust our physical and emotional feelings. Wondering about the status of your own embodiment? Think about the following:

- Forgetting to eat until we are starving, rest until we are exhausted, or exercise before we atrophy may be ways of pretending we are not embodied at all, we are "above" such petty concerns, or we should not have to be responsible for taking care of ourselves.

- Addictions to drugs, alcohol, sleep, shopping, cleaning, work, food, sex, abstinence, perfectionism, or even small habitual movements or gestures may all have a component of avoiding the soul's legitimate physical and emotional needs or messages, leading us to crave addictive substitutes instead.

- Uncertainty about who we are or what we want may stem from a lack of awareness of what we feel, physically and emotionally. When cut off from our physical selves, we lose touch with our deepest desires, joys, and creativity.

- When we rarely cry, avoid people who are emotional, or pride ourselves on objectivity or intellectual insight, we may risk becoming disembodied observers rather than full participants in our own lives.

- When we find ourselves feeling emotional for no apparent reason or feeling flat and unemotional recalling traumatic events in our past, we may be dissociating from our body. Trauma can split the mind, body, and emotions so they seem to operate independently, prohibiting the integration that accelerates healing.

- Excessive exercise or avoiding exercise, eating compulsively or rigidly avoiding food, craving sex or having sexual anorexia— all can be ways to avoid body awareness. Physical discipline and lawful pleasure in reasonable balance are essential to healthy embodiment.

- When we dislike or distrust our body and become preoccupied with its flaws and imperfections, it is difficult to value ourselves. Every mortal body is flawed. These flaws, like all weakness, are part of, not impediments to, our mortal mission.

The more we integrate our body's realities, the more whole and free we can become. Gospel ordinances, performed in the body, invite us back into our truest, fullest selves.

A Healing Inn

The healing journey eventually calls upon us to reclaim our embodiment with all our feelings and capacities and to make the marriage of spirit and body an eternal union. Embodiment is not simply a mortal confinement that lasts only until death or dissociation. Like a good Samaritan, Jesus invites us to the temple as to an inn of sanctuary where our spiritual and psychic wounds are cleansed, anointed, and dressed. He says to the Nephites whose less righteous comrades had been destroyed prior to his coming, "O all ye that are spared because ye were more righteous than they, will ye not now return unto me, and repent of your sins, and be converted, that I may heal you?" (3 Nephi 9:13). Conversion, repentance, and healing are intertwined.

To claim more fully the earthly body, despite its wounded state, we need healing balm, safe and respectful touch, soothing words, and appropriate boundaries. Whether or not we are *cured*, we can *heal* in the ways that matter most as we await our promised resurrection.

Traditional stories and ceremonies from other cultures underscore these principles and point us toward temple truths. The haunting story of "The Handless Maiden" reiterates both our need for cleansing and the value of our feelings as instruments of healing. See if any of the themes in this old, traditional story sound familiar. The story begins as a young woman's father unwittingly agrees to sell her to the devil in exchange for wealth. When the devil comes to take her, she has washed and dressed in white, and in that state the devil has no power to claim her. In frustration, he dirties her hands and forbids her to wash, but her weeping cleanses her hands with tears, freeing her again from his grasp. Enraged, he commands that her hands be cut off, but as her tears wash her bloody wrists, she is again cleansed and freed, this time completely, from the devil's power. Her honest feelings become her portal to healing power. With white dressings on her maimed arms, she sets off on a journey of initiation into spiritual power, eventually regaining her lost limbs and much more.[2]

In like manner, we are bloodied as a result of both others' and our own bad bargains with the devil. The gospel provides the cleansing and healing ointment to change us from victims into spiritual initiates who willingly claim embodiment—even wounded embodiment—as we set off on a journey of learning and empowerment. Healing involves first cleansing mind and body from blood-guiltiness and submitting to the potentially instructive qualities of suffering. Of course, we can suffer without learning anything, but it is difficult to learn the things that matter most without suffering. The gospel helps us turn our suffering into not only compassion for others but also a new and deeper level of seeing and knowing what is real, true, and good.

In ancient Egyptian temples, the ceremony of Opening of the Mouth initiated the "seven gateways" of the eyes, ears, nose, and mouth into fitting vehicles of sensory perception. "The Opening of the Mouth, in which the organs of the senses are first washed and then anointed, is to make the organs efficient conveyors to a clear and active brain, by which the mind evaluates, structures, and comprehends reality."[3] Exploring the symbolic value of our various limbs and organs can help us appreciate both ways we may need healing, and ways we can more fully receive the wondrous gifts of the body.

The Body's Symbols

Eyes

Dreams use symbols to communicate deep truths. In Crisp's analysis of one thousand therapy patients' dreams, the most commonly occurring word was *see*, which occurred 1077 times.[4] Our eyes allow us to get our bearings in the world and to discern what world we are even in.

> And the Lord spake unto Enoch, and said unto him: Anoint thine eyes with clay, and wash them, and thou shalt see. And he did so. . . . And he beheld also things which were not visible to the natural eye; and from thenceforth came the saying abroad in the land: A seer hath the Lord raised up unto his people. (Moses 6:35–36)

Enoch's eyes, anointed and washed, could see things accurately, including truths others would not perceive. This is the gift of being a Seer with a capital *S*: one who Sees God and invisible worlds and testifies of that vision with special authority. But each of us has the capacity through God's blessings to be "lowercase" seers, those who see for our own lives what the natural eye does not perceive. To open our eyes is to understand what is real from an eternal perspective and to live in that reality, which we cannot do when our eyes are not yet opened. Seeing is not only an act of physical capacity; it is also an act of faith and volition. When we have been hurt or deceived, we may struggle to "see" clearly.

Becoming a seer requires not limiting ourselves to what people have taught us is acceptable to see. After spending years in Western schools far from his home and family in Africa, Patrice Malidoma Somé miraculously finds his way home. Tutored in the ways of the West, he is moody, troubled, and far removed from the maturing wisdom of his culture. His elders conclude he must undergo the traditional initiation into manhood of his tribe, even though he is far past puberty. During Somé's initiation into these mysteries, he is given the task of learning to "see" a tree. He sits for hours staring at his assigned tree, but he is incapable of seeing whatever it is the elders are waiting for him to see. One of them remarks:

> Whatever he learned in the school of the white man must be hurting his ability to push through the veil. Something they did to him is telling him not to see this tree. But why would they do that? You cannot teach

a child to conspire against himself. What kind of teacher would teach something like that? Surely the white man didn't do that to him. Can it be that the white man's power can be experienced only if he first buries the truth? How can a person have knowledge if he can't see?[5]

After a second torturous day of sitting, contemplating, struggling, and humbling himself, Somé eventually learns to "push through the veil" (his words) to "see" the tree. As he does so, he experiences the tree in a new and unanticipated way. Akin to Lehi, Somé not only sees the tree, but he partakes of it, becomes enraptured with it, and is enveloped in its nurturing presence, which he experiences as a pure, profound, and immeasurable love. He later comments:

> There is more to sight than just physical seeing. I began to understand that human sight creates its own obstacles, stops seeing where the general consensus says it should. . . . There does, however, come a time when one must learn to move between the two ways of "seeing" reality in order to become a whole person.[6]

I may never "see" a tree as Somé did, but his experience has opened my eyes to the possibility of living in a world in which nature surrounds me with love, abundance, and life. I see trees differently because Somé did, and I long for eyes to see more of the hidden evidences of God's goodness in the created world. Even more, I long for eyes to see the hidden life in other people. I want my eyes to be open to the truths others broadcast with only their hearts, while their mouths say other things. When I pray for eyes to see God's children as he sees them, I see them with my heart as well as my retinas, and my understanding is enlarged. Nothing changes my interactions with others more quickly than this perspective.

Consider: Where are you on the road to empowerment as a seer—one who sees truths that are hidden from ordinary sight? Do you willingly linger over the visions open to you each day?

Ears

The ears as dream symbols often represent more subtle communications with God or other people than hearing alone.[7] Hearing includes ability to discern the unspoken message in the spoken word, and the truths and falsehoods in our internal dialogues. When our ears are blocked up with harsh words that echo in our self-appraisals, we struggle to perceive the subtleties of the still, small voice of God. Voices that feel loud, sarcastic, shaming, forceful, mocking, or disrespectful do not come from God. God does not yell, belittle, or deride. Voices in my head that tell me to give up, feel hopeless, or indulge in self-hatred are not divine.

Most of us would never talk to someone else as critically as we talk to ourselves. We know a constant barrage of shaming criticism is not constructive. Yet we may fear if we don't constantly berate ourselves, then we will not improve, even though this internal barrage serves mostly to make us despair. God is the bringer of hope, not despair. When Satan tempts us with jealousy, pride, or fear, and then with self-hatred for even being tempted as if those temptations were really our truest character, it is good to remember that being tempted is simply part of being human. Gently, smilingly turning our heart back to truth is more effective at thwarting the accuser's voice than self-castigation.

Consider: What do you hear when you tune your ears to the calmest voice within?

Nose

The nose in dream language represents our sense of curiosity, our intuition, and our capacity for enjoyment. While cameras can duplicate the functions of an eye and tape recorders the functions of an ear, the sense of smell is so finely articulated as to virtually defy mechanical replication. Symbolically, damage to our sense of smell suggests trouble making fine discriminations, enjoying legitimate physical pleasures, or nurturing ourselves. Giving ourselves permission to "smell" includes delighting in the radiance of the evening sky, the bounties of good food, or the warmth of a friendly touch.

Consider: Do you give yourself permission to enjoy all of these sensations within their proper bounds? If not, at what cost does this happen?

Mouth

We know what we know as we put words to our truths. A common dream image involves trying to speak or scream and being unable to utter a sound, which is usually a terrifying experience. Many things interfere with our ability to articulate. We may not have learned the names for some of our feelings or wishes. We may occasionally experience needs so primitive as to be prelingual, returning us for a time to the raw experience of a child without language. We may struggle to really understand what we have never named or put into a story. We may have been ignored or ridiculed for our words and so stifle them.

What we cannot say with words, we often "say" by developing symptoms or by acting badly. We might shoplift in an effort to communicate feelings of deprivation for which we have no words. We may suddenly get sleepy when we unconsciously don't want to listen but don't want to say so. We may "forget" to take out the garbage when we feel overloaded but hate asking for help. We may unconsciously touch our once-broken collarbone whenever we feel threatened. Words give form to our feelings so we can better recognize and meet our true needs and negotiate fairly with others.

Joseph Smith taught that faith is the power to create by words instead of physical action.[8] The power God extends to his greatest prophets is the right to speak and have their words fulfilled (see, for example, Moses 6:34; Moses 1:25; Doctrine and Covenants 21:5). We practice these powers when we pray, teach, bless another through our faith, or persevere to express a spiritual insight accurately. Words are a potent tool of creation.

We learn Adam and Eve were taught to speak and write by the spirit, and their language conveyed truth with such power that it may be termed a Priesthood (Moses 6:6–7). In contrast, Enoch and Moses each worried that his ability with words was inadequate to his prophetic call. Moroni complained to God that his own language was weak compared to the Adamic tongue of the brother of Jared, a language "mighty even as thou art, unto the overpowering of man to read" (Ether 12:24). True, our degenerate language can obscure meaning as well as reveal it. Still, God invites us to articulate our desires, to ask that we may receive (Matthew 7:7; Doctrine and Covenants 4:7). When God asks us to make records, exhort, teach, or sing praises to him, our words not only reflect but also create new realities.

Saying or writing what we feel helps us process those feelings and move them along in ways that merely thinking about them does not, and spoken language and written language are even processed differently by the brain. Vocal prayer can have a different emotional quality and power than prayers we only think. Prayer is an act of bringing something into being through articulating our faith, intentions, and desires and committing to them.

Consider: What realities are you creating with your words? What worlds do you make as you speak? To what actions do you commit with your petitions to God?

Neck

The neck is a weak point in the body, easily damaged yet crucial. It represents the connection between the mind and the rest of the body with all its emotions, appetites, and sensations. Without a firm connection between mind and body, we lose vitality. We can't tell what we want or feel.

As discussed previously, some people who exude calm and objectivity have really become watchers instead of livers of their lives, distanced from their feelings and physical power. When the head rules the body with an iron fist, the body's blessings are lost on us. When the body rules the head, psychological chaos may ensue. When the neck holds the head in proper relationship to the whole, life takes on richness and completeness.

People who have been injured or neglected are often especially adept at living out of their heads, unwilling to admit painful feelings into awareness. They may run on autopilot, unconsciously acting out feelings and beliefs the mind will not acknowledge. Or they may experience some types of physical sensation but not others (for example, pain but not pleasure). Reestablishing a loving connection between mind and body requires a kind of atonement, or "at-one-ment," between the body and the spirit. The Atonement of Christ not only brings us back into the presence of God; it also brings us back into our own presence. "Presence of mind" requires presence of body. The neck represents this healthy unity.

Consider: When emotions or physical sensations seem to take on a life of their own or turn off altogether, how can you feel safe enough to reconnect body and mind so as to reintegrate your life?

Bones

The skeletal framework supports the physical body and keeps us from collapsing into a pile of mush. Bones are not only strong but also enduring: we don't find much dinosaur skin around, or many primordial eyes or ears. We find bones. In many cultures, bones represent the indestructible life force within us, our spiritual essence. Marrow is the source of blood cells that fight off infection and death. Bones and marrow, like winter trees that still bud in the spring, represent the latent source of life within something that appears dead.

Bony joints like knuckles, elbows, and knees become symbolic of an ordering process joining part to part to allow movement and stability. Like other ordering principles, joints provide a fundamental structure to the body so all the parts may operate in harmony. "The whole creation is to be understood as a synthesis: the imposing of inner order on outer material," says Clement of Alexandria.[9] The ordering of the body, the ordering of the universe, and the ordering of the house of the soul—all proceed according to a structured inner pattern that joins parts in meaningful relationship to each other. The temple borrows from these concepts to teach us in many ways.

Christ's body of flesh and bone represents to his disciples the physical reality of the resurrection (Luke 24:39). His bones, never broken, symbolize the eternal nature of the spirit, indestructible as bone. We too have an everlasting part of ourselves to be discovered and named anew in mortality, even though it is the most fundamental part of who we are.

Bones and flesh ordered together form the foundation for human life, while the dividing asunder of joints and marrow implies a complete disorganization of physical existence. Apparently God places himself in both of these processes. We do not always consider the ways God's truth can completely disorient us and cut us asunder. God does not mince words when he says his word is like a two-edged sword, both protecting us and piercing us to the bone. When God is at work in our lives, we may at times feel like nothing but dry bones scattered on the desert floor, shattered, broken, cut off from our parts. At such times it is crucial to remember God can and will make even dry, lifeless bones live (Ezekiel 4). But sometimes our old order has to come apart before we can be reorganized and reordered in God's image. God can be in such death as well as in life.

In American Indian myth, the Wolf Woman gathers the bones of a dead wolf and assembles them into a skeleton, which she sings over until the flesh and sinew re-forms and the creature springs back to life.[10] In another story, a maiden restores the life of her father by singing over a single vertebra until his body re-forms around it.[11] We see similar imagery in the Old Testament story of Ezekiel's vision of a valley full of bones. In language with a poetry we can easily miss, he is commanded to "prophesy upon these bones, and say unto them, O ye dry bones, hear the word of the Lord" (Ezekiel 37:4).

> So I prophesied as I was commanded: and as I prophesied, there was a noise, and behold a shaking, and the bones came together, bone to his bone.
>
> And when I beheld, lo, the sinews and the flesh came up upon them, and the skin covered them above: but there was no breath in them.
>
> Then said he unto me, Prophesy unto the wind, prophesy, son of man, and say to the wind, Thus saith the Lord God; Come from the four winds, O breath, and breathe upon these slain, that they may live.
>
> So I prophesied as he commanded me, and the breath came into them, and they lived, and stood up upon their feet, an exceeding great army.
>
> Then he said unto me, Son of man, these bones are the whole house of Israel: behold, they say, Our bones are dried, and our hope is lost: we are cut off from our parts.

Therefore prophesy and say unto them, Thus saith the Lord God; Behold, O my people, I will open your graves, and cause you to come up out of your graves, and bring you into the land of Israel. (Ezekiel 37:7–12)

In each story, the bones provide the basis upon which the body is reconstructed, but the spirit—the song, the breath, the wind, the words of the prophet—is the animating force that makes the bones live. Bones represent either death and lost hope or potential and new birth, depending on the covenant relationship we hold with God. Bones are tokens of our immutable connection with heaven through our spirit that will never die. They remind us that even though alienation from God, self, and others is inevitable here, we are not permanently cut off.

To summarize, bones represent at a psychic level our deep, instinctual self, the bone-deep knowledge we bring with us from the premortal world of who we are and what we want. Our yearning for God, our longing for spiritual knowledge, our deep resonance with truth all reside, as it were, in our bones. When destructive forces of coercion and deception bruise our flesh and sicken us, God can restore and heal us, as from the marrow in our bones. He wants to restore to us our premortal, bone-level understanding of who we are and can be.

Consider: What are the vital patterns that order your life to reflect your deepest truths (for example, meditation, gratitude, morning prayer to prioritize your day, journal writing, attending church)? What aspects of your eternal identity are most crucial for you to magnify here?

Internal Organs

Our physical internal organs have messages for us about our spiritual and emotional life. The gastrointestinal system, lungs, heart, and other vital organs nourish, oxygenate, and cleanse the body. When these vital systems fail to perform properly, food and air do not nourish us and our own internal toxins poison us. Symbolically, the internal organs represent our ability to both nourish our souls and rid ourselves of the soul-equivalent of toxins and wastes.

Children and those in delicate health may need simple, mild, easily digestible foods in order to grow. When we are children in the gospel, we may also do well to stick to the basics and give ourselves time to grow before taking on coarser spiritual challenges. As we mature, we need to ingest the spiritual roughage of honest questions and real-life problems. We benefit from the oat bran and raw celery of life and not just spiritual white bread.

This principle can be taken too far, of course. Oat bran may be good for us, but without many other nutrients vital to our growth and health, we will not thrive. This is true spiritually as well.

I once had a client who grew up in a large family under conditions of appalling neglect. As a child, she would go to the barn and gnaw on insect-infested horse feed to fill her empty stomach, ruining her teeth and overloading her internal organs. As an adult, when she is stressed or afraid, she continues to crave the raw, unmilled grains that provided what nourishment she could get as a child. So it is with many wounded children who may continue to crave the familiar taste of abusive relationships, inappropriate touch, or brutalizing shame, even when there is healthier food available. When unhealthy relationships also provide our only comfort or security, their pull can be confusingly strong. None of us flourish when our systems are overwhelmed with the toxins and infestations of neglect, violence, or apostasy. We need solid, nourishing spiritual food to sustain the spirit's life.

Consider: Do you generously nourish (not just feed) your physical and spiritual life, or are you constantly running on empty? Do you have a proper balance of roughage and nutrition, or do you lean to either horse feed or over-processed bread? Do you easily release the wastes from your life, or are you constipated with past hurts or fears and afraid to let anything go? Do you think about your experience so as to learn from it, or rush it through undigested?

Shoulders, Arms, and Hands

In dreams, shoulders symbolically and physically carry the weight of our burdens. People whose life burdens feel too heavy often take that stress into their shoulder and back muscles. John Sarno, MD, a professor and attending physician of clinical rehabilitation medicine, asserts that the modern epidemic of shoulder pain, back pain, neck pain, carpal tunnel syndrome, migraine headaches, and so on, reflects our stress-laden lifestyles and the anger, resentment, and internal conflict we feel (but don't consciously acknowledge) about all the pressure we are under.[12] Even when X-rays suggest herniated disks or other structural abnormalities, his research suggests that hidden resentment and anger are often the real culprits, producing the muscle spasms that lead to pain. Many people he treats can resolve their pain by acknowledging the underlying feelings, which their pain both expresses and distracts them from facing head on. His work is a powerful reminder of the inviolate oneness of mind and body.

A friend of mine is an extraordinarily talented musician who developed such severe pain in his arms and hands that he had to stop playing. He consciously agonized over this loss. But as he considered Sarno's hypothesis, he decided he might be harboring some hidden resentment about the things his music had taken away from him (despite all it had given him). As he allowed himself to see and feel these resentments, work through them, and develop a different relationship to his gift, the pain stopped and his talent once again soared.

Arms and hands represent our ability to act—to love, to give, to receive, to create, and to defend. Hands are the part of the body we dream of most often.[13] Ultimately, the entire body supports the creative life work of the hands—molding, writing, drawing, building, cooking, holding, diapering, cleaning, touching, healing, sewing, hammering, typing, or music-making.

I remember a client whose hands went numb when she talked of certain early experiences. Exploration revealed the rage she felt toward those who had hurt her as a child. She also came to acknowledge the extreme powerlessness she had felt, and her enormous fear of hurting others with her rage. The numbness in her hands both expressed her sense of powerlessness and constrained the dangerous impulses she feared. Another individual's left arm became achy and almost lifeless when she was overwhelmed by sadness. When she allowed herself to feel the true feelings she had buried, the pain subsided and her arm functioned freely again. Another client felt little in most of his body except a vague sense of exhaustion. Only his stiff shoulder muscles cried out loudly enough to signal how overwhelmed he felt with the excessive load of all his tasks. Symptoms like these speak to our relationship with our power, our creativity, and our life work.

Consider: What do your shoulders, arms, and hands teach you about your relationship to your mission, talents, labors, and creative life?

Reproductive Organs

In addition to procreation, sexuality represents our larger capacity to create, engender life, and bear fruit of many kinds. We create by engaging deeply with one another's ideas, experiences, or dreams. Our creativity and thus our identity are inexorably interwoven with our sexuality. We create out of who we are.

Healthy sexuality, like health in any appetite, allows us to fully enjoy enriching sexual experiences and calmly avoid spiritually dangerous ones. Finding joy in our sexuality and its literal or symbolic fruits is not always easy, however. Nor is it always easy to sort out or even discuss the ways sexuality becomes painful, addictive, or unfulfilling. Understanding our sexuality involves noticing what we want and don't want, how we know, and what it means to us, rather than pretending sexual arousal happens or doesn't happen entirely beyond our control.

We use sexuality to express a variety of thoughts and feelings, such as what we idealize, what we hope for, and what we want to get rid of. When we feel inexplicably infatuated or attracted to someone, we may be drawn to physical or personality characteristics that remind us of something we value but do not acknowledge in ourselves, or that symbolize some quality we wish for but lack. Far better to consider what such an attraction might communicate to us than to assume an illicit attraction should be acted on.

Some people have been deeply injured in sexuality, either by their own sexual failures or sins or by the sexual misconduct of others (or both). Sex seems to cause them more pain than it is worth. Under such circumstances, one resists seeing sexuality as a spiritual gift. Such individuals may tend to black-and-white thinking: sexual self-denial means self-worth and sexual expression means worthlessness. Or sexual enjoyment means victory and sexual disinterest means failure. Or sexual satisfaction is either all-important or not worth worrying about at all. Sexual health is a process of finding a healthy path through these extremes, and learning from both appropriate sexual expression and gentle but firm sexual discipline.

Consider: What does your sexuality suggest about your willingness to be vulnerable and connected? To be disciplined and independent? How might your sexuality reflect your other creative dreams and efforts?

Hips, Legs, and Feet

Through our legs and feet, we feel our connection to the world, the ground of our current reality. We use our lower limbs to navigate in the world and move forward on our mortal journey with balance and grace. Figuratively, our legs represent our sense of purpose, independence, and motion, our willingness to be the movers of our own life.

I am fascinated by the differences in people's styles of running and walking. I notice differences in gait, posture, rhythm, and intensity. I notice also that my feelings change when I change how I walk. I experience the world differently when I stretch or shorten my gait, loosen or tighten my hips, relax or straighten my shoulders, or try to copy the gait of someone else.

I need a balance of strength and flexibility in my walk through life. When I lack the literal and figurative muscle to accomplish my goals, I can persistently build strength through pushing myself a little more to do hard things. When I overdo and then want to give up, I can remember to practice within my real range of ability. When I lack sufficient adaptability and range of motion to adjust to my circumstances, I can practice stretching and flexibility instead of relying on rigid muscle power alone. If a poor sense of balance makes it hard to recover from missteps, I can practice physical and spiritual grace and centering.

Consider: As you examine your physical gait, strength, and flexibility, do you see any correlates with your psychological style?

Skin

Skin is our outermost boundary, the demarcation between what is us and what is not us. Human skin is both more sensitive and less protected than the scaled, furred, shelled, or feathered exteriors of animals. Clothing enhances the protective power of our skin.

God gave Adam and Eve coats of skin to protect and cover them when they were cast out of the Garden of Eden (Genesis 3:21), perhaps symbolic of the physical body itself that gives us power over Satan as long as we stay fully present in it. Skin and clothing also symbolize our need for spiritual sensitivity and spiritual protection so we can stay "in our skin" until our missions in life are completed. Our skin will not always succeed in warding off invaders, yet we are protected nonetheless. Through our obedience to our covenants and our acceptance of the saving Atonement of Christ, destructive powers will not prevail against us forever.

The symbolism of skin also reminds us of our need to establish appropriate boundaries in relationships. In popular psychological jargon, "boundaries" refer to limits on how much others influence our thoughts, feelings, behavior, and identity. Weak boundaries leave us "thin-skinned," easily hurt, offended, influenced, and confused. We have trouble holding on to our beliefs when opposed. We let others take advantage of us, get closer than we are comfortable, or manipulate us to do what they want. We give in too easily because we are afraid of conflict or abandonment. We become confused, annoyed, even resentful when others do not think, feel, or act as we do.

In contrast, fear may cause us to create overly rigid boundaries, like thick armor that limits movement and flexibility. We may become angry and combative if opposed, inwardly fearful that we are powerless to protect our psychological space. We may refuse to allow others to get close or resist feeling vulnerable in relationships. We have trouble with compromise and negotiation. We become inflexible and defensive, as if we were living in armor instead of skin.

Healthy skin and appropriate clothing symbolize appropriate, flexible boundaries that allow us to sense the world without being overwhelmed by it. Healthy boundaries allow us to calmly say, even when others disagree: "I can do this but not that." "I would enjoy 'a' or 'b' but not 'c.'" "I believe in this principle." "I want to pursue that goal." "I see reality this way." "I feel this way." "I claim my ability to perceive what is true and respond to it from my highest values." Healthy boundaries also allow us to say, "What do you think? How do you see it? What would you like? How could we work this out?" without feeling swamped or invaded by the answers we receive. Boundaries strengthen an identity grounded in what we want, feel, believe, choose, and value.

Consider: Do you need to strengthen or loosen your personal boundaries? In what ways?

Clothed and Named

As we continue the journey of new life beyond the new birth of baptism, we open our hearts and souls to receive the Holy Ghost. We are nourished and soothed by the Comforter. We walk in his light. He welcomes us into God's kingdom. We receive his testifying witness. We are healed, protected, and sanctified through his gifts. We shine. Our bodies, created in the image of God, become tabernacles of the Spirit.

Olive oil was used in the ancient world for many pragmatic purposes, including food, medicine, ointment for wounds, and soap. It was used as a soothing gesture to welcome guests or receive new infants, as fuel in lamps for light in the dark, and even as a cosmetic to make the skin shine. We see all of these uses reflected in the influences of the Holy Ghost listed in the listed in the preceding paragraph. Anointing with oil thus became a symbol of pouring the influence of the Holy Ghost upon a person. Kings, priests, and prophets were anointed as a sign of their being consecrated to God and filled with the Spirit to perform their roles. *Messiah* means "the Anointed," or perhaps more accurately, "covered with oil." The Messiah, Christ, was completely covered or filled with the Spirit, which was poured down upon him by God himself, not just symbolically but in fact. By proper authority, we too can be blessed that we might be filled with God's spirit—not just influenced or healed or fed or enlightened or confirmed—but *filled* with its constant companionship. Oil can be used symbolically for all these purposes.

God is not just about making us whole, but holy. We are to become priests and kings and prophets, to receive our anointing call. We all emerge from the temple as the Lord's anointed ones, prepared to stand at the door of the tabernacle, where God promises to meet us:

> And Aaron and his sons thou shalt bring unto the door of the tabernacle of the congregation, and shalt wash them with water.
>
> And thou shalt take the garments, and put upon Aaron the coat [tunic], and the robe of the ephod, and the ephod [embroidered waistcoat with shoulder pieces on which were engraved the names of the twelve tribes of Israel], and the breastplate, and gird him with the curious [skillfully woven] girdle [tie] of the ephod:
>
> And thou shalt put the mitre [turban] upon his head, and put the holy crown upon the mitre.
>
> Then shalt thou take the anointing oil, and pour it upon his head, and anoint him.
>
> And thou shalt bring his sons, and put coats upon them . . . and the priest's office shall be theirs for a perpetual statute: and thou shalt consecrate Aaron and his sons. (Exodus 29:4–9; information from Bible Dictionary added in brackets)
>
> [There] shall be a continual burnt offering throughout your generations at the door of the tabernacle of the congregation [also translated as "the tent where God and his people meet"] before the Lord: where I will meet you, to speak there unto thee.
>
> And there I will meet with the children of Israel, and the tabernacle shall be sanctified by my glory. . . .
>
> I will sanctify also both Aaron and his sons, to minister to me in the priest's office.
>
> And I will dwell among the children of Israel, and will be their God. (Exodus 29:42–45; Bible Dictionary; bracketed information added)

These preparations symbolically fit Aaron's sons to enter the Holy Place as priests, and fit Aaron to cross the veil into the Holy of Holies, where the throne of God was kept. In the apocryphal Gospel of Bartholomew,[14] Mary, the mother of Christ, was given a similar opportunity. She describes her experience in the temple at the annunciation: "I was washed and anointed and wiped off and clothed in a garment by one who hailed me as a 'blessed vessel,' took me by the right hand and took me through the veil." As Aaron's priestly anointing takes him to the door of the tabernacle and Mary's angelic ministrations take her through the veil, so we prepare to take the next steps toward God at the door of his holy abode.

When body and spirit are cleansed and anointed, we more fully claim and willingly dedicate each part of our embodiment to him. We hold sacred the boundaries with which our spiritual nakedness is clothed. We receive the salutations that proclaim our eternal identity. We prepare as priests and priestesses to meet with the Lord. We embrace this embodiment as we learn to see spiritual dimensions to life that others do not, claim our voice and speak our truths, and rejoice in the appetites and passions that, properly bounded, do not set us apart from God but rather co-identify us with him.

The story of the good Samaritan concludes:

> And on the morrow when he [the good Samaritan] departed, he took out two pence, and gave them to the host, and said unto him, Take care of him; and whatsoever thou spendest more, when I come again, I will repay thee. (Luke 10:35)

The Savior has not only brought us to his healing house, but he has also fully and personally paid the price for our healing care. In Gethsemane he willingly offered "whatsoever" it cost to save us. Because of his healing ministry, we can afford to be in our bodies more fully now, and we can look forward to having them for eternity—consecrated and prepared by him for all our priestly duties and parental opportunities.

We have previously noted the idea others have expressed that the Church is not a museum for saints but a hospital for sinners. How grateful I am for the healing inn of the temple. It teaches us the importance of recovering our embodiment and invites us to stop walking in the redundant and truncated circles of woundedness and fear. We can learn to see and work through old feelings that were once too painful to stick around for. We can learn to be present in our life. We can be prepared to go down with our whole soul into the chaos of cosmic creativity through which the earth itself and all life upon it come forth.

HEALING PRACTICE FOR CHAPTER FOUR: CLAIMING MY FLESH

Many of us have learned to divide thoughts and feelings as a way of managing painful experiences. We learn to tune out awareness of our body, which carries emotion, and stay focused instead on insights, thoughts, ideas, and a constant barrage of internal dialogue. We think about life more than experiencing it, leaving us feeling detached from ourselves and from others. The exercises below help us heal this internal split and learn from our fleshly tutor. The first four are especially appropriate to introduce us to the body and help us practice being more comfortable in our flesh. They focus on healing the split between thought and experienced feelings.

- *Relaxation and mindfulness.* First and foremost, in the stress-filled world we live in, everyone needs to learn and practice the skills of relaxation, just to enhance the quality of life and decrease its toxicity. Practice whatever form of deliberate relaxation and mindfulness is familiar to you, or get familiar with one. Consider deliberate muscle relaxation, deep breathing, yoga, breath meditation, and positive imagery. If you are not familiar with any of these techniques, take a class or get a book and practice the exercises in it until you are skilled at it.

- *Reading avoidance.*[15] Make a decision to not read anything (that's right, *anything*) for at least three days (a week is even better). Push yourself to engage in alternative activities that are more actively embodying, such as

gardening	painting	needlework	sports
cleaning	crafts	puzzles	car repair
woodworking	sewing	cooking	raking leaves
making repairs	playing games	singing	other?

  Why? Because reading can be a kind of addiction, cutting us off from the natural world and distracting our restless mind from genuine reflection and aliveness. While reading is a wonderful skill, it can interfere with the development of other skills of conscious living. If you are a computer junkie, you may wish to try a similar period of fasting from computers, or anything else that fills large chunks of your day.

- *Get physical.* Engage in activities that unite the mind and the body, and be aware of that connection as you do them. As you engage in the activity, move back and forth between conscious awareness of your body and just losing yourself in the pleasure of the experience. Try

  - Exercising or walking to music, tuning your rhythm to the music

  - Dancing, with or without a partner, embodying the emotions the music stirs in you

  - Any kind of artwork that requires the hands and the eye to work together

- Playing musical instruments with feeling and motion

- Moving furniture to make a room more appealing, feeling your muscles enact your eye's design.

- Planting and weeding to create a garden with an artistic blend of color and shape

- Martial arts or sports, done with consciousness and attention to movement, feelings, and how they are embodied

- Yoga or meditation, with specific attention to the processes of deliberate relaxation and increased awareness and presence

- *Chop-chop.* The mind and body crave a certain amount of relatively mindless, repetitive activity like chopping, brushing, digging, sorting, sewing, weeding, or sawing. Many people today have lost touch with these natural life rhythms. Getting into a rhythm frees the creativity of the mind to work at a different level on problems and goals, as well as being soothing to the spirit. One friend of mine discovered walking around her yard mindlessly picking up after her two large dogs was actually good for her creative side. She lovingly refers to this as "dog-poop therapy." Other friends prefer quilting therapy, painting therapy, tile-setting therapy, or gardening therapy as times to reflect and relax.

- *Exercise.* Walk, swim, bike, work out—find something to get yourself moving in regular rhythms on an almost daily basis. Find a friend to do these things with if that makes the activity more likely to happen, but at least occasionally do them alone so you can feel yourself doing them and experience the world they connect you with.

As we become more aware of our embodiment, we begin to notice how we "do" certain emotions, how we give form and shape to our self-image, how the body responds to the world and articulates how and where we hurt, struggle, or desire. Memories and reactions to them are stored in the body as well as in the mind, and whether or not we are aware of it, we shape and move our body to both express and create our worldview. As we attune to our body, we can learn more about who we have been, and begin to imagine alternative forms, shapes, and movements to embody a different worldview if we desire to change.

CHAPTER FIVE

THE CREATOR'S CHILD

One does not discover new lands without consenting to lose sight of the shore for a very long time.

—ANDRÉ GIDE[1]

When the world we inhabit feels flat or barren, the baptistry invites us to consider if we have reached the limits of how far our ancestors' worldview can take us. Perhaps it is time to set sail for a new promised land, oriented to a different longitude and sustained by a different ecology—even if others tell us we'll drop off the edge if we try. To begin this brave journey, we show up at the temple doors to obtain our errand from the Lord. We strip off familiar defenses and comfortable addictions to don new identities and come alive in the world. Healing blessings and protections welcome us into our flesh. God offers to heal our blindness, and everything starts to look different. We begin to see.

So what does God show to those who have eyes to see? He shows them his creations.

> And [God] called upon our father Adam by his own voice, saying: I am God; I made the world, and men before they were in the flesh. (Moses 6:51)

> And when the Lord had said these words, he showed unto the brother of Jared all the inhabitants of the earth which had been, and also all that would be; and he withheld them not from his sight, even unto the ends of the earth. (Ether 3:25)

> And God spake unto Moses, saying . . . behold, thou art my son; wherefore look, and I will show thee the workmanship of mine hands. . . . Moses looked, and beheld the world upon which he was created . . . and the ends thereof, and all the children of men which are, and which were created. (Moses 1:3–4, 8)

Thus I, Abraham, talked with the Lord, face to face, as one man talketh with another; and he told me of the works which his hands had made; And he said unto me: My son, my son (and his hand was stretched out), behold I will show you all these. And he put his hand upon mine eyes, and I saw those things which his hands had made, which were many; and they multiplied before mine eyes, and I could not see the end thereof. (Abraham 3:11–12)

And now, after the many testimonies which have been given of him, this is the testimony, last of all, which we give of him: That he lives! For we saw him, even on the right hand of God; and we heard the voice bearing record that he is the Only Begotten of the Father— That by him, and through him, and of him, the worlds are and were created, and the inhabitants thereof are begotten sons and daughters unto God. (Doctrine and Covenants 76:22–24)

As we consider the Creation, we first begin to see ourselves and our potential more clearly. Second, our trust in God's goodness and power deepens. Third, we begin to imagine what it would be like to become more like our Father, whose ability to bring new life out of chaos and confusion is endless.

First: Seeing Ourselves and Our Potential More Clearly

In showing us his creative work, God shows us both who we have been and who we may become. If we are created in his image, then we are created to create. We are not just children watching an adult sew a dress or drive a car while being told, "Don't touch. You're too little." God puts us in the driver's seat and lets us fashion our own lives. Amid his endless works, we also have a work to do, both here and in eternity (Moses 1:5–6). We may not know a lot about what heaven will be like, but we do know we will not spend it passively playing harps and endlessly repeating "Hallelujah." If we become like God, then apparently we will live in a state of perpetual, exuberant creativity.

That we come to mortality with premortal lessons in creativity embedded in our souls is suggested by Elder Bruce R. McConkie: "In Christ's creation of this earth he was assisted by Michael and other noble and great spirits."[2] Scriptural references and prophets throughout the ages add "our glorious Mother Eve, with many of her faithful daughters" to the list of "noble and great ones who were chosen in the beginning" (Doctrine and Covenants 138:38–9, 55). The creation story stirs our memory of our eternal identity. The perspective we gain by contemplating God's creations is crucial to our understanding of who we are, why we are here, and the purposes of our personal creation. The story of the Creation, the Fall, and the Atonement is not just another story in the scriptures; it is *the* story—our story. This story begins long before we were born, and extends into eternity. It helps raise our eyes from the sidewalk we are fixated on to contemplate from loftier peaks who we are and where God is trying to take us. This mountaintop perspective is the one offered us in the mountain of the Lord's house, encouraging us to observe, plan, intervene, and evaluate our lives.

Second: Trusting God More Deeply

Seeing his astounding creative capacities, our trust in the Lord begins to become as expansive as his handiwork. From the beginning, Adam and Eve found joy—even in their fallen state—as they grasped the astounding truth that God had prepared all things necessary to (a) turn them loose to create and (b) redeem the messes they would inevitably make in the process (Moses 5:9–11). They taught these promises to their children (Moses 5:12). Satan always presents a different view of things, insisting God is not involved in these processes or that redemption is either impossible or insufficient, and from the beginning, people have believed him (Moses 5:13). Whom we choose to believe becomes our god. If we believe what God places before us, then he becomes our God, and we become his people. If we believe the versions of reality described by Satan or by mortals, they become the object of our worship and the influence behind our decisions.

Satan shouts in our ears about the inevitability of our failure, the futility of trying when we are so weak, the silliness of trusting a God who lets bad things happen, the flimsiness of the evidence that God can truly make us happy. God speaks to us of forgiveness, love, and a land of promises fulfilled (another way to translate "promised land") to which he will bring the faithful. Whom do we choose to believe? It seems obvious in theory to bet on God as my only hope for lasting joy. But in the practical living of my life, it astounds me how readily I forget who I am dealing with—the Creator of all I see. I ignore what God says is real and trust instead my own puny vision or Satan's insistent babble.

So God speaks to me of his creations. As I witness the processes and outcomes of his creativity, everything testifies I can afford to believe and trust him. My heart and mind quiet. I see love of variety, abundance, beauty, order, and vastness, and I am filled with awe as I compare his vision with my limited perspective. I see the evidences all around me of his power, wisdom, and goodness. I become as one who sees—even in the sights commonly available to everyone—things others do not always see.

Recently I asked a friend how he deals with disappointment. He wrote back:

> It is hard to let go of resentments and disappointments. Yet the alternative is so completely stupid, it's ridiculous! Who, in their right mind would not believe and trust a being who has created millions of earths and billions of people, and glorified just as many—and over a selfish resentment? That really is the stupid side talking.
>
> For me, it's as if I am standing in a room of my making with all the things I love: travel, cars, airplanes, strength, beauty, adventure, fun, laughter, fulfillment, and friends. It's my ideal, everything I love and want to experience and have in this mortal life. But on the other side of the room there is a simple wooden door with nice trim, maybe a little plain, and an average, well-used knob. When I open that door, I realize it goes to God's room, and I have to choose whether to trust him and believe him. When I look in his room, I don't see any of the things in my room! That surprises, shocks, and even scares me a little bit because I know my things will make me happy. Will his? So I stand there with Jesus at the door, and I get to choose. Do I leave all my things behind me and let him take me in his arms and follow him, without any knowledge of what is in store, except his will for my soul, period? Do I choose to live my covenants? In his arms, the resentments seem to fade away for me.[3]

This is what it means to truly believe and trust the Lord, and that trust makes all the difference in how we approach life.

Third: Bringing New Life Out of Chaos

We see in the Creation the provisions God has made to bring beauty, hope, peace, wonder, and joy to our lives—even in the midst of the confusion, uncertainty, and difficulty inherent to mortality. Creativity, then, is more than a luxury for the artistically inclined; it is a mandate to every soul on the path to godliness. Our daily opportunities to solve problems, plan projects, build relationships, live morally, and exercise spirituality call for daily acts of imagination and innovation as we create ourselves, our work, our families, and the Zion communities that will greet the Savior on his return.

God invites us to do more than copy old blueprints or relive past itineraries as we fashion our lives. In fact, our great challenge is to act, love, relate, enjoy, and dream in ways that transcend the ways we have been acted upon, or the ways we have always acted in the past. Will we, like God, choose order, beauty, and endless variety, or will we prefer the false hope, false control, and false security of our defenses, addictions, and refusals to try? Will we accept God's invitation to become something new instead of something old and to live joyfully, purposefully, meaningfully, gloriously—even amid the outcomes of others' uninspired choices? What can God's creative processes teach us about the process of creating our lives?

I still remember the dream of Ivan, who feared to risk creating something new out of a life that seemed mired in old patterns. Ivan dreamed he was on the roof of his parents' house, which had many gables, peaks, and steeply sloped eaves. He was trying to navigate around this roof. He worked really hard at planning and maneuvering his way around, and he had a real sense of accomplishment as he got past one peak safely and moved around to the next one. He felt safe up there because if there were trouble on the street down below, then he would see it coming. But then he started to notice that for all his effort, he was really just going around in circles.

Like Ivan, we can spend much time circling the same problems and solutions. Unable to break away from an old worldview to take on the more risky challenges of an unknown world beyond, we have the illusion but not the substance of progress. We cherish the imagined safety of our rooftop perspective, believing it allows us to see trouble coming and prevent it. Up there we feel powerful and big; down on the street walking out toward the wilderness, we imagine feeling small, unskilled, and overwhelmed. But the dream doesn't mince words: we make no progress conquering and reconquering the same familiar territory using the same familiar strategies. Our rooftops are not just sites of familiar challenges and comforting perspectives; they become prisons of our own making, and it takes courage to leave them behind.

We are our most important creation. We have the capacity to

- Create and embody our values—what we want and what we love

- Create our body—with health, strength, flexibility, and passion

- Create our relationships—with friends, parents, siblings, spouse, and children

- Create beauty and abundance—in our home, in our workspace, in our art

- Create our work—through special projects or daily use of our skills

- Create our church callings—to bless individuals and families

- Create our communities—as places of peace, service, and problem-solving

- Create our spiritual life—through discipline, integrity, humility, and joy.

What are you trying to create? To what unorganized matter (raw materials, ideas, emotions) do you wish to bring order, beauty, and purpose? What are you trying to do with your life? What relationships are you building? What life patterns need an overhaul? What are your hands eager to pursue? Pause for a moment and make a list.

The Days of Creation

The temple and the scriptures tutor us in our godlike capacity to create. "Watch and see how this is done," God seems to say. "I intend (Abraham 3:24), I descend (Abraham 4:1), I speak (Moses 2:5), I appraise (Moses 2:31). That is the process of creating an earth—or a life."

I try to follow. I intend—imagine, visualize, and plan. I descend—go down into unorganized matter and undifferentiated darkness to bring order, variety, light, and life. I speak—bring to life with words, name, describe, make stories of, report on, and communicate about. I appraise—evaluate, judge the worth of, appreciate, value, and delight in. And then I, like God, joyfully rest.

Well, that's the theory.

Gratefully, the creation story reminds me that, even for God, creation proceeds in steps, with alternating periods of pondering from a cerebral distance and descending into the chaos to get our hands dirty. We do not create in a flash of light but a little at a time, forging gradually our new identity, relationship, or work. We spend much of our creative time in the dark. And we need help from others along the way.

Each of the seven days of creation suggest distinct aspects of the creative process of organizing a glob of matter into a work of art, a collection of information into a story, a collection of insights into a new identity, or a collection of people into Zion. The days of creation unfold in time as the earth is constructed in space. The seven rooms of the temple overlap in instructive ways with the seven days of creation: (1) Baptistry, (2) Initiatory, (3) Creation, (4) Garden, (5) World, (6) Terrestrial, and (7) Celestial/Sealing. We can learn more about the application of the seven days to our lives by comparing them with these seven rooms, but to simplify this chapter, I will only touch on this overlap.

Each of these days/rooms has implications for not only building our creative projects but also as we create the temple of our soul.

Day 1: *Without Form and Void*

When we set about to create (a belief system, a career, a marriage, a ward), there is a certain tension in the air. There is both excitement and fear as we start something new, the end of which we cannot yet fully envision. Indeed, there is anxiety to be faced in every step of the creative process. What shall we make? What raw materials will we use? What patterns might we draw on? Where do we begin?

We begin by brooding in the dark.

> And they, that is the Gods, organized and formed the heavens and the earth. And the earth, after it was formed, was empty and desolate, because they had not formed anything but the earth; and darkness reigned upon the face of the deep, and the Spirit of the Gods was brooding upon the face of the waters. (Abraham 4:1–2)

The initial organization of the earth has a parallel to physical birth and spiritual rebirth, as does the start of any creative endeavor. Creativity begins with everything in an unorganized state, and something may have to die or come apart, literally or figuratively, for new life and new connections to begin. We don't need to be unsettled about being unsettled—this is just the way it is when we face something not yet formed. Our first day of creation requires tolerance for unorganized matter. Indeed, nothing new can occur when everything is numbered and named and categorized. "Without the random there can be no new thing," said psychotherapist Gregory Bateson.[4] Sometimes when we are most frightened by the possibility, we need to simply brood.

If this is true of creation in the physical world, it is even truer when we are attempting to create our lives and relationships. Apocryphal writings describe the beginning of new creation as a time when "all spaces were broken and confused," in a state of instability and chaos too frightening and disorienting for humans to view.[5] Creating our lives also may require us to face swirling, raw feelings—chaos and anarchy in their most painful forms. As we sit with such feelings calmly, curiously, and compassionately, we get more and more precise about what these feelings are, what they remind us of, when they began, and eventually, how we might order them into some new story that better defines what happened, what is possible, who is responsible, and why.

Abraham's account of the creation confirms the importance of descent in the creative process—any creative process, whether of healing, art, identity, work, or love:

And there stood one among them that was like unto God, and he said
unto those who were with him: *We will go down*, for there is space there,
and we will take of these materials, and we will make an earth whereon
these may dwell. . . .

And then the Lord said: Let us *go down*. And they went down at
the beginning, and they, that is the Gods, organized and formed the
heavens and the earth. (Abraham 3:24; 4:1; italics mine)

While we accept the rhythms of light and dark in the natural world,
we tend to resist our own dark hours of descent, trying to always stay above
it all, in control, happy, knowledgeable, and safe. But darkness is an inevitable starting point. Darkness can give depth and grounding to our souls
and our creativity. In fact, even after the Lord brings light to the earth, light
and dark alternate in regular rhythms throughout its existence—and ours.
We are meant to spend some of our time here in the dark.

And the earth, after it was formed, was empty and desolate . . . and
darkness reigned upon the face of the deep. . . . And they divided the
light, or caused it to be divided, from the darkness. And the Gods called
the light Day, and the darkness they called Night. (Abraham 4:2, 4–5)

Some people become fascinated with the dark side and focus too much
on the inevitability of overwhelming struggle, forgetting there even is Day.
They may have learned by hard experience to be suspicious of hope, pro-
activity, and vision for fear of disappointment. But most of us get nervous
in the dark. We need others to go with us when the darkness is vast and
the elements unstable so we don't get lost out there. The further down we
have to go, the more we need company if we can get it. And if we can't get
it from our fellow mortals, God is not afraid of the dark, whether in the
world or in us.

We also see in the creation story that sometimes when we are most
unsure of how we will do it, we simply need to begin. We need to take
responsibility, impose some order, try something unexpected, and persist
to maintain that new effort against the pull of old patterns or the black
holes of chaos until our will is accomplished and the elements obey. Or
until we realize we need to try something else. Whether we are trying to
restructure a relationship, write a novel, form a company, or live with less
depression, the process seems to start with an idea and some unorganized
matter. Then it proceeds to beginning tentative steps of order and light, and
then it invites evaluating the results, which gives direction for more steps
through alternating periods of darkness and light, which results in some
creative outcome we must eventually decide is good—or in our case, good

enough for now. This is the creative process put in play by the initial Day and Night of creation.

Day 2: Dividing Land and Sea

After the first day of creation, the earth is shown as a bare planet, floating untethered in space. Without additional creative investment, its capacity to bring forth new life would be limited indeed. The remaining days of creation each add to the earth's life-giving capacity and metaphorically, to ours. Having chosen our creative project and set up the loom, it is time to get to work on the weaving.

> And the Gods also said: Let there be an expanse in the midst of the waters, and it shall divide the waters from the waters. . . .
>
> And the Gods ordered, saying: Let the waters under the heaven be gathered together unto one place, and let the earth come up dry; and it was so as they ordered;
>
> And the Gods pronounced the dry land, Earth; and the gathering together of the waters, pronounced they, Great Waters; and the Gods saw that they were obeyed (Abraham 4:6, 9–10).

In the creation of our lives, adulthood brings new skills and tasks. As the earth takes on the beauty and variety of its magnificent landscapes, so our bodies and minds take on the beauty and variety of physical maturation, and so our creations begin to take shape within our hands and in our hearts. We may need to protect our still-evolving work from critical eyes for a time, just as the atmosphere that drapes the earth protects it from solar storms and wandering asteroids, or as temple clothing protects and nurtures our spiritual life. As the Gods give the names of Earth and Great Waters to their burgeoning creation, so our creative work is imprinted with our unique style, message, and truths.

As we begin to work in earnest, we need an observing, thoughtful part that can remain, Elohim-like, in an objective place above the fray—planning, evaluating, reminding us of our intentions, and keeping a cool head. Other people can help us hold this perspective, as can writing about our thoughts and feelings; reading other people's ideas about the problems we wrestle with; deliberately remembering what is good, ordered, and provident in our lives; or just taking a break and getting on with our day for a while. Another part of us needs to willingly tackle the hard, sometimes tedious work of molding the mountains and rivers of our particular opus.

As the Creation unfolds, the simplistic division of land-sea gives way to the beauty and intricacy of the real world, where land contains water and water brings life to land in dynamic, changing patterns of infinite variety. So our simplistic divisions of good-bad, right-wrong, and black-white must give way to a more complex understanding of the world if our creativity is to flourish. We learn to distinguish right from wrong and truth from error, while also enlarging our capacity to accept ambiguity, paradox, and balance. We come to understand that blood cleanses, submission empowers, and the thinnest garment provides the mightiest shield.

When we are stymied in our creative process, sometimes it is because we are looking for a black-and-white solution to a many-colored challenge. Our creative efforts are often enriched by bringing some shadows into our painting, some paradox into our script, some spontaneity into our relationship, some playfulness into our week. We can afford to explore solutions that may not solve our problems once and for all but that blend just a little more beauty and variety into our landscape, one day at a time.

Day 3: Sun, Moon, and Stars

> And the Gods organized the lights in the expanse of the heaven, and caused them to divide the day from the night; and organized them to be for signs and for seasons, and for days and for years. . . .
>
> And the Gods organized the two great lights, the greater light to rule the day, and the lesser light to rule the night; with the lesser light they set the stars also;
>
> And the Gods set them in the expanse of the heavens, to give light upon the earth. . . .
>
> And the Gods watched those things which they had ordered until they obeyed. (Abraham 4:14, 16–18)

These verses underscore the message that all things on earth have been carefully planned and prepared for us, God's children. We are not alone among the stars. We live in our appointed place within the universe. There is order and purpose in all the Creation, and there is order and purpose to our lives as we submit them to God. As the earth is placed in its orbit around the sun that rules our days, we recall our heavenly Parents also rule amid all the heavenly hosts, and we are among the bright stars of their known and numbered children. When we cannot directly see their love and light, we can still feel hope from those who reflect their glory to us while we are in the dark. Looking at the starry sky, we remember this larger perspective on our mortality, a perspective that imparts courage and peace. We begin to imagine processes by which we too may create, order, and engender life.

As the sun sets and the stars emerge, we see the evidence of our nothingness amid the vastness of creation, and evidence of our "everythingness" in the simple fact that the God who numbers the infinite stars numbers us too and knows us by name. We also see in the predictable patterns of the heavens an order to be discerned in all of life. The rising and setting of the sun and the waxing and waning of the moon suggest our need for rhythm, structure, and predictability to shape our days and nights. Indeed, night-time encourages us to seek solitude, rest, and introspection to balance our purposeful and goal-directed days. The consistent unfolding of the days and nights of creation reminds us not to dread the dark nor give up on the sun on cloudy days. There are rhythms and patterns that support our creative life, seasons and cadences to be respected and followed.

Creative work is hard, and it takes courage to keep working when we aren't sure what we are doing. We get discouraged, we get stuck, and we second-guess our motives and our vision. Periodically we need to reconnect with our guiding lights, to view our creative works from a larger perspective, and to remember our finest creations must be expressions of the Holy Spirit and not the human ego. Who we become through our creations and how the Father can use them to his ends may be more important than the product itself. We need to be in proper proximity and relationship to his light and to the lesser lights of the people around us for our creative work, creative relationships, and creative personal development to flourish.

Day 4: Plant Life

> And the Gods said: Let us prepare the earth to bring forth grass; the herb yielding seed; the fruit tree yielding fruit, after his kind, whose seed in itself yieldeth its own likeness upon the earth; and it was so, even as they ordered. (Abraham 4:11)

As the Creation unfolds, plant life greens the earth. Its rich variety recalls the abundant world of the Garden of Eden, an idyllic world where fruit and flowers proliferate spontaneously, and humans may eat their fill each day without worrying about tomorrow's winter or next month's drought. Attitudes of innocence, abundance, and trust feed our creative life and provide the feelings of safety and security we need to create well. In the garden, abundance is assumed.

We also need a garden in the temple of the soul, a place of renewal and abundance. Without it, life becomes lonely and dreary indeed. We cannot stay there always, to be sure, but if in our hardest hours we can find ways to tend and cultivate that which nourishes us (a walk in the woods, the serenity of the scriptures, an honest conversation, a ripe peach), then our sense of trust in life and God and ourselves can be restored.

Children surrounded by emotional abundance generally grow up trusting life will bring them what they truly need. In the absence of such care, we may feel forever like orphans who must scrounge in garbage cans to survive. We may barely notice when real food is offered, or we may clutch at it like starving animals gorging themselves today on what may not be available tomorrow. We may give up on other human beings as a source of help, withdrawing into icy self-reliance, or we may passively insist we are helpless to care for ourselves, sure our only hope lies in getting someone else to do it for us. Sometimes we alternate among these positions, confusing even ourselves.

When our experience suggests distrust is the wiser course, rekindling some sense of innocence and connection becomes a major challenge. It can feel risky indeed to trust in the continuity of abundance, or in our own capacity for resilience in the face of scarcity. We have to learn both to accept the help and care that are available from others, and that taking care of ourselves does not have to mean abandoning hope of being cared for. We have to invest a little less energy into staying safe and a little more into getting back up when we fall. Even when painful experiences have undermined our trust in the goodness of the world or in us, it is not too late to cultivate a garden for our soul.

Stuck in a plot that won't gel, an insight just out of reach? We can nurture our creativity with small acts of delight, small interludes of pleasure, small forays into nature and the goodness of the world. We replenish our creative stores with fresh images, new possibilities, and a good night's sleep. It helps to walk a bit with God in the cool of the day.

Day 5: Animal Life

We want to believe our creativity would flourish best if surrounded only by Eden-like abundance and safety, but our creative capacities are also honed by scarcity and want, pruning and competition. The establishment of animal life on the earth foreshadows the harsh realities of a telestial world dominated by hierarchies of prey and predator.

> And the Gods said: Let us prepare the waters to bring forth abundantly the moving creatures that have life; and the fowl, that they may fly above the earth in the open expanse of heaven. . . .
>
> And the Gods said: We will bless them, and cause them to be fruitful and multiply, and fill the waters in the seas or great waters; and cause the fowl to multiply in the earth. . . .
>
> And the Gods organized the earth to bring forth the beasts after their kind, and cattle after their kind, and every thing that creepeth

upon the earth after its kind; and the Gods saw they would obey. (Abraham 4:20, 22, 25)

All these beasts feel like playmates until we realize they eat each other, and us! We can feel on the verge of being devoured as we contemplate showing our creative efforts to others. We may have felt more creative as children before someone told us our poem didn't rhyme or our picture didn't look like a person at all, but we can learn to find satisfaction in learning and mastering the rules of the telestial world of work and competition. The skills of critical thought that can be used to degrade and shame can also be used to improve and enrich our products and our lives. Creative discovery often occurs when we are emotionally or literally hungry, for then we seek new solutions to old problems. The creative outcome is improved as we submit to the scrutiny of our fellows and learn to appropriately critique our work, figuratively killing off the feeble and unfit parts of it so the dynamic and fitting parts may live. Ruthlessness has its place.

Creativity always requires pruning. Even our brains don't really begin to function well until we start pruning neurological connections down, not just building more up. We can't ever do all we set out to do. If we never prune the apple tree, then its fruit will be plentiful but underdeveloped, and if we are not careful, the limbs will break beneath their weight. Nature has ways to thin the herd and the forest, and we need not worry when we must settle for something less than what we had hoped. Staying humble is the prerequisite for all learning, and limits and failings can be among our most powerful teachers. As we soldier through, we learn to rely on ourselves and feel our strength, to ask more clearly for what we want, and to acknowledge more fully our limitations. Our animal bodies find both the power of our muscles and the limits of our speed.

In dreams, animals represent aspects of our emotional life, our sexuality, our family relationships, and our personal identity. According to Crisp's research-based *Dream Dictionary*, "the animal represents *all* our biological needs and responses, which include survival and hunger; reproduction; parental urges; need for exercise and rest; social drives; fear reactions; anger; urge to provide (for young and mate); home/nest building; territory protection; social hierarchy, etc."[6] This biological heritage provides the energy for our creative and procreative drives.

For example, Crisp finds dreamers use horses to represent their own power, exuberance, and sexuality. Elephants represent the self and our great inner potential and strength. Bears suggest one's powerful maternal drives of protecting young as well as the capacity to bring new life out of periods of hibernation and rest. Lions epitomize our aggressive instincts, either when aroused by jealousy or hunger, or when needed to protect or compete. Birds represent the freedom of independence, as well as our imagination, intuition, and all our spiritual longings. Fish may represent "the wisdom we have not yet brought to consciousness, regarding our personal journey in time and eternity." Insects may represent irritations at the edge of consciousness, reminding us of instructive awareness we might prefer to ignore. Reptiles suggest survival impulses from the deepest part of our brain.[7]

As we cloak our spirits in the animal skins of our mortal flesh, we experience firsthand our humanity: emotion, sexuality, power, empathy, independence, and sociality. The animal creation reminds us of the power in our passions and desires and to take our place in the world of competition and survival. We submit to the opinions and counsel of others. We show our work to the world even if we are afraid of being eaten alive. We stare down our jealousies and fears and try again. We limit how much we take on and learn when to stop. And we can grow in our creative capacities as we do.

Day 6: Human Life

> And I, God, said unto mine Only Begotten, which was with me from the beginning: Let us make man in our image, after our likeness; and it was so.
>
> And I, God, said: Let them have dominion over the fishes of the sea, and over the fowl of the air, and over the cattle, and over all the earth, and over every creeping thing that creepeth upon the earth.
>
> And I, God, created man in mine own image, in the image of mine Only Begotten created I him; male and female created I them. And I, God, blessed them, and said unto them: Be fruitful, and multiply, and replenish the earth, and subdue it. (Moses 2:26–28)

On the sixth day, man and woman are created, brought together, and commanded to replenish the earth. Symbolically, this day suggests our possibilities for transcending the dreary world of predator and prey to contemplate a terrestrial realm of consecrated cooperation with other people. The ideas and care of other people are seminal to our creative life. Only when we connect can we be fruitful in every sense of the word. Within the safety and challenge of committed relationships and communities we become free to be all of who we are. Uniting in purpose to give voice to our prayers and direction to our acts, we commit both our faith and our hands to the intentions of our hearts.

As we connect our creative efforts to the needs of other people, our creativity serves the world. I love a video produced by Playing for Change.[8] It starts with a seasoned street musician strumming a guitar, his head bobbing as he sings soulfully, "No matter who you are, no matter where you go in life, you gonna need somebody to stand by you." His name and "Santa Monica, California" appear on the screen. Guys with dark glasses and baseball caps pull on headphones and fiddle with computers, recording his song. Tourists amble by, and one man in the background is holding a child and dancing along. The guitarist keeps strumming, but the scene changes to a bearded old man in overalls and a floppy hat, sitting on a bench, headphones connecting him to the rhythm of the first man's guitar as we hear his deep, rich voice. His name and "New Orleans, Louisiana" flash on the screen. "When the night has come and the land is dark, and the moon is the only light I see, I won't be afraid, no I won't be afraid, just as long as you stand, stand by me." The two singers in two cities, connected by technology, harmonize and tap their feet through the pounding chorus as we catch glimpses of the music mixers' grins. The intensity builds with a brief shot of an airplane taking off. A fervent young rocker with dreadlocks in an alley in Amsterdam belts out the next stanza, the others harmonizing from across the globe. Next, we see an American Indian drum group in New Mexico link up with the rhythm, then a sober cellist in a Moscow plaza, a rapturous bass player with a child playing in the dirt at his feet in a village in Guguletu, and a soulful saxophonist from Pisa. The end product, skillfully edited and mixed, is a fervent, joyful blend, "Darlin', darlin', stand by me, oh stand, stand, stand by me." I can't listen to this without moving, grinning, sometimes tearing up, always wanting to sing along. This is creativity of global proportions, gently nudging us toward peaceful cooperation, respect, and harmony.

Each of these musicians sings or plays alone, not even a visible audience to urge them on. But I urge them on. Even when creativity is a solitary process, it reaches out to someone, connects with a larger movement, or shapes a new one for others. It is fostered in writers' groups, committees, families, political parties, companies, and guilds that enlarge our creative purposes and strengthen our creative identity. Creativity at its best melds our creative efforts with those of others to become something more than the sum of our parts. We play to change the world.

Day 7: Day of Rest

Thus the heaven and the earth were finished, and all the host of them.

And on the seventh day I, God, ended my work, and all things which I had made; and I rested on the seventh day from all my work, and all things which I had made were finished, and I, God, saw that they were good;

And I, God, blessed the seventh day, and sanctified it; because that in it I had rested from all my work which I, God, had created and made. (Moses 3:1–3)

Inasmuch as entering into God's rest is to enter the fulness of his glory (Doctrine and Covenants 84:24), the day of rest described at the end of the earth's creation also suggests the celestial promise of exaltation and eternal lives. More than relaxation alone, this "rest" implies a fulness of joy and rejoicing in all the *life* that we have created on the journey.

As mere mortals, it is always hard to know when our creation is finished and we can rest. Anxiety creeps in again as we face the decision to stop. Is it enough? In fact, we will never be done, but at some point we must move on before we ruin the picture with too many erasures. God pronounced his work good, not necessarily perfect. Still, he turns it loose to have a life of its own. We can do the same, trusting Christ's redemptive work applies to it all.

The rest God took on the seventh day speaks to us of not only knowing when to quit or knowing how to rejuvenate, but also knowing God. We do not merely rest from our labor on the Sabbath to nap, but to turn our heart to entering God's rest. This is a time to turn our creative efforts over to him to bless and to breathe with life. At some level, this means our work will take on a life of its own that we no longer fully control. We trust it into his hands for the accomplishment of his purposes, and we detach our ego from the outcome. Our attachment and veneration are to God, not the workmanship of our hands—something easy for the idolatrous within us to forget. We find our approbation from him, not the pride-driven response of the world in the "great and spacious building" (see 1 Nephi 8:25–28). When we can do this, we can rest indeed, grateful for what we have been able to do and even more grateful for what he has done with us in the process, bringing us another step closer to him:

But if ye receive me *in the world*, then shall *ye know me*, and shall *receive your exaltation*; that where I am ye shall be also.

This is eternal lives—to know the only wise and true God, and Jesus Christ, whom he hath sent. (Doctrine and Covenants 132:23–24, italics mine)

If we receive and come to know the Lord while we are yet in the world, we can begin to enter celestial promises while we yet live in telestial surroundings. We can pronounce our work good, beautiful, even hallowed, without it having to be perfect.

Beginner's Mind

A few months ago, I was recovering from a somewhat lengthy illness just as some work demands increased substantially. I was physically exhausted and emotionally depleted. Yet there was still much more to do. I felt discouraged and overwhelmed. In the midst of all this, I felt almost compelled to begin a complicated woodworking/art project as a gift for a friend's birthday just a few weeks away. I knew what I wanted to make, sketched out the design, and gathered some materials, but I knew almost nothing about woodworking and even less about painting. I had no idea where to begin. Yet this project felt like more than a whim—it felt like a spiritual imperative. With all the "Very Important Work" I would have to ignore and all the humiliation I would undoubtedly suffer in the process, I wondered if that "spiritual imperative" part could possibly be right.

A dear friend set up his chop saw and sander in my garage, showed me how to use them, and got me started. He arranged with another friend to let me borrow a table saw, router, planer, band saw, and biscuit joiner (I love that I know what these things are!). They both spent an entire afternoon helping me, teaching me, and encouraging me as I merrily cut up wood and planed and glued and joined and routed it. I spent hours on my own time covering myself in sawdust as I sanded it all down. And I began to feel the life come back into my body as I felt the power of the tools and shaped the wood to my desires. I wrote,

> Why is it that cutting up a bunch of wood with a chop saw, making a big messy pile of sawdust and breathing it in until I'm coughing, sanding off little pieces of wood until they are smooth and my hand hurts and my arm is tired makes me feel like I'm swimming in a warm ocean? I feel so much better I don't even know how to describe it.

Once I had the wood nailed and glued and prepped, I asked an artist friend what kind of paints to buy, trying not to convey my terror about how I would actually use them. She took off work early, showed up at my house with her acrylics collection, and spent the good part of three days patiently teaching me techniques and helping me accomplish my goal. We chatted and laughed as we worked into the night. For the first time in months I felt connected, present, happy. In the end, the project turned out as well as I could have ever hoped—for the wood, and quite unexpectedly, for me.

I still wondered if I had really been justified in taking on this project, which consumed me for weeks when I had so many other things I "should" have been working on instead. Then I went to a Deseret Book–sponsored dinner at which two senior General Authorities were speakers and guests of honor. To my astonishment, the first speaker's entire talk was on the importance of getting out of our comfort zones and trying creative things we were not good at. Emphasizing his point by jabbing his finger our way, he firmly counseled that if we wanted to keep our creativity alive and our spirits growing, we needed to try utterly new things. He told us about his own efforts with watercolor and poetry, both of which he professed minimal ability in. He reminded us of the importance of being a beginner again, feeling the joy of learning and creating unburdened by high expectations. The second General Authority took up his theme, also talking about his fledgling efforts at watercolor paintings, which were so bad the person at the frame shop required him to pay the full amount up front instead of the usual 50 percent because she was afraid he would not really come back for them otherwise!

I felt amazingly confirmed. Creativity is not always about what we produce. Sometimes it is simply about whom we produce. Who would have thought power tools could be catalysts of God's healing blessings and so much joy.

Standing By

I wasn't having a great day—I can't even remember why. But I had recently seen the video of "Stand By Me" I mentioned earlier in this chapter, and I went looking for it again. As I watched and listened, something shifted inside me. I saw something and heard something I don't imagine the producers ever intended. I found myself weeping as I thought of the chaos and ugliness of the world, transcended by these musicians' creativity and soothed by the hand of the Lord, who "stands by" us. In this joyful noise, I realized that through all of us, God is creating still—bringing new life into old forms, touching the music with light that goes straight to my heart.

One of God's most defining characteristics is his ability to create. This includes his astounding power to work all things together for our good—music, technology, sin, loss, relationships, to-do lists, misunderstandings, economies, pain, evil, *all things*—if we love him and remember our covenants with one another (Romans 8:28; Doctrine and Covenants 90:24).

He invites us to learn this astounding creative power, this ability to see what is chaotic and unorganized in the world and in us and weave it into a new story, a new meaning, and a newness of life. In the myriad choices we make about how we will give form to the raw materials of our lives, he invites us to create. We are not just trying to duplicate his vision. He enters into ours.

As the creation story concludes, the earth is poised for the fulfillment of its purposes. And so are we. With the peaceful perspectives obtained by considering the beginning and the ends of our creation, we see ourselves more clearly. We know more deeply whom we trust and follow. We are more prepared to tackle the creative work of our life's journey. We remember we are here to learn to engender creative life in the world and in others in the all the ways God models. We begin to imagine how we, like God, might learn to turn all kinds of straw into gold.

Having recovered our creative power, our perspective on where and who we came from, and our awareness of the unseen threads that still tie us to God, we go with Adam and Eve and all the "noble and great ones" who helped form the earth into the garden, where we learn by our own experience about Satan's deadly redundancies, God's creative capacity to bring life and hope to any situation, and the choices we make between them. And we see it is good.

HEALING PRACTICE FOR CHAPTER FIVE: THE CREATOR'S CHILD

- *Harnessing creative goals.* Give quick answers to the following and then go back to consider how your answers might provide direction for creative change. (I ask for a specific number not only to encourage a little brainstorming beyond what readily comes to mind but also so you will not get bogged down in creating a lot more ideas than you can really work with.)

  - What are five classes you'd take if you had a chance?

  - If you had nine lives, what would you do for a career in each of them?

  - What are five little changes you'd love to make in your life right now?

  - What are three recurring problems you would like to solve in your family or in your personal life?

  - What are five questions on any subject you'd love answers to?

- What three things have you been worrying about for a long time that need resolution?

- What is one thing you might explore or do differently as you consider your answers to these questions?

- *Finding creative balance.* When involved in a creative project, consider the balance needed between immersing yourself in the chaos of the creative process and finding the distance and objectivity to evaluate and plan. If you feel stuck, is it because you have stayed alone in the darkness too long without getting the opinions and help of others? Do you need distance and objectivity by leaving for a time and resting from your labors? Or do you need to more trustingly immerse yourself in the unknown, not forcing closure prematurely?

- *Acknowledging goodness.* Take a few minutes to consider how you created your life today. Review what you accomplished, how you related to others, and ways you ordered your life according to God's commandments to you. Which of the choices you have made today can you acknowledge as good? Consider spending a few minutes in prayer each evening *only* focusing on what you are grateful for and what you enjoyed about the day.

- *Resting.* How can you find time for rest in your life? What kinds of rest do you enjoy or would you like more of? What would it take to arrange more time for such restful pursuits? Choose from and add to this list:

spend time in nature	take a walk
listen to music	sit quietly and think
look at the stars	take a long shower
daydream	canoe
dance	attend the temple
read the scriptures	garden
play with animals	write in a journal
visit with a friend	read a book
paint, draw, or sculpt	breathe deeply and slowly

CHAPTER SIX
NOT ASHAMED

—⊗⊗⊗—

Each man is questioned by life, and he can only answer to life by answering for his own life; to life he can only respond by being responsible.

—VIKTOR FRANKL[1]

So far on our journey we have recovered truths about our history, a deeper presence in our body, and awareness of our creative power. Next we will grapple with the garden story of how to recover our sense of trust and hope in the face of betrayal and self-deception. But first, a more personal story.

When I was four or five, I graduated from the bathtub to the shower. My parents delighted in this "developmental milestone" of their firstborn and got out their camera to record the event. Me in a shower cap, slippery gray tile, the mottled glass shower door propped open. I remember posturing for the camera, smiling shyly, my mom and dad grinning the way parents grin to get children to do likewise for a picture. I also remember vague confusion as to why it was okay to have my picture taken in the shower, or why they thought it worth recording that I do something so ordinary. But I was young and modesty was only a vague concept without much relevance in my world.

One day when I was about twelve, fully and newly grown up, I was walking through my grandparents' house in a city far from where I grew up, with a couple of older male cousins, and there in my grandparents' bedroom on my grandmother's dresser mirror for all the world to see was that picture—*that* picture of me, age whatever, grinning naked in the shower. My cousins hooted to each other before I even recognized what they were looking at. Then I saw what they were laughing at. Utter humiliation and sudden rage shot through me, fueled by the howling question *why?* Why, of the million photographs my parents must have taken of me, had my grandparents chosen this one to display on their mirror? I grabbed the picture, slammed it down on the dresser, and wanted to yell or cry. I did neither. I just felt ashamed.

Shame is a nebulous emotion, instantly spotted but variously defined. It includes the natural human response to being seen in a negative light, a compromising pose. Different from guilt for having violated one's moral code, shame has more to do with a feeling of smallness, a perception of oneself as an object of contempt, unworthy of others' care, and thus under threat of abandonment. We feel ashamed because we are seen in our nakedness when clothes are called for, seen in our neediness when independence is praised, seen in our ignorance when we didn't even know we didn't know. Shame is the natural response to deception or betrayal but also to realizing we have participated in our own deception, our eyes not yet open to what others could see. We feel ashamed to recognize we were once so naïve and childish as to stand in front of a camera naked, or ashamed of having exposed a child to embarrassment because we never thought about her becoming modestly twelve when she was innocently five.

Our experiences with shame vary greatly, ranging from mild embarrassment to mortifying humiliation. We risk feeling shame any time we try something new or show our work to the world—yet some people seem to tackle such tasks without shame. Once shame is triggered, we just want to cover up, so shame is a catalyst for lying, running, and blaming. In contrast, genuine guilt leads us to take responsibility for our errors and want to make things right when we violate our moral values or hurt another person. Guilt leads us to repent and change, while shame leads us to get defensive or ignore the problem. Shame is also different from humility. Genuine humility helps us hone, improve, grow, and see what others see so we internalize society's ethical, artistic, and technical standards. Humility helps us acknowledge our limitations and accept counsel from others. Guilt and humility come from a highly developed sense of conscience and empathy, while shame undermines both.

Shaming others is a potent way to correct bad behavior, but it can backfire if overdone or if not quickly followed with loving reconnection. Some people have had their emotional psychic skin burned so raw with shame that the slightest additional blush feels unbearable, and the normal risks of life feel fraught with danger of utter and singular mortification. Other people may not feel a lot of shame, even in the face of failure or public censure; either life has not forced them into a painful obsession with worrying about what others see that they do not, or they have learned to self-protectively block that awareness from consciousness. At the extreme, they may block out empathy as well and not develop a conscience.

Ideally, we learn to experience and tolerate some shame because we recognize it as a normal human experience, worth learning from but not worth obsessing about. If you are one who does not overdo shame, more power to you. Perhaps you will be better served to plumb the story of Eden for its lessons on loss, ambition, anxiety, or love. But if shame is at least a passing problem in your life or the life of someone you love, Eden might hold a lesson or two worth noting.

That I see in the story of Adam and Eve a composition on personal shame probably says much more about me than it does about the story. The story says only that in the beginning Adam and Eve are not ashamed in their nakedness, and that in the end they see their nakedness and try to hide from the eyes of God. Hiding seems to be the natural response to shame or is perhaps an inherent component of it. If I hide, then I don't have to see your disappointment if I failed you or your gloating if you outwitted me.

Hiding one's nakedness seems like a reasonable idea until we recall that God has all-seeing eyes. Perhaps Adam and Eve do not just hide because they are now psychologically closer to twelve than five and have suddenly acquired modesty; perhaps they also hide because what moments ago seemed like such a good idea now fills them with the particular shame of having been betrayed. Their eyes have been opened, and they suddenly see their own nakedness in a new light—as a glaring sign of their previously unrecognized vulnerability and naïveté.

Eugene England's personal essay "Easter Story" exposes the shame we feel when we have been duped into thinking we can see, only to realize we have been blind.[2] He tells of being tricked into a game with some "friendly" con artists in Manhattan who appear to be conning someone else instead—someone naïve and not too bright who can't seem to catch on to what looks so obvious. Only when England has lost—twice—a considerable amount of cash does the dark betrayal sink in. Too late. When one who pretended to be our brother deceives us, we yearn to undo the sickening fact of being made a fool. We feel our blindness like an ugly deformity. Moments before, we felt rather smug in our superior wisdom. Now the world is full of predators and mockers, people malevolently smarter than we are. To be deceived by another is hard, but recognizing how we have colluded in our own deception by not trusting God's wisdom is much harder.

The garden story is not foundational just because it explains the start of the human race; it is also foundational because it teaches us about our lives. Experiences of self-deception or betrayal are nearly universal. We misunderstand, we are blind, we fall, each in our own way, although in that collective moment we may feel painfully alone amid an imagined circle of pointing fingers. Gratefully, the story also teaches us what God advises us to do when we fall versus what Satan advises, for on this distinction the plan of salvation turns. "Were it not for our transgression we never should have had seed, and never should have known good and evil, and the joy of our redemption, and the eternal life which God giveth unto all the obedient" (Moses 5:11), says Eve after her betrayal, and we long to learn the secrets of her hope.

As we consider the moral lessons of the garden, we can profitably consider ourselves as if we were Adam and Eve (1 Nephi 19:23). Not limiting this comparison by gender, I find I benefit from considering how Adam, Eve, God, and the serpent may each represent different voices in my internal world. One of those inner voices is rigidly cautious, obeying obvious rules while ignoring less clear ones. Another jumps to conclusions too quickly to escape the tension of this moment's ambiguity. One part of me is grandiose, another timid. One part is honest, another deceptive. One part can observe with mercy and justice from an eternal perspective. Another gets caught up in preserving the illusion of this moment's power.

At this level of comparison, I note men are not always or even primarily cautious or stubborn, and women are not always rebellious or naïve. We each have characteristics of all the players here. We each need lessons in casting off voices within us that entice us to evil, and we each need to bring our whole soul to Jesus to redeem. As we attend to the garden plot, we see analogies to our own experience with temptation, deception, sin, shame, and redemption.

Let's look more closely at three temptations apparent in this story.

The First Temptation—Forbidden Fruit

Initially we note that the abundance of the Garden of Eden promotes innocence and trust. While no parents create a perfect paradise for their children, fortunate indeed are those who spend childhood immersed in an abundance of all that nourishes: predictable companionship, peaceful solitude, beauty, pleasure, meaningful responsibility, and just a few clear rules, with more imperatives to create, care, and find joy than to do what we're told and stay out of sight. One can afford to be trusting in such circumstances. That capacity to trust provides a wondrous foundation to the development of conscience and the ability to love. But one cannot afford to be ignorant under any conditions that permit choice, as events soon prove. Ignorant as we are, turning to God for counsel is our only safety. Even in paradise.

In this place, the trees of life are everywhere, and God apparently comes and goes and returns again. He allows his first children to take his recurrent presence for granted, as children should. All that is deathly can be reduced to one clear option, available simply because agency is God's way, his only way. God describes his laws straightforwardly to Adam and Eve, not as threats to make them afraid or to bully them into submission, but so they can feel secure predicting the consequences of their choices. That God tells me an apple may fall on my head if I stand beneath the apple tree is not a threat but a statement about cause and effect that allows me to make informed choices about how to accomplish my will. Shake the tree and the apple will fall, not suddenly decide to fly into the sky or turn into a hammer. If God were to "overrule" these laws, then we would lose capacity to choose the outcomes we desire and to plot a course to arrive at them. How much more effectively we attempt to influence others when we also describe consequences to help others feel *secure* as they make choices, not to make them *insecure* about our love if they don't choose as we would prefer.[3]

Within this idyllic world, God both commands Adam and Eve to multiply and replenish the earth (Moses 2:28) and forbids their eating from the tree of knowledge, the fruit of which apparently initiates that reproductive possibility (Moses 5:11). I used to find it both unusual and unfair that God describe two laws that apparently could not both be kept. But life has taught me that we face choices among seemingly contradictory laws constantly: Think for yourself, but be absolutely obedient. Fulfill your personal goals and mission, but sacrifice yourself for others. Stay out of debt, but get an education, pay tithing, and provide for a family on one salary. Be meek, but stand up for what is right. Get enough sleep, but read the scriptures daily. In a thousand areas of life, we have to make hard decisions on how to balance, prioritize, do two things at once, or choose among good alternatives. In that decision, that agency, we choose who we are and what we love most, and we learn the evils of rigidity or omission as well as the evils of rebellion. And just when we think we have figured out how to stay as far away from the edge of the cliff as we can, another cliff shows up on the other side of the road. We can't stay in Eden for long.

So this con man, Satan, comes along, gives a slick story, and decides to divide and conquer. Eve listens to the con man and is convinced to take matters into her own hands. Adam listens to Eve and is convinced to take matters into her own hands. But the bottom line is that each listens to someone other than God about what is true and good. We, their progeny, make similar choices. We ignore God's descriptions of reality and believe the adversary's instead. Sometimes we do this maliciously; most often we do it, as Adam and Eve did it, ignorantly. But we do it. And when we do, we distance ourselves from the God we have not comprehended or not believed or not trusted.

Most of Christianity blames Eve for eating the fruit and bringing death and evil into the world, contrary to God's plans for humankind. Latter-day Saints see it differently. We honor the mother of all living for a choice that brought us the chance for mortal life and all its opportunities for growth and learning. We know God was not thrown off course by her act, and opposition is necessary. Sometimes in our exuberance to exonerate Eve, however, I think we are in danger of falling off that other cliff, so to speak. We may insist she knew what she was doing all along and acted from intentional self-sacrifice when the text implies otherwise. There is no mention of her choosing her course in order to become a mother, only in order to get knowledge. Nor, when God returns, does Eve confidently assert, "No problem here. I've got this all figured out! We have to eat this fruit to have children as you commanded, so I did. Aren't you proud of me?" Nor does Adam respond to God's voice in the garden by enthusiastically announcing, "Father, I'm so glad you're back. Guess what I did? At first I thought Eve had made a real mess, but I finally realized what we needed to do all along was get out of here so we could multiply. Pretty clever, huh?" No. They are not so confident of their decisions when the Lord comes for a walk in the cool of the day.

Eve doesn't mince words: "The serpent beguiled me, and I did eat" (Moses 4:19). The Hebrew word translated as "beguiled" means to deceive and implies to distract, give false hope, cheat. Whatever may be necessary or beneficial about this course of action, Satan has lied to her, and she has believed him, and believing Satan over God is always a problem. Latter-day revelation affirms Adam was also tempted and also yielded: "Wherefore, it came to pass that the devil tempted Adam, and he partook of the forbidden fruit and transgressed the commandment, wherein he became subject to the will of the devil, because he yielded unto temptation" (Doctrine and Covenants 29:40; see 2 Nephi 9:9). Modern scriptures further clarify that repentance on their part (Moses 5:8) and forgiveness from God (Moses 6:53) are now in order, steps we would not assume necessary if they merely transgressed a natural law.

Perhaps the problem lies not in what they did but on whose counsel. God had never told them they must figure out this dilemma without any further help. In fact, the God we know is constantly inviting us to pray, to ask, to seek, that he might answer. It is difficult to imagine he would not have invited Adam and Eve to do the same. We can't know now what might have happened had Adam and Eve asked God for more instruction or waited for his return because apparently they did neither. Neither Adam nor Eve stopped to counsel with the other or with their lawgiver as to how they might reconcile what appears irreconcilable, or if they might find another way. Adam, it seems, fails to initiate any discussion with Eve about how to keep God's command to multiply, or with God about the best response to Eve's choice. Eve never seeks either's counsel about eating the forbidden fruit or the true sources of knowledge. Each acts on his or her own limited understanding. Each is tempted. Each ultimately yields to temptation. Each is poisoned by the fruit eaten as each chooses to believe Satan's description of reality ("You must eat of this fruit; you shall not die.") over God's ("I forbid it; you shall surely die.") (see Moses 3:17, 4:10). And each brings similarly devastating—and potentially growth-enabling—consequences to their progeny.

I bring these things up not to argue about doctrine, however, but to assert that the story of Adam and Eve is our story. We are the ones who are deceived, either by the great con artist or some beguiled but well-intended fellow mortal, and we must figure out what to do about it. The garden story helps us see, reminding us we are not justified in sinning just because we are deceived. Nor, the story assures us, does God forsake us in disgust because we could not see before and now we can. He is always one step ahead of the con man.

When that heart-sinking moment of clarity comes, we wonder how we could have been so blind as to fall for the con man's trap despite our good intentions. We may then take some comfort in recalling life's complexity, and precedents. Things are not as simple for anyone as they sometimes appear to outsiders or as we would like to believe. God has not singled us out as the class dunce while everyone else gets *A*s. We are each blind in our way, beginning with our noblest forebears. It is not by accident, I assume, that the temple does not tell us stories from the life of the perfect Savior, but stories from the lives of our imperfect parents. These are the stories we need here because this is who we are too.

The problem is not that the knowledge Eve seeks or the companionship Adam desires or the initiative they take is bad. It is even true that sin can lead us toward some valuable things. The problem is that sin will also lead us and many innocent bystanders to some other consequences we may not want mixed in the bag. Perhaps the benefits of forbidden fruits are worth those consequences, but God alone can give us trustworthy counsel on such a question. Listening to Satan while ignoring God is always a kind of idolatry. It will always lead us away from Eden and toward the dreariness of a dying world.

The Second Temptation—Do Unto Others

At first, Eve doesn't fully grasp the problematic elements in the plan the serpent proposes. She acts. Then, as all of us are prone to do, she follows Satan's advice one step further and invites Adam to follow her. Although there is no suggestion that she deceives him (as Satan deceived her), neither of them seems to grasp that they are acting on Satan's counsel and not on the Lord's. The story thus reminds us of our human proclivity for perpetuating with others some version of the deceptions that have been perpetrated on us. This is not some special perversity of Eve's or of mine or of yours; it is the most common of human tendencies. We are often blinded to the ways we hurt others until we face how we have been injured ourselves.

Sometimes this realization comes only slowly. Sometimes we see with sudden clarity we have followed the golden rule in a most tarnished and distorted sense, doing to others, often those we love dearly, what has been wrongfully done to us. When a mother realizes she is damaging her children with the anxiety that maimed her own upbringing, when a father recognizes in his anger with his children the anger he was subject to, when a husband understands he is ignoring and neglecting a spouse within the pattern of his own neglect, when a roommate catches herself drawing a friend into the same self-destructive patterns undermining her life—these are terrible moments of recognizing our capacity for evil.

Until Eve brings it up, Adam has avoided grappling with the command to multiply. Relying exclusively on rigid determination to obey the command to not eat of the fruit of this tree, he has ignored the first instruction to procreate. Now, realizing Eve will be cast out and he will be alone, Adam chooses the first commandment and ignores the second. In the most human of responses, he decides he can fix this problem by taking matters (and fruit) into his own hands. He tries to mitigate the consequences of Eve's choice by participating in it instead of letting her take it to God for healing and redeeming. He too eats the forbidden fruit (apparently a crucial and necessary step), but he does so on the counsel of someone other than God—and that's the problem. He acts on his own judgment of what must happen to right this wrong.

A naïve "forgetting" that God knows more than we do seems to underlie the acts of both Adam and Eve. Though her intentions are good, Eve's choice suggests she believes Satan's portrayal of how this tree works over

God's, and she acts on her self-deception. Adam also seems to trust his own judgment over the Lord's forbidding, and he takes actions that will separate them from God, just as Eve's actions would have separated her from Adam. Despite their intentions, when each comes up against the second temptation to act upon others as they have been acted upon, each yields. But for repentance and the Atonement of Christ, each would become nothing more than an instrument in Satan's plan as well as a victim of it.

The Third Temptation—Hide

Satan's third temptation is suggested only subtly in the text: to hide. Adam and Eve hide from God among the trees of the Garden and hide their nakedness by sewing fig leaves into aprons as cover-ups (Genesis 3:7). The text cites fear as their motivation: "I was afraid, because I was naked; and I hid myself" (Genesis 3:10). The Bible Dictionary expounds, "Sin destroys that feeling of confidence God's child should feel in a loving Father, and produces instead a feeling of shame and guilt. Ever since the Fall God has been teaching men not to fear, but with penitence to ask forgiveness in full confidence of receiving it."[4] While shame and guilt are consequences of sin, Satan adds fuel to this fire by telling us to hide, either to wallow in our shame or to try to avoid sin's consequences. Hiding is the antithesis of repenting.

Commenting on this phenomenon, LDS psychologist Burton Kelly writes, "Who told them to hide? The adversary did. Why? His two primary objectives are that we fail to reach our potential and that we be miserable in the process. Hiding is a marvelous tool for Satan to achieve both of these objectives. His introduction of it in the very beginning was not an accident."[5]

Kelly goes on to enumerate the many ways we also are tempted to hide, either to try to cover our shame or to wallow in it. Satan's primary tool for accomplishing his goals is to destroy our agency. When we fail, he tries to convince us he has destroyed our agency and that we cannot change. Instead we can only hide. Kelly's lengthy list of ways we hide includes

- Lying, exaggerating, withholding relevant information, giving a false impression

- Employing psychological defenses of rationalization, denial, fantasy, repression, projection, dissociation, and so on

- Controlling and manipulating others to cover up our own fear or inadequacy

- Participating in addictive lifestyles that generally include extensive denial

- Dwelling on past failures or successes to avoid current challenges, risks, or possibilities

- Using self-pity or self-blame to manipulate others or avoid conflict or responsibility

- Getting angry as a way to blame, control, and punish others while denying our true power to respond more helpfully and humbly

- Using inaccurate language, such as saying, "I can't" when "I don't want to" is meant, or saying, "mistake" or "accident" when "avoidable result of poor judgment" is meant

- Sinking into obsessive-compulsive behavior that often covers unacknowledged anger or resentment, or denies agency

- Procrastinating to avoid facing the possibility of failure

- Being excessively busy so as to avoid intimacy or self-awareness

- Waiting for others to solve our problems rather than taking responsibility for them

- Creating all-or-nothing overgeneralizations that deny the complexities of reality

In all varieties of psychological pathology, a major contributing factor is our refusal or inability to know what we know. Instead, we hide from ourselves or others what is real either in the outer world or within our hearts, minds, or bodies. Kelly describes the extensive negative effects of hiding on physical health, relationship intimacy, and self-esteem. He concludes,

> In the intrapersonal realm, hiding is so destructive because self-awareness is the initial basis of all change and hence is requisite to personal growth, development, and fulfillment. As painful as the revelation might be, becoming aware of our weaknesses is essential to overcoming them (see Ether 12:27). To the degree we avoid or hide that awareness, we have no basis for change and [eventual] well-being.[6]

Ironically, shame researcher Brené Brown reminds us that even though we *think* others will be drawn to us for our accomplishments and perfections, we are *actually* more drawn to people we see as authentic, down-to-earth, and comfortable with their flaws. Our imperfections connect us to one another by reminding us of our shared humanity. They help us grow in compassion and the courage to be real. The best antidote to the pervasive (and probably inescapable) feeling of shame is sharing it with someone we trust. She reminds us, "Owning our story and loving ourselves through that process is the bravest thing that we will ever do."[7]

Sometimes, each of us, like Eve, is deceived by one who claims to be our friend, and we deceive ourselves in the process. Each of us, like Eve, perpetrates a certain amount of our own ignorance on others, knowingly or naïvely leading them away from God. Each of us, like Adam, sometimes chooses human companionship over God's, or believes we can fix things only God can fix. Each of us, like Adam, sometimes thinks the best course now is to hide from God and encourage others to do likewise. In short, each of us, like Adam and Eve respectively, is tempted to think we or someone else knows more than God about what is fair or real or good. We act in forbidden ways, encourage others to do the same, and then hide when reality begins to assert itself. We may also mimic the devil's responses when we get called out on our choices: ranting, raving, complaining, blaming, and threatening (Moses 1:19–22).

Taking action, with its inherent risks, is vital to God's plan of agency. If we are to grow, we will have to act, and if we don't act, that will be its own kind of failure. Taking action means taking a chance you will fail and a chance you will succeed. Some choices are riskier than others, but every choice carries a risk. We could avoid some risks by never leaving our cribs and doing nothing at all, but that doesn't seem to be the point here. Faith is a risk. Skepticism is a risk. Obedience is a risk. Rebellion is a risk. God tells us faith and obedience are less risky than skepticism and rebellion, but even skepticism and rebellion have a place, and even faith and obedience can get us in trouble. The scriptures attempt to delineate those choices with gravest consequences. We can pretend these consequences are optional and try to circumvent them, or we can try to protect others from the consequences of such choices (especially tempting with our children). But to the degree that the laws we break are not human inventions but divine descriptions of reality we will only dig ourselves in deeper when we do.

The internal or external voice that tells us to hide, whether in an intentional effort to sidestep the law or out of "simple" shame, is not the voice of God. God not only calls us out of hiding and upholds the choices we have made to leave him, but he also tells us how we may change our minds (repent) and make our way forward to find him again. So back to the story, the story of hope for God's hiding children.

The Plan of Healing Salvation

Adam and Eve make a brief foray toward hiding and shame. But then they turn around. When God invites them to come forward and tell him what has happened (Genesis 3:9) they are absolutely honest. Some people see evasion and blame in their responses, but I see only truthful descriptions of exactly what happened, acknowledging both the actions of others and their own complicity. Then, when the consequences of their choices unfold as God had previously described, they don't say, as I have been known to, "But we were just trying to obey your law to multiply! You are not fair! We didn't know any better! Why won't you protect us? And why are you now sending that deceiver exactly where you are sending us? How many times do we have to go through this?" Nor do we have any record that they say these things when they get to that lonely, dreary world where God is *still* allowing Satan to tempt them to think he can answer their prayers (Moses 4:3–4), where they *once again* must wait and wait and wait for God to send more instruction, and where they have to learn *one more time* the difficult art of spiritual discernment (Moses 5:2–6, 12–13).

This is what they do instead: They tell the truth. They covenant with God and each other to try again. They don't blame God or each other in the process. They submit without complaint or self-pity to all the consequences of their choices. And then they go to work to make the best of things, stick together, take another chance on obedience, and wait for as long as it takes for God to send someone to tell them what to do next (Moses 5:1–8).

What a concept. Quite different from the course we often take—the one that involves liberal expressions of humiliation or anger or fear, as if these might get God to change his mind or turn back the clock or make the world safer than it can be if agency is to be upheld here. In following such a course, we remake God in our human images, imagining a punishing, vengeful God who needs to be appeased by our shame and self-flagellation; or an ineffectual, truth-rescinding God who can be stopped by our anger and threats; or a relentless, controlling God who will never quit pushing us unless we put the foot down and refuse; or an indifferent, absent God we can't trust to return. Though *I* can behave in all these ways at times, and therefore imagine God does too, the God I have come to know is not like these false idols at all.

For example, after a period of soul-searching in which I asked God to help me be closer to him, an uncomfortable awareness of a particular sin came to my heart. I tried to put my life in order and then went to God to ask forgiveness. No feeling of forgiveness came. I went back to the drawing board of self-examination again and again, trying to learn my lessons. For the first few rounds of this, I could eventually identify things I yet needed to change. The sensibleness of what I was learning helped me avoid my tendency to see God as punishing and relentless for requiring all this painful self-reflection. But after several rounds of this "try again" approach my capacity for rational thought got swamped. I imagined an endless stream of demands for insight and change I could never pull off. I wondered how long it would go on. I wanted to either whine pitifully about my worthlessness or get angry about the futility of trying. I unconsciously hoped one of these two approaches might get God to ease up.

Somehow, at about this point, I managed to remember that I had, after all, asked God to teach me, so it made little sense to complain about being forced. This gave me a toehold on a tiny faith that maybe God was not the demanding, never-satisfied critic I was making him out to be, but an honest coach in my self-selected growth project. I went back to the drawing board once more. I began to see a deeply impactful pattern I needed to change in order to stop hurting myself and others. Then clearly, quietly, but definitively I received the peaceful assurance of forgiveness I had been seeking.

I was reminded again that God is humble, patient, and full of love, particularly toward those who desire to live his laws. I believe he wants to help us learn all we can about the ways we have wrongly imagined how the world is put together, including our inner world and including his world.

God does not spare Adam and Eve the consequences of their choices. Nor does he leave them comfortless. He offers them the protection of covenant clothing, symbols of his ongoing presence, and promises that through obedience and sacrifice, the redemptive power of the Savior can be activated on their behalf (Moses 5:5, 8). He can do this for them because they come out of hiding, lay aside shame and blame, and covenant in remembrance of Christ. There is an appropriate place for a kind of hiding that is really about privacy, boundaries, or even secrets—but not from God and not from ourselves. Knowing ourselves, owning that knowledge, and living out of it with integrity is the path to consciousness and freedom.

This is where Adam and Eve absolutely deserve the honor we as Latter-day Saints give them—not because they never mess up, but because they act with such nobility and courage when they do. They don't disintegrate into hubris or shame, exaggerated self-sufficiency or despairing self-flagellation. They don't blame each other or God. They take responsibility for their behavior without denying the circumstances that influenced them. They trust God can and will save them. They submit to his tutoring and judgment. They renew their covenants with him and each other. They walk out into the world. They do this not passively but actively, making choices, trying to figure things out, speaking their truths as best they can, accepting their absence from God, waiting and looking for God's messengers when they surely would prefer he speak to them face-to-face as he once did. They do not demand God demonstrate they are special by sparing them, or think themselves sought out for unfair persecution when he does not. They do not wallow in self-pity that God does not lighten up because, after all, they were the first people to come this way, and how were they supposed to know? They trust the Lord. They get on with business.

If Christ provides a perfect model of how to live, Adam and Eve provide us with a perfect model of how to die—to die to one worldview and embrace another, to let go of sin without letting go of hope, to yield to justice without despairing of mercy, to walk into the lonely, dreary world of personal sin and interpersonal betrayal and not shrink from the challenge. They do not lose trust when they lose innocence. They do not lose faith when they lose access to God's presence. They do not lose charity for each other when they become victims of each other's less than perfect decisions. They continue to choose hope even when hope is a frightening choice, fraught with the potential for disappointment. And they teach us, their children, how we also can hold on to what is real in the midst of our letting go.

Aprons of Fig Leaves

Like Adam and Eve, we must face the painful consequences of our naïve bargains with the devil and the choices we made to not wait for God's promised but as yet unrealized return. We fall when we see for the first time, or yet again, that we alone cannot conquer our sins, wounds, or grief; that, despite our best intentions, we have been blind and foolish and filled with hubris and self-deceit; that we do not know the way; and that all the answers we have are insufficient to the problems we face. We fall when we are filled with shame to suddenly see ourselves in the nakedness others have seen all along. We didn't know. We misunderstood. We failed the test we thought we were so cleverly acing. We want to run and hide, making aprons in some vain hope that God's all-seeing eye will be stymied by the sight of fig leaves, like Superman's vision is confounded by lead. But this is not a time to run and hide. It is a time to slow and speak. Multiplying old words is not the answer. Speed is not the answer. Hiding our ignorance is not the answer. Slow. Speak. Sort the wheat words from the tare words after both have been allowed to ripen together. Ask God to hear our words (Psalm

55:16–7). As we yield to God's instructive voice, he will provide us with tokens and signs, names and covenants, clothing and power to sustain us on our journey and help us find the way home.

The clothing Adam and Eve construct for themselves at first is the clothing of "quick, hide." We wonder if they do not feel a little foolish in it once they step out into the open. Fig leaves don't last long once cut off from the tree that gives them life, and neither do we. Yet there is no mention of God asking them to abandon these aprons they make, nor does he mock their efforts. Perhaps we can give these aprons new meaning, beyond something to hide behind, as we take them off and put them on again as part of a larger purpose. They can remind us of our weakness and insufficiency without the Lord, but also that he can make true on his promise to work *all* things together for the good of those who search, pray, trust, repent, and remember their covenants with him (Doctrine and Covenants 90:24)—all things—even this apron, encouraged by the adversary, and the mortal weakness it suggests.

The word *endow* comes from the Greek word *endevein*, meaning "to clothe." This first clothing Adam and Eve create may also become symbolic of an endowment of power if reclaimed and repurposed in response to God's voice and not Satan's. What power can there possibly be in flimsy leaves, scant covering, soon to wilt and crumble away? Perhaps it is the power of the "beginner's mind," as Buddha called that state of innocence that eschews pride and all claims to having the answers. This is the power we start with: the power of knowing our vulnerability. It is the power of humility, the power of the question too trusting to be hopeless, the muscle too ignorant to tense against a fall. New life emerges from questions, not answers; from the random, not from the ordered; from risk, not from safety. God honors this power, and we will take it with us into his presence. Without it, we can get too cocky or terrified to wander fasting into the desert in search of questions not yet formulated, answers not yet imagined.

Coats of Skin

There is a second item of clothing needed for shielding and protection in the desert wilderness outside the garden. The Lord provides it to Adam and Eve when he makes coats of skin to clothe them. Have you ever considered what has to happen to make a coat of skin? Quite simply, the previous owner of the skin has to relinquish it. Something had to die for Adam and Eve to be thus clothed, just as they will be subject to death, and just as Christ will die for them. Along with the rest of earth's life-forms, Adam and Eve will now be both prey and predator for the rest of their mortal lives. There is power in knowing we cannot claim our skin forever and that we live off the bounty of others' flesh, animal and divine. Awareness of the potential for life's loss is the price we pay to live gratefully, fully, close to the bone.

Coats of skin remind Adam and Eve of their need for protection, personal boundaries, and claiming as fully as they can the power and wonder of their own skin for as long as they are in it. These coats remind us of our dependence on the atoning death of Christ to save our skin and to cover and protect us adequately from life's vicissitudes. Awareness of Christ's willing submission to humiliation, suffering, and death—all for us—is not intended to heighten our sense of humiliation but to fill us with gratitude and hope.

The coats given Adam and Eve remind us some things must die so new life may be sustained. They remind us of our true identity as immortal spirits encased in the skin of animal bodies, which are vehicles of spiritual protection and teaching. They remind us to anchor our sense of safety in God's power to save, heal, and protect us after, not before, we are lost and wounded. They remind us of his power to keep us spiritually whole in the midst of the furnace, though our heart is faint at the sight of the flames.

In J. K. Rowling's novel *Harry Potter and the Sorcerer's Stone*, Harry, a young apprenticed sorcerer, learns the hidden secret of his mother's death when he was an infant, and the reason the evil ones recoil from him. The description is reminiscent of the way coats of skin may have provided our first parents with a powerful reminder of God's parental love. Harry is told by his headmaster,

> Your mother died to save you. If there is one thing Voldemort cannot understand, it is love. He didn't realize that love as powerful as your mother's for you leaves its own mark. Not a scar, no visible sign . . . To have been loved so deeply, even though the person who loved us is gone, will give us some protection forever. It is in your very skin. Quirrell, full of hatred, greed, and ambition, sharing his soul with Voldemort, could not touch you for this reason. It was agony to touch a person marked by something so good.[8]

The coat of skin seems to represent the soul-identity closest to our heart, shining with the lingering touch of God's deep and abiding love. It may be stained with our sweat and marked with our scars, but it also represents our covenants of faith that God will (eventually) provide us the compass to find our way in the wilderness though we are constrained to wander here. Where the apron might represent the power of confessing we do not know the way, the coat of skin could represent our faith that there is a way to be known and that we will find it by getting as close as we can to our own essence, and to God's. In fact these two sentiments go together: we are ignorant, and we are powerful—powerful when capacitated through Christ's Atonement to find and create the ways God knows. We can combat Satan's stultifying assertion that there is no other way but the ways we have always known—deadly, circular paths to false hopes for control.

Lessons Learned

Wisdom does not come, as the serpent implies it might, from sitting around eating delicious fruit as revelation after revelation drops upon us from heaven. Nor does wisdom come, as the serpent implies it will, from disobeying God's laws and ignoring his counsel. Wisdom, knowledge of good and evil, comes as we pass through the sorrow of trying to do the best we can, making mistakes anyway, experiencing the painful consequences of our choices and those of others, grieving the losses of innocence that leave us breathless at our human capacity for disobedience and self-deception—and repenting. This is Adam and Eve's great testimony to all their dying children: "Because of my transgression my eyes are opened . . . and again in the flesh I shall see God. . . . Were it not for our transgression we never should have had seed, and never should have known good and evil, and the joy of our redemption, and the eternal life which God giveth unto all the obedient" (Moses 5:10–11). Wisdom distills as we realize that the power of Jesus to save us is greater than the power of Satan to destroy. This is the vision that opens our eyes to who God really is, and how we may see his face with joy.

Adam and Eve turn away from the voice of Satan and come out of hiding, accepting God's invitation to speak the truth and begin the process of change. This is the first step in their repentance and in ours. Their conduct in the fallen world reveals they have learned the lessons they missed in Eden.

In the garden they acted impatiently on their own understanding. In the fallen world they demonstrate that they have learned to wait, "call[ing] upon the name of the Lord . . ." (Moses 5:4), obediently making sacrifices unto God even without understanding their significance, and patiently enduring until further explanation is revealed to them "after many days" (Moses 5:6).

In the garden, they acted independently of each other and then enticed each other to sin. In the fallen world, we read of their unity:

> Adam began to till the earth. . . . *And Eve, also*, his wife, did labor with
> him. . . . And *they* began to multiply and to replenish the earth. . . .
>
> And *Adam and Eve* blessed the name of God, and they made all
> things known unto their sons and their daughters . . .
>
> And *Adam and Eve*, his wife, ceased not to call upon God. (Moses
> 5:1–2, 12, 16; italics mine).

Fulfilling Adam's prophecy, "Therefore shall a man leave his father and his mother, and shall cleave unto his wife; and they shall be one flesh" (Moses 4:24), Adam and Eve cleave to one another as well as to the Lord.

In the garden, they trusted Satan's version of reality over God's. In the fallen world, they understand that "as many as believed in the Son, and repented of their sins, should be saved; and as many as believed not and repented not, should be damned; [for] the words went forth out of the mouth of God in a firm decree; wherefore they must be fulfilled" (Moses 5:15).

In the garden, they trusted Satan to keep them safe and alive. In the fallen world, they dare to be uncertain and to die, trusting in God's power to save and resurrect them as they submit to the certainty of his love.

Losing Innocence without Losing Trust

The garden story foreshadows the loss of innocence we too experience as we face betrayal and self-deception. It is no small project to lose innocence without losing the capacity to trust. The less reason life has given us to trust in the first place the harder trust is to retain. Yet Adam and Eve show us a path through this universal challenge of mortality, a path marked by both humble acceptance of their capacity to sin and unapologetic trust in God's will and power to redeem. They rightfully reclaim their status as "noble and great" leaders in the kingdom, teaching us in the process what we can do when deception, sin, and shame threaten our trust in ourselves and in God.

Shame is one of the forms our fear takes, but of course there are others. We can also fear loss, failure, the future, death, life, speaking up, holding still, being alone, getting too close—and the garden can teach us about each of these. Whatever our fears are, the occupants of the great and spacious building that represents the pride of this world will attempt to use them to keep us away from the tree of life (1 Nephi 11:35–36). God guards the way to that tree as well, but only until we have repented (Moses 4:31). Then he draws us to it and allows us to beckon to others as well (1 Nephi 8:9–15).

The Pearl of Great Price records, "And the Lord said unto Adam: Behold, I have forgiven thee thy transgression in the Garden of Eden. . . . Behold, thou art one in me, a son of God; and thus may all become my sons" (Moses 6:53, 68), and a later prophet adds, his daughters (Mosiah 5:7). Forgiveness is available to all who seek it and extend it to others.

Adam and Eve leave the garden just once, but we leave it many times throughout our lives. It is tempting to hang around the gates of Eden, trying to find a way back to the way things were before we knew we and others were capable of soul-wrenching mistakes and before we knew God would let us make them. The cherubim drive us off, not because God is vindictive, but because there is no going back to the illusion of safety once we have caught on to reality. Happiness is not found, as we think it can be, by turning back the clock to reclaim lost innocence, flawlessness, and proximity to God, but it is found by moving willingly into, and ultimately through, the fallen, dangerous, telestial world, which is the subject of the next chapter.

HEALING PRACTICE FOR CHAPTER SIX: NOT ASHAMED

Questions on Shame

- What is one thing about yourself you are ashamed of?

- Who taught you this was shameful, or what experiences led you to that conclusion?

- How do you try to hide it from others' and your awareness? (See list above.)

- What sins does hiding make you prone to?

- What do you miss out on by hiding from other people? How do you feel about that?

- To what extent does your shame reflect a false pride that you should be above making mistakes? What problems does that create for you?

- What image, phrase, or experience captures for you the mind-set of true humility?

- How can you increase humility and constructive guilt and reduce shame?

Shame and Pride

- Which of your personal traits and characteristics do you particularly value?

- How much did your parents or others take pride in your traits to build their own self-esteem or to serve their own needs?

- How do you traffic in these gifts to get what you need at the expense of a greater wholeness?

- Are these sources of pride also sources of particular shame when you fail?

- What do you want to do about your shame and pride?

Shadows

As you consider your "negative" traits, what strengths might be considered the other side of the coin of each weakness? (For example, a weakness of being easily bored with routines might have a corresponding strength of being creative.)

Corresponding Weaknesses	Strengths
•	
•	
•	
•	

- What would it take for you to live more honestly with your "shameful" weaknesses—to accept the strengths that go with them and take more responsibility for reigning in or working around the weakness rather than hiding?

CHAPTER SEVEN

THE DESERT OF DISCERNMENT

*Prone to wander, Lord, I feel it, prone to leave the God I love;
Here's my heart, O take and seal it, seal it for thy courts above.*

—ROBERT ROBINSON, "COME, THOU FONT OF EVERY BLESSING"

We replay the brave departure from Eden every time we face our losses and failures with grace, support the plan of agency even though it hurts, and humbly submit to the God who sends us away. The world we enter when we have seen our capacity to betray and be betrayed, deceive and be deceived, feels lonely and desolate. We wander in the dark with only the sporadic light of the moon to guide us. How did the world that at the end of the creation was glorious and beautiful become this dreary wilderness? Because wilderness is by definition the place where we cannot see God—"that which you hear is as the voice of one crying in the wilderness—in the *wilderness*, because you *cannot see him*—my voice, because my voice is Spirit." (Doctrine and Covenants 88:66; italics mine)—we too must rely on acute spiritual hearing, attuned to this still, small voice, to find our way. This is not as easy as it sounds, for there is a cacophony of voices here. But as Adam reassures us, if we learn our lessons well, "in this life [we] shall have joy, and again in the flesh [we] *shall see God*" (Moses 5:10; italics mine).

God doesn't send us away to punish us. We are here to gain practice in discerning good from evil, resisting the tempter's voice, and following the light of personal revelation to guide us home. We are here to learn to desire Christ and be perfected in him. In so doing we gain a measure of joy and power unknown to us before. In a universe infused with agency our ultimate safety does not lie in being kept out of harm's way. It lies in acquiring wisdom and self-awareness to detect, resist, comprehend, defeat, avoid, reform, cope with, heal from, and transcend evil. Mortality provides us with this crucial experience. Here we are truly in the driver's seat of our lives. We must navigate rough terrain at high speeds in the proximity of other drivers as inexperienced and reckless as we are. The gospel provides such maps, rule books, and manuals as can be communicated to people just learning to drive. Jesus Christ provides, if you will, the GPS, pit crew, and tow truck to get us home despite wrong turns, breakdowns, and collisions.

Who to Believe?

In Eden, Adam and Eve choose to believe Satan rather than God about what is real and true, a choice Satan would rather we not see for what it is. He whispers to us to do not just wrong things, but also to do right things at the wrong time and for the wrong purpose. The Hebrew word *nachash* translated as "serpent" in the Genesis story also means "shining" or "bright," implying that the being who spoke to Adam and Eve in the garden was Satan appearing as, and trying to assume the authority of, an angel of light. This idea is reiterated in 2 Nephi 9:9, in which Nephi refers to the devil as "that being who beguiled our first parents, who transformeth himself nigh unto an angel of light." One of our challenges in mortality is to figure out what about us is drawn in by Satan's deceptions so we can better detect and dismiss him.

Outside the garden, Adam and Eve gratefully teach us, their children, about God's mercy and plan of redemption, but Satan teaches us something else, and the choice is played out again as to whom we all will believe:

And Adam and Eve blessed the name of God, and they made all things known unto their sons and their daughters.

And Satan came among them, saying: I am also a son of God; and he commanded them, saying: *Believe it not; and they believed it not*, and they loved Satan more than God. And men began from that time forth to be carnal, sensual, and devilish.

And the Lord God called upon men by the Holy Ghost everywhere and commanded them that they should repent;

And *as many as believed in the Son, and repented of their sins, should be saved*; and as many as believed not and repented not, should be damned; and the words went forth out of the mouth of God in a firm decree; wherefore they must be fulfilled. (Moses 5:12–15; italics mine)

This is the crux of our earthly probation: Will we believe Satan, or will we believe the Lord? We play out this choice in a thousand ways as we try to decide what will make us happy or help us heal: Drugs? Scriptures? Money? Faith? Anger? Patience? Insistence? Submission? In this lonely world the threat of our being hungry, ignored, and powerless is constant, and Satan's loud insistence that he can keep us safe and in control is tempting indeed. He is eager to answer our prayers and draw our adoration. Receiving light and knowledge from God requires patience, trust, putting off the natural man, and responding to whispers heard with our heart, not with our ears. Receiving revelation is not optional if we wish to grow spiritually.

The themes of this telestial experience echo the experiences of Jesus Christ in the wilderness, where he encounters both angels to be believed and followed and the devil to be detected and ignored. As we learn these telestial lessons, we learn to seek truth, recognize it when we find it, and follow it home. We come back to Life, moving a little further toward the God whose face we seek. "But the path of the just is as the shining light, that shineth more and more unto the perfect day" (Proverbs 4:18).

The Anointed One

Just as Jesus was baptized to fulfill all righteousness, I assume he was anointed to his sacred office and endowed with all the identities we learn of today through the temple. *Messiah* means "the Anointed One."[1] We see elements of an endowment experience in Jesus's retreat to the desert wilderness following his baptism. He is taken by the Spirit to the *desert* to commune with angels and with God (JST Matthew 4:1; Mark 1:13; italics mine). The Spirit then takes him to the Holy City, to the pinnacle, the Aaronic priesthood *temple* (JST Matthew 4:5; italics mine). Finally he is placed on an "exceeding high *mountain*" where the Spirit shows him all kingdoms with their different glories (JST Matthew 4:8; italics mine). Wilderness, mountains, and temples—all are traditional sites of endowment revelation by which we too are prepared to commune with angels, reject the devil, gain power and glory, and find the holy ones we seek.

Though sketchy, the scriptural details of Christ's wilderness experience suggest ancient temple themes catalogued by LDS scholars, including a retreat into solitude; descents and ascents; communing with God's messengers; obedience and sacrifice; preparing for the missions of adulthood; learning true identities; experiencing telestial, terrestrial, and celestial glories; expelling Satan; and communing with God.[2]

The wilderness to which Christ went was, according to tradition, an area of desert and cliffs bordering the Dead Sea. This was the lowest spot in the ancient world. It is still a bleak place almost devoid of life, for all its stark beauty. In the temple, we also descend in many ways—into the baptismal font, another kind of dead sea, "instituted as a similitude of the grave,"

(Doctrine and Covenants 128:13); into the vulnerability of the washing and anointing rooms; down and down again to the earth as we review the events of creation; into the garden of our earliest mortal experiences, where we forget our former status and relationships; and finally into the lonely, telestial world. Descending to the desert floor, we begin to contemplate the depths of who we are. Out of such descent, Christ can bring healing, wisdom, discernment, and spiritual strength.

Curiously, the Dead Sea, this lifeless place of ultimate descent, is sought out even today for its great healing power. People go there to soak in sooth-ing, restorative water that has a texture like oil. Bitter and mineral-laden, these waters can choke the life out of a person, or they can wash, anoint, and buoy up, depending on the respect or reverence with which they are entered. Perhaps this is true of any experience of descent.

The Deceiver's Voice

Christ's wilderness retreat includes both communion with angels and experience with Satan's false claims. First the scriptures record: "Then was Jesus led up of the Spirit into the wilderness to be with God" (JST Mat-thew 4:1) "and was with the wild beasts; and the angels ministered unto him (Mark 1:13). Whatever Jesus was taught about heavenly beings is not recorded. Perhaps it could not be. We can only assume this forty-day initia-tion included new understanding of his identity, his earthly mission, and the plans of his Father. Perhaps he was shown his role in the Creation, or the unfolding of the Fall, Atonement, and Restoration. Of these things we can only guess, but the pathway to them is clear: "Jesus was led up of the Spirit." This must be our course as well—to follow every shred of light we can find.

Hard on the heels of these forty revelatory days, the tempter makes his entrance. It is hard to imagine the Messiah, fresh from this holy commu-nion, being impressed much by a face-to-face confrontation with the evil one. I wonder if Christ's temptations came in forms similar to mine, Satan's voice barely discernible from my own thoughts. Perhaps these temptations sounded more like such almost-reasonable notions as, "If I am the Son of God, I could turn these stones into bread. I really am tired and hungry." Or even, "Wait, what am I thinking? How horrible to even consider using my power so selfishly! Who do I think I am!" The deceiver calls to us in simi-lar terms: *I don't deserve to be hungry given all I'm trying to do. Why hasn't anyone cooked dinner? Do I have to do everything around here?* Or perhaps: *I can't believe how selfish I am. Where did I get the crazy idea I could be a decent Mormon? I should give this whole thing up now. God must be disgusted with me.* We take Satan's voice for our own and become angry at others' inconsideration of our special status, or ashamed of believing in our worth against a barrage masquerading as deserved self-condemnation. "And thus he flattereth them, and leadeth them along until he draggeth their souls down to hell; and thus he causeth them to catch themselves in *their own snare*" (Doctrine and Covenants 10:26; italics mine).

As we enter the complex and paradoxical adult world, all our anointings bless us to discern truth and live by our values. Meanwhile, Satan encourages our self-deception and self-betrayal. He lulls us into believing all sorts of lies and exaggerations: *I shouldn't have to tolerate disappointment or being made afraid. Money can buy anything. God has abandoned me anyway. Power can keep me safe. I am hopelessly lost if I do not live up to every covenant perfectly.* Amid this disorienting chorus, some part of us keeps searching for a clearer, truer, more hopeful voice.

How do we recognize the voice of Satan, either externally in the world or internally in the mind and heart? There is no simple answer. Even when we have discerned the con man once, he shows up again in new guises. We are deceived by the righteous intent of blind guides, the moral failures of the otherwise decent, and the selfish goals of the willfully sinful. We are deceived by our own ignorance, hunger, pride, fear and jealousy, and we deceive others in turn. With Adam and Eve, we often learn only at great cost that God means what he says and means it to us personally, and that other portrayals of reality will fail us in the end. We are just as likely to doubt his merciful love for us as we are to doubt his truth-telling condemnations of evil.

The voice of God is also virtually indistinguishable at first from our own thoughts, but it is quieter and less dramatic than Satan's. Some significant revelations simply occur to us, unpretentious and unremarkable. Many do not come in words at all, but in quiet feelings of hope, acceptance, delight, warning, or direction. While I rarely mistake God's voice for Satan's, I often mistake one of their voices for mine, mine for one of theirs, or Satan's for God's.

Of course, much of the time I know what is the decent thing to do—the brave, loving, honest, responsible thing—I just don't want to. But not every decision is readily classified into good or evil, right or wrong. Sometimes our search for truth requires peering into shadows, struggling with paradox, wrestling with angels. If attending one temple session is good, would staying for a second one be better—or a way to avoid pressing duties? Is that nudge I feel to talk to the taxi driver a revelation or a distraction?

Should I tell my friend she hurt my feelings or handle it myself? Is that urge to fast from revelation or from a anorexic superstition?

Tolerance for ambiguity is widely regarded as a sign of maturity, but ambiguity provokes our anxiety. We scramble to create little personal rules to calm our fears: *You should try harder. Always avoid conflict. Expect God to be disappointed. Don't trust women.* After a while, we hit the limitations of such approaches, however. Our wariness doesn't just keep us safe; it also keeps us stagnant, lonely, and insecure.

So let's say we catch on. We decide to try to be more trusting, more courageous, more open. The next step is to find our betrayals and self-deceptions repeated, seeming to prove our rules were warranted: *You idiot—you just blew it again! You were right to be wary!* What's a person to do? We must learn more than "trust" or "don't trust," but "trust whom, for what, under what circumstances." We also learn we can tolerate disappointment, heal from betrayal, and recover from loss. We do not have to put all our effort into avoiding them. Indeed, if we do, then we will have nothing left to invest in creativity, closeness, or growth.

People around us may imply this is all easy: *You should know you can trust me. I can't believe you fell for that old con. How could you doubt this inspiration? Can't you see this child needs some discipline?* These are easy to say from the viewing stands. But we seldom enjoy the luxury of making hard life decisions from lofty perspectives. We make such judgments down in the swamps, hungry and alone, on moonless nights, whistling in the dark to stave off our fear of predators. If we are lucky, distant warning voices of those who have been here before will echo to us. We may or may not have the presence of mind to heed them, especially when their advice seems far removed from the experience at hand. We may hear no echoes at all for the pounding of our hearts, the rumbling of our stomachs. Our fears and hungers run so deep, and they can make us blind even when we think we are trying hard to see.

Christ's experiences in the wilderness suggest guidelines for detecting the voice of the deceiver and the voice of the Spirit—with a caveat to us lesser mortals: unlike the Savior, we will all fail at these things, and that is when the real trial begins. What will we choose to do when we feel angry that God has let us get hurt, when we doubt he could still love one so blind, or when we can't imagine how to ever trust others or ourselves again? Will we learn, grow up, forgive and be forgiven, fine-tune our "rules" or transcend them altogether and try anew? Or will we protest instead that God should turn back the clock, restore us to Eden, and make us as if we had never known about con men, never hurt someone we love? Will we choose to trust God's will and power to save us, or put all our energy into trying to get so safe as to not need saving? These are some of the difficult choices we face when we follow Adam and Eve into the lonely world on the other side of betrayal and transgression.

Principles of Discernment

God invites us to seek spiritual guidance to navigate our murky world, but our prayers draw to us messages and messengers of many kinds. Christ's experience in the wilderness suggests four principles for discerning truth from versions of reality that will fail us in the end.

- We learn discernment by *experience*, not intellectual understanding alone.
- *Scriptures, covenants, and counsel* reinforce true messages.
- True messages bring us *power*, while false messages offer us *control*.
- *Self-awareness* enhances discernment.

In the abstract, these four principles may seem obvious, but discerning in those dark swamplands amid the chaos of conflicting voices is hard. If we are willing to walk with patience this tutoring course God sets us on, learning from mistakes without despairing, we will eventually come out into the light with our instincts honed and our spiritual muscles strong. These are not casual, optional pursuits. If we want the spiritual blessings the temple points us toward, this is the only path. We must obey the light of Christ each of us has been given, not doing the thing God has told us not to do and waiting for him to tell us more. When no answers come, we follow as best we can the light we have, doing what is most consistent with our most enlightened understanding of who God really is.

This is not an obsessive-compulsive, frantic, fear-based pursuit of every item on the to-do list, but a thoughtful willingness to seek and do what the Spirit of the Lord guides us toward, one thing at a time. The goal is not to keep every one of the 642 commandments with perfection each day, but to keep the one commandment God invites us to keep right now. Obedience to the light we have will eventually bring us more light, which will eventually bring us to our perfect Savior: "That which is of God is light; and he that receiveth light, and continueth in God, receiveth more light; and that light groweth brighter and brighter until the perfect day" (Doctrine and Covenants 50:24).

Let's consider these principles in more depth.

Principle One: We Learn Discernment by Experience

Joseph Smith taught that the process of personal revelation, discerning God's voice, is learned by *experience*, carefully pondered over time: "the things of God are of deep import; and time, and experience, and careful and ponderous and solemn thoughts can only find them out."[3] It is hard to accept that experience is the only way to learn some things, however, because some experiences really hurt. Some of that pain is avoidable through obedience to God, but even when we try hard to hear aright, we misstep, we fall, and we get scraped up in the process. So do the people around us, even when they try hard, sometimes taking us down with them. And that doesn't even take into account the people who are not trying hard, or Satan, who is trying hard to destroy us.

Apparently even Christ had things to learn by experience that could not be learned in any other way "that he may know in the flesh how to succor his people according to their infirmities" (Alma 7:12). Did Jesus fully understand who he was before hearing the voice out of heaven proclaim, "Thou art my beloved Son" (Mark 1:11), or did he, like us, live for years with premonitions but not certain understanding of his identity and mission? Paul writes to the Hebrews:

> Forasmuch then as the children are partakers of flesh and blood, he also himself took part of the same. . . .
>
> For verily he took not on him the nature of angels; but he took on him the seed of Abraham.
>
> Wherefore *in all things* it behooved him to be made like unto his brethren, that he might be a merciful and faithful high priest in things pertaining to God, to make reconciliation for the sins of the people.
>
> For in that he himself hath suffered being tempted, he is able to succour them that are tempted. (Hebrews 2:14, 16–18; italics mine)

If Jesus was made like unto us "in all things," learning by earthly experience and not just by remembering his role in heaven, perhaps the forms his temptations took were not vastly different than ours. If even Christ could be tempted and Joseph Smith fooled by Satan appearing as an angel of light (Doctrine and Covenants 128:20), then surely we too will have to confront conflicting voices and learn discernment through experience, effort, and in our case, mistakes.

We would never expect to learn to play the piano without ever hitting a wrong note, or to qualify to play professional basketball by merely reading the rule book. Yet sometimes we think if our intentions are good and we are trying hard, then we should never make a mistake at discernment. If we want to play with the pros, then we have to be willing to not only learn the rules but also learn how to apply them while playing the real game. Sticking to spiritual "Chopsticks" is one way to reduce our error rate, but that is hardly a good strategy if we are trying to learn to play spiritual Beethoven. If there were an effective substitute for personal experience in learning good from evil, why bother with mortality?

A client was deeply hurt when a trusted church leader deceived and betrayed her. She spent a long time trying to figure out why God did not protect her when she was trying hard to discern his will and follow it. I do not claim to fully understand the answer to that honest question. It is hard to accept how vulnerable we are to being deceived or hurt, even by others who also try hard to discern (at least, in my most generous moments, I assume they do). But scripture never refers to the Lord as the Great Preventer, only as the Savior. His offer of salvation follows, but does not preclude, others' errors or our own. He will keep us saved but not always safe. These are lessons we have to learn again and again in a world where things that go bump in the night assault both our bodies and our imaginations.

Principle Two: Scriptures, Covenants, and Counsel Reinforce True Messages

In a religion that relies so heavily on personal revelation, what keeps us from all flying off in a hundred directions while trying our revelatory wings? The safeguards God gives us include intensive study of the scriptures, personal integrity, and counsel from others.

Scriptures. The Savior models reliance upon scriptures when, at the moment of decision, he uses them to answer each of the deceiver's temptations: "*It is written*, Man shall not live by bread alone, but by every word that proceedeth out of the mouth of God" (Matthew 4:4). "It is *written again*, Thou shalt not tempt the Lord thy God" (v. 7). "*It is written*, Thou shalt worship the Lord thy God, and him only shalt thou serve" (v. 10; italics mine). Satan also touts scripture to the Savior, however, reminding us that the intent of the law, not just the letter, is key.

I love that the scriptures are full of stories, not just penal codes. Some psychotherapists assert that telling people what to do makes clients become more like the therapist, while telling stories that clients can apply as they see fit helps them become more fully themselves. Scripture stories help us use true principles to become more fully ourselves. They tell us about real people playing the real game with real opponents while trying to stay in bounds and not foul out.

Stories like Nephi killing Laban are tricky, however. Sometimes they give us courage to follow revelation unique to our circumstances, but some people use them to justify "revelation" that is self-deceptive. How do we know the difference? Frankly, sometimes we don't. We can realize too late that we have rationalized stepping out of the bounds the Lord sets, or that we have been too timid to take a bold stand in his name. We can sometimes feel good about poor choices, and God will usually let us learn these lessons the hard way. He does not always rush in at the moment of decision to nag us to not do something he has already warned us against through scriptures or living prophets. He lets us choose. Then if we get it wrong, he humbly asks, "Will you turn around? Will you try again?"

Integrity. God's covenant with Israel was that he would be their God and they would be his people. He promised to provide for, preserve, and sanctify them. They promised to become a holy people, set apart from the world by their obedience and worship. Today we make promises at baptism and in the temple that qualify us for this covenant relationship.

Even Christ does not become a god unto himself, but operates with integrity within a covenant relationship with the Father. He responds to the adversary's temptations, saying: "Man shall not live by bread alone, but by every word of God," and "Thou shalt worship the Lord thy God, and him only shalt thou serve" (Luke 4:4, 8). Christ turns to the Father for sustenance, safety, and purpose. True messages invite us to be true to covenants we have made within our relationship with God.

Counsel. Christ's superior wisdom in all things probably precluded relying on the counsel of anyone but his Father, but when we are in doubt, counseling with other people provides a safeguard for our efforts to discern the Father's voice. We can get counsel from families, home and visiting teachers, presidency counselors, teachers, quorums, bishoprics, stake leaders, conference talks, and other living sources.

The more difficult it feels to subject our conclusions or choices to someone else's scrutiny the more likely we are acting self-deceptively. I've seen well-intentioned, active members ignore counsel all the way to apostasy, adultery, bankruptcy, spouse abuse, abandoning children, job loss, and jail. They are not monsters or idiots. Or if they are, then so am I. They are generally otherwise decent people who ignored or avoided counsel, became over-reliant on their own unchecked revelation or overconfident of their own powers of resistance. They started to miss things, to rationalize, to blame others, and to hide. To be sure, our human counselors also have human frailties, biases, and blind spots, but "it is written" in Proverbs 11:14, "Where no counsel is, the people fall: but in the *multitude of counselors* there is safety."

Principle Three: Truth Brings Us Power, Not Control

Power seems to be the coin of this earthly realm we live in. Power struggles, whether between spouses or nations, underlie most of our problems. In the Joseph Smith Translation of Luke, after Christ rebuffs the temptation to turn stones to bread, he is blessed with a great spiritual vision of all the kingdoms of the world from the top of a high mountain. After this glorious manifestation from God, "the devil said unto him, All this power will I give thee, and the glory of them: for that is delivered unto me; and to whomsoever I will give it. If thou therefore wilt worship me, all shall be thine" (Luke 4:6–7).

I'm not sure how such a temptation might have come to the mind of Christ—perhaps as a thought to skip the agony of the Atonement and go straight to the glorious Second Coming? In any case, power over other people is something not even the Son of God can rightfully take. Such dominion must descend upon us as the dews from heaven, without compulsion, drawn to us by love and righteousness alone (see Doctrine and Covenants 121:45–46). When we forget this truth and try to take control over other people, we relinquish our true spiritual power. Once again, Christ recognizes and dismisses the deceptive pull, trusting in God's timetable. God will bring him glory and honor at the conclusion, not the outset, of all his earthly trials. Meanwhile, even Christ must trust in our willingness to be drawn by his love, without compulsory means.

Satan's voice inside of our heads speaks to our longing for control-based power, while Godly voices teach us the basis of true power. In the Topical Guide in the LDS scriptures, when *power* and *Satan* are found in the same verse, the power referred to is almost always *power over* (or control over) another person. This is the kind of power Satan both claims and offers us.

In contrast, when *power* and *God* are found in the same verse the preposition used is almost always *to* or *of*. God's power is the *power to* accomplish and bless through the *power of* the Spirit. Godly power is the *power of* an eternal perspective on the challenges of our lives, the *power of* peace amid paradox and ambiguity, not the control we imagine in having all the right answers. Spiritual power seems to include *power to* nurture, subdue, and learn from our bodies rather than ignoring the needs of our flesh. *Power to* lies in risk-taking with its inherent messiness and falls, not in the clean, hard control of doing only what is easy. *Power to* is often enacted from curiosity and humility, not in the controlled conditions of satiation and conclusiveness. We can discern the influence of Satan in the pull to be in control, while true spiritual power is *power to bless* others and bring them to Christ. In the following by M. Catherine Thomas, note that the greatest mysteries do not give us privilege or power over others, but show us how to bless and bring others along:

> The urge to know the mysteries of godliness is no idle curiosity; rather, it is a divine drive to acquire that level of *godly power* modeled by Christ and others of his holy order. It is in addition the means of increasing one's power to bring others to Christ: "And if thou wilt inquire, thou shalt know mysteries which are great and marvelous . . . that thou mayest bring many to the knowledge of the truth." (Doctrine and Covenants 6:11; see also Alma 26:22)[4]

Many circumstances challenge our commitment to God's plan of agency, including the dangerous choices of others. Agency is a wonderful thing until someone uses his or hers against us. We may try to control them in turn, but the harder we try to control what we cannot control (like other people), the more out of control we will feel. We fail to find and exercise our true power when we clamor instead for control. We learn more about the difference between godly power and unrighteous control from the Doctrine and Covenants:

> The powers of heaven cannot be controlled nor handled only upon the principles of righteousness. That they may be conferred upon us, it is true; but when we undertake to cover our sins, or to gratify our pride, our vain ambition, or to exercise control or dominion or compulsion upon the souls of the children of men . . . behold, the heavens withdraw themselves; the Spirit of the Lord is grieved; and when it is withdrawn . . . ere [we are] aware, [we are] left unto [ourselves] to kick against the pricks, to persecute the saints, and to fight against God. (121:36–38)

We are stripped of whatever spiritual authority we had clothed with and are left to ourselves, at enmity with others and with God, when we seek to exercise unrighteous control. We persecute the Saints and fight the Lord's plan of agency even if we never leave the Church, and we find ourselves stinging from the pricks of our conscience and others' resentments.

Where there is agency, violence and intimidation are within our power to perpetrate upon one another. If we insist on a god who purports to always keep us safe and in control, we will be worshipping an idol of our own making. The God of truth tells us plainly that here death and pain are inevitable but surmountable. Our true freedom lies not in restricting choice, ours or anyone else's, but in the Atonement of Jesus Christ, which provides a freedom that circumstances cannot constrain.

In the premortal world, we were free to choose evil once we had chosen good, but only through our acceptance of the Atonement of Christ are we free to hope to be good once we have chosen evil. This is the agency Christ offers us, as Lehi explains:

> And the Messiah cometh in the fulness of time, that he may redeem the children of men from the fall. And *because that they are redeemed from the fall they have become free forever, knowing good from evil*; to act for themselves and not to be acted upon. . . . And they are free to choose liberty and eternal life, through the great Mediator of all men or to choose captivity and death according to the *captivity and power* of the devil; for he seeketh that all men might be miserable like unto himself. (2 Nephi 2:26–27; italics mine)

Christ does not promise us control, whether over our children, our leaders, or our enemies, but he does assure us that if we will choose him and his ways, his power to save is greater than the deceiver's power to destroy. Our salvation is never in the imagined safety of control, but in the pilgrimage path toward atonement.

It is a righteous desire to seek the holy power of God, to want to come into his presence, and to bring with us all who will be drawn there by love. True messages empower us in our search for God's promised blessings. The most trustworthy voices in our minds do not overpower us, flatter us, belittle us, threaten us, yell at us, trick us, or make grandiose claims. Instead they are respectful and uplifting; they testify of Christ; they ask questions such as "What do you think?" (Matthew 22:42; Acts 8:30); "Are you being true to what you already know?" (Abraham 3:25–26; Genesis 18:19–21); "Do you traffic in your identity and gifts, bartering them away for wealth, security, or other illusions of control?" (2 Nephi 26:31; Acts 8:20); and "What additional light and truth do you want?" (Helaman 13:29; Ether 2:25). True messages are spiritually empowering (Doctrine and Covenants 38:32) and remind us not to relinquish our true spiritual power for the illusion of control (Doctrine and Covenants 121:36–37, 46).

Christ's calm, reasoned response to his adversary contrasts with our own responses to those who oppose us. We are more prone to attempt to control others with anger, self-pity, jealousy or fear than to exercise the true power in humility, quiet self-assertion, and responsible action. Anger is often a disguise for such an effort at control as we puff ourselves up with threats and rages. We are especially prone to such puffing and huffing when what we really feel is small, powerless, and out of control. When we feel threatened by another's rage, it pays to remember that the angrier someone appears, the more threatened he or she might feel. Self-pity is another indication that some part of us is trying to gain the illusion of control by blaming others and choosing powerlessness rather than taking the risks that go with claiming our true power. Jealousy is a way to sidestep the demands of our personal gifts and mission. Envy lets us ignore the price others pay for their gifts, allowing us to pretend we should not have to pay such prices either. Anxiety is often escalated by a misguided effort to control the unknown; the more we try to control what we cannot control, the more out of control we feel.

What can we do instead? We can get back on the throne of our life, wearing the apron of mortal weakness with humility but dignity, admitting our ignorance or hurts and living in expectation that we and others can change. We can wear our God-given coat of spiritual power close to our skin, claiming the power that is ours to receive and to bless amid the power that is not ours. We can ask to be treated with respect and fairness, offer our gifts with love, ask in good faith for what we want, and counsel with others about how to effect change. We can wear our creative gifts joyfully and chuckle at the ignorance and pride that makes us think one person's gifts matter more than another's. We can choose to trust the Lord.

When we long for the control of perfection, God invites us to grow in the power of humility. When we get down on ourselves for not being enough, God invites us to join the ranks of those who progress toward godhood through hungering and thirsting, losing the popularity contest, flunking the test, feeling sullied by others' sins, enduring pointing fingers, being less than amazing. Our place in God's heart is ours by virtue of our covenants and desires, independent of today's accomplishments.

> After the devil's offer of earthly power and glory is resisted, true power and glory come:
> And when the devil had ended all the temptation, he departed from him for a season.
> And Jesus returned in the *power of the Spirit* into Galilee; and there went out a fame of him through all the region round about.
> And he taught in their synagogues, being *glorified* of all. (Luke 4:13–15; italics mine)

Principle Four: Self-Awareness Enhances Discernment

Although we often speak of three temptations faced by Jesus, there is a fourth more insidious than the rest. It is hidden in the word *if.* "*If* thou be the Son of God," the deceiver intones, "command that these stones be made bread." "*If* thou be the Son of God, cast thyself down" and let the angels bear you up (Matthew 4:4, 6). The temptation is twofold: First, will he traffic in his identity for his own gain, selling out on his name simply to satisfy his hungers or flaunt his power? *Or* will he abandon his identity, ashamed of trusting in its power and hoping in its promise. After all, it *is* quite preposterous to the rational mind to claim kinship with deity. Yet deity's voice proclaims us his. For some it is the struggle of a lifetime to trust that assertion. Jesus models such trust without fanfare, quietly refusing to either debate or prove by dramatic means his naming as God's Son.

Satan's third temptation begins with this provocative, "*If* thou be the Son of God," followed by a taunt to Christ to cast himself down from the pinnacle of the temple and let the angels rescue him. I've certainly tried such Houdini feats, trying to call forth some wondrous, rescuing sign of my mission or of God's love, demanding nothing bad happen to me when I take dangerous risks so as to prove I am special or at least visible to God. I too am tempted to try to get God to change the realities of the world to fit my purposes—changing self-neglect into nourishment, inactivity into results, or spiritual sloth into spiritual power (but it's an emergency!). I have thrown tantrums of anger or pleading when I have to wait too long for answers, as though if I act miserable enough I can compel the angels to come. And when things get bad enough, I can sink into hopeless despair that I am not who God claims I am, that I was foolish to trust him, or that perhaps there is no God to father me at all.

I didn't always know I do these things, but having spent several decades now asking the Lord to show me my sins and weaknesses, I have less trouble identifying which antics I am prone to. Jesus shows me the better path. He does not place himself above the rest of us when it comes to living within the prescribed limitations of mortality. He counters the "if" temptation with scriptures available to us all: "It is written again, Thou shalt not tempt the Lord thy God" (Matthew 4:7).

The more clearly we know our own internal voices, the more accurately we can distinguish them from deceptive or divine ones. True messengers will honor our truest identity, inviting us to be more of who we are, not more of who they are.

Trusting God

In the crucial but challenging task of discernment, there are no guarantees. We are so dependent on the whisperings of a still, small voice to compensate for our spiritual blindness. Experience is reliable only after our failures, scriptures can be twisted to justify almost any conclusion, counsel from others can sometimes mislead, covenants are too broad to easily apply to every specific decision, and personal revelation is not always available on demand. We must learn about our blind spots, become familiar with our internal voices, tame our desire for control, and combat our tendencies to anger, self-pity, jealousy, and fear. Only then can we discern with confidence.

Unlike Christ, we will all fall short of victory over Satan. We will be deceived, we will deceive, and we will then face the biggest question of all: will we trust in God's will and power to save us? One of the biggest temptations, especially for basically good people, is to doubt the power of forgiveness when we fail the tests of mortality and yield to the tempter's voice. As my daughter once taught me, repentance is not the backup plan for mortality; repentance *is* the plan. Satan is "*the accuser* of our *brethren . . .* which *accused* them before our God day and night" (Revelation 12:10; italics mine). His voice in our mind is often accusatory, threatening, sarcastic, blaming, belittling. This is the voice to ignore. Christ is our advocate, the one who is always on our side (1 John 2:1). The voice of his spirit, even when corrective, is hopeful, affirming, and kind. Our challenge is to trust in the sanctifying power of the Spirit, and to trust that his sanctifying power is not just for those already holy but also for those who are broken beyond mortal repair. We trust in this forgiveness not because we deserve it, not because it makes sense, and not because it is an easy out. We trust it because we choose to believe God tells us the truth when he tells us he is on our side and that his grace is sufficient, even for us. Ultimately, faith is a choice we will always make among competing voices and perspectives; it is not a conclusion we come to after all the options have been neatly eliminated.

Where Satan offers satiation, Jesus chooses spiritual hunger as the precursor for true nourishment. Where Satan suggests proving one's specialness, Jesus opts to submit like everyone else to the laws of this mortal sphere and to God's as yet unproven power to save him. Where Satan offers power over mortal exigencies, Jesus models submissive discipleship. Where Satan offers the forced adoration of the masses, Jesus claims only his right to learn compassion by the things he suffers, taking a chance on our willingness to be drawn to him by his love.

Power in the Desert

There is another desert story of temptation and choice, short and seldom referenced by Christians, that touches me deeply. It is the story of an Egyptian slave woman who belongs to Sarai, wife of Abram. Abram and Sarai have been promised by God that Abram will be the father of God's covenant people, an endless posterity, but as yet the couple has no children. Marriage contracts recorded at this time period sometimes specify that if the wife does not produce an heir within so many years, she can purchase a slave to bear children for the couple. Apparently children from such an arrangement were considered to belong to the couple, not to the slave.[5] Sarai apparently acquires Hagar to perform this function.

Apparently Hagar is treated by Abram and Sarai in such a way that she learns to trust the God they worship and prepare herself to follow him. But when Hagar becomes pregnant, she takes a little too much pleasure in her new status for barren Sarai's comfort. (These are such human stories!) Sarai complains to Abram, who tells Sarai to handle this matter with her handmaid as she sees fit. Sarai "deals hardly" with Hagar. Hagar flees into the dreary desert wilderness to wander in her own testing ground until an angel (also translated "messenger") finds her. Their dialogue is brief but poignant (Genesis 16:8–11):

> "Hagar, Sarai's maid, whence camest thou? and whither wilt thou go?"
>
> "I flee from the face of my mistress, Sarai."
>
> "Return to thy mistress and submit thyself to her hands. . . . I will multiply thy seed exceedingly, that it shall not be numbered for multitude. . . . Behold, thou art with child, and shalt bear a son, and shalt call his name Ishmael, because the Lord hath heard thy affliction."

This is high-magnitude personal revelation. *Ishmael* means "God hears." Apparently Hagar does indeed feel heard and answered in this encounter, for she in turn hears God and heeds him. We don't know what experience prepared Hagar to gratefully receive this messenger rather than fleeing or swooning or doubting. But there in the desert, probably facing down internal voices of abandonment, self-pity, jealousy, and fear, Hagar is visited, and she hears. She does not insist on control, even though she is sent back into the fray of a turbulent family triangle. She shows integrity in her promises to God, Abram, and Sarai. She trusts in the power of forgiveness. In turn, God does not leave her comfortless. He knows her by name, enlarges her identity, and expands her vision of what she may yet become as a mother of nations.

The scriptures record: "And she called the name of the Lord that spake unto her, Thou God seest me." Another translation renders it: "She gave this name to the Lord who spoke to her: 'You are the God who sees me,' for she said, 'I have now seen the One who sees me'" (Genesis 16:13, New International Version).[6] From the sound of things, like Jacob in a generation to come, Hagar understands this messenger she sees, and who sees her, to be God (see Genesis 32:24, 30).

This may be the best candidate for an Old Testament story of a woman's direct encounter with God, and it is a slave, an Egyptian, out of sorts with her mistress and alone in the desert, who is thus encountered. He promises to her as to Abram an endless posterity, and gives to her, not just to Abram, the name to give this child who would not legally even be hers. God hears her affliction, knows her name and her circumstances intimately, and though he does not release her from bondage, he opens her eyes to see the One who sees her, and to see herself more clearly in the process. Like the traveler left by the side of the desert road, Hagar receives the ministrations of the Holy One, who does not pass by on the other side but instead sees her, has compassion, and comes to her (Luke 10:33). What mortal servitude would we not endure to obtain such an inheritance? She knows that whatever else she is, she is his.

So this is the desert journey, following Adam and Eve and Abram and Sarai and Hagar—and Jesus—into the water, out to the wilderness, up to the mountain, into the holy city, back to the private chambers, descending and ascending again and again for every dead part of ourselves that needs redeeming by name. On the journey, we learn about taming our anger, quieting our self-pity, redirecting our envy to get back to our own life, humbling our pride, and calming our fear. We find the power of both our ignorance and our true identity as daughters and sons of God with bodies, parts, and passions. Not hiding in shame but humbly veiling our glory, we take our place in the circle, at the altar, at the veil, finding our voice and our dance, and walking not back into God's presence, but forward toward God's presence, bringing with us every soul we can love enough to convince to come along. In doing so we not only see reality accurately and respond to it from our deepest values, we gain power to change reality. We use what we have learned through hard experience to engender new life into old realities, coming to know God in the process. These are the powers God offers us through the wilderness journey of mortality.

HEALING PRACTICE FOR CHAPTER SEVEN:
THE DESERT OF DISCERNMENT

It Is Written

One way to know if we are listening to the Spirit is if we feel consistently directed to meaningful study of the scriptures. Especially if scripture study is difficult, pray for the Spirit before you start (even if you only have five minutes). Start small, and include general conference talks in your study.

If you don't get a lot out of reading, try memorizing some passages. Try listening instead of reading sometimes. Don't rush. Studying a few verses for fifteen minutes is generally better than racing through three chapters in fifteen minutes.

Write, speak, dance, or draw a key idea each from your study. Apply the scriptures to you, reading with your specific concerns in mind. Look for the character and attributes of Christ in what you read. Try putting each verse into your own words to clarify what you understand.

Responding to What Really Is from Deep Values

Pick a problem in your life right now and write it down.

- What aspects of this problem do you actually control?
- What values do you hold about how to behave in such situations?
- What other values do you hold that seem to be pulling you in a different direction?
- If you were to ask for 100 percent of what you want, what would it be?
- What stops you from asking for 100 percent of what you want?
- Would waiting with patience or giving someone else what they want take you to your growing edge?

Living Our Values

- Who have you tried to control this week through anger? How did you do it? What did your anger look and sound like? What fear underlies the anger?
- Who have you tried to control this week through self-pity or unexpressed resentment? How did self-pity look and sound—how

did you "do" self-pity? What were you trying to avoid by doing things you resented doing? What were you trying to gain?

- Whom do you envy, and for what? What risks or self-doubts do you try to avoid by focusing on this envy? What part of your mission could you get back to instead?

- How can you tell in your posture, facial expression, activities, or words that pride is active? Does pride show up for you more in personal perfectionism or in criticism of others? What would true humility require?

Reality Checks: Claiming the Power of Mortality

If you really claimed your mortality, really let yourself know you will die, what would change in your life? If you had only a short time to live, how would you respond to that reality from your deepest values?

- What would need to be in order so your family could go on without you?

- What relationships would you want to mend or nourish before you go?

- What would you want to make sure you left the world? What work would you want to complete this year?

- What experiences would you want to have while you still can?

- What traits would you want to work on developing before you leave?

- What would you want to repent of while you still have a body to help you?

- What spiritual preparation would you want to make to meet God again?

- How would you perform your church callings during these last weeks or months?

- How would you order your daily life now?

Reality Checks: Claiming the Power of Eternity

Then, if you knew you were going to live at least a hundred more years . . .

- What would you want to do physically to preserve your body or cope with pain?

- What would you need to change financially so your resources would last?

- What would you do differently to take care of your home and belongings?

- What would you change about your career if you would be at it for a long time?

- What relationships would you put more time into if you had plenty of time?

- How would you order your daily life now if you had all the time in the world?

- What would you go ahead and try if there were lots of time?

- What would you want to learn if you had all the time you needed?

- What would you stop worrying so much about if time were not pressing?

- What would you make time for that you don't now?

EXPERIENCES CLIMBING THE MOUNTAIN

CHAPTER EIGHT

LEARNING TO LOVE

———∞∞———

The structure of community is a circle . . . the appropriate social structure for a "pilgrim people," a people on a journey together.

—MARY ANN CEJKA[1]

After the long night of soul work, the lights eventually come up. With the breaking of this quiet dawn, the time has come to pursue in earnest the God we can only find in the tops of the mountains. To our amazement, however, our long experience with descent has actually brought us very close to the summit. We thought we were falling and falling, but we have been climbing all along. We glimpse the misty veil that hides the peak from our view. We know it can't be far. Maybe there is hope after all.

As our eyes adjust, we find ourselves in a world untethered to scriptures and stories from the past, but which grounds us in the present. It is a world of work to be done. The sick need to be healed, the hungry fed, church leaders sustained, missionaries protected, and friends and neighbors served. Terrestrial space invites us to tackle the myriad challenges of our wards and communities, committing our hands and our faith to blessing others out of all we have received. As we do so we enter a portion of the terrestrial realm of the Millennium. Perhaps that future Zion state will not simply descend with Jesus when he comes again, like a giant Emerald City landing upon us from above. Perhaps, under Christ's direction, we will first work together to solve this world's problems and create the holy cities of Zion. We can begin that work here and now. Our collective acts, touched by Christ's present grace, can lift the human race closer to the God we seek.

But work is not the heart of the gospel of Jesus Christ. Love is. Love is the central law of God's habitations. Love is the factor that turns ordinary work into sanctifying labor. This is a daunting notion to those of us who never feel more inadequate than at love. How do we prepare to live in Zion, and to unite our love-poor hearts with those that are rich in love? Having recovered our history, body, creativity, hope, and discernment, how do we now take our place in the community of Zion? Are we up for this climb after all?

Bearing the Burden of Loving

Trying to love well keeps us humble for many reasons. We can't help but notice the pettiness of our preoccupations, the selfishness behind our generosity, and the coolness beneath our warm façade. The great gospel laws to love our neighbor and our God bring us up short against our scrawniness at love. We love too sparingly or too greedily, too rigidly or too loosely, too jealously or too distantly. We are already weighed down with calendars, finances, houses, and jobs. Life piles on additional loads of illness, despair, trauma, or sin. When we add to this the weight of caring relationships and service to others, the strain can feel backbreaking.

Jesus promised, "Come unto me, all ye that labour and are heavy laden, and I will give you rest. Take my yoke upon you, and learn of me; for I am meek and lowly in heart; and ye shall find rest unto your souls. For my yoke is easy, and my burden is light" (Matthew 11:28–30). How can we experience the yoke of Christian discipleship as rest and respite to our love-burdened souls rather than as heaviness and guilt?

A yoke is not just an additional burden, I remember. Yokes make it possible to balance the weight of a load and shift it from the weaker muscles of hands and arms to the stronger muscles of shoulders and back.[2] The yoke of Christ is also designed to help us rebalance, gain perspective, and carry our burdens from our strengths.

Still, sometimes I struggle to make sense of Christ's assertion that his burden is light. I imagine his back in Gethsemane, bent with anguish under the burden of his mortal mission. There, he shouldered all it means to be human, including being injured and demeaned in ways that leave us feeling distinctly unloved, maybe unlovable; losing things and people we love; feeling overwhelmed by the world's suffering; struggling to love when neglect or injury have left us love-impaired. He shared in all our mortal suffering from the lovelessness of this world and found it as bad as we know it can be (Doctrine and Covenants 19:18). When I imagine him turning his back to the smiters who flogged him without mercy or carrying the cross through the mocking crowds to Golgotha, I so want to ease the burden he shouldered. But of course, I am his burden too:

For he said, Surely they are my people . . . so he was their Saviour. In all their affliction he was afflicted, and the angel of his presence saved them: in his love and in his pity he redeemed them; and he bare them, and carried them all the days of old. (Isaiah 63: 8–9)

His burden was not light, but I trust it was lighter than the alternatives—lighter than letting us all die without hope, lighter than loving us less than was his nature to do. Love creates burdens for me as well, heavy with the weight of potential and blessing. Christ is the master carpenter, who knows how to make an "easy" yoke for me.[3] Now it is my task to take it up, so he and I together can carry our burdens of love—carry them long and well, all the way to the very top of the mountain.

Principles of Love

Picking up the yoke of Christ is not an esoteric, symbolic exercise. The loads I face are as jarringly present as a neighbor's cancer, a brother's discouragement, a leader's need for support, or a spouse's wounded faith. Some of the heaviest loads are my own fears. What might happen if I let myself be cared for, if I came to trust, put down my guard, and exposed my flaws? Love is the greatest source of blessing in our lives and the place of comfort, learning, and joy. But love is also where we feel most vulnerable to being rejected, mocked, ignored, or abandoned. We long for emotional intimacy, but we fear it. We resist getting too close. We can't trust people with our hearts. We can't be trusted with theirs.

Four principles stimulate my imagination as I join the circle in striving to shoulder the yoke of Christ and build Zion as a place of unity and love that will fit us to enter God's presence. They are principles by which love is learned and practiced:

Order that makes us trustworthy. As we order our lives on true principles, we become people of honor, trustworthy for relationships with people and with God. We build out lives to the square of obedience with exactness and integrity, thus gaining confidence that our will aligns with God's

Receiving that strengthens humility. The more deeply we receive God's love the more humbly we can acknowledge our weakness, confident that God loves us still. We humbly make a receiving place for all God is willing to give.

Blessing others through our strengths. As we receive God's compassion, our compassion for others multiplies. We reach out our hands to bless, liberate, and heal others out of the store of gifts we've received.

Prayer that invokes miracles of charity. While we can practice love in many ways, its highest expression, charity, is a gift of the Spirit given in response to prayer. As we come before God to plead for charity, we access the powers of heaven to change the world with our words as well as our hands.

The processes of ordering, receiving, blessing, and praying increase our capacity for both human love and the charity that comes as a spiritual gift. This is the work of building Zion, briefly discussed below.

Order

Putting our lives in proper order is an initial step in making us safe to love. The order we seek is the Order of the Son of God. The words *order, ordain,* and *ordinance* share a common origin. These words show up frequently in the scriptures and in the writings of early Church leaders.[4] People of many faiths join religious orders patterned after exemplary religious leaders and take vows of silence, celibacy, and poverty to increase their devotion. Latter-day Saints make covenants to follow a religious order prescribed by Jesus Christ. We vow to conform our lives to Christ's gospel. We order our speech instead of being silent, order our affections and sexuality instead of renouncing them, and consecrate our resources instead of embracing poverty. Such disciplines give parameters and substance to love, which is built through what we say, how we touch, and what we give.

The original name of the Melchizedek priesthood was the "Holy Priesthood, after the Order of the Son of God" (Doctrine and Covenants 107:3), implying that the Melchizedek priesthood is "after" this Order of the Son, but not precisely equivalent to it. In the temple, both men and women enter the Order of the Son of God. President Ezra Taft Benson teaches:

> To enter into the order of the Son of God is the equivalent today of entering into the fulness of the Melchizedek Priesthood, which is only received in the house of the Lord. Because Adam and Eve had complied with these requirements, God said to *them,* "Thou art after the order of him who was without beginning of days or end of years, from all eternity to all eternity" (Moses 6:67). . . . This order is . . . an order of family government where *a man and a woman* enter into a covenant with God—just as did Adam and Eve—to be sealed for eternity, to have posterity, and to do the will and work of God throughout their mortality.[5]

Within the Order of the Son, love can be experienced and practiced. In fact, the best description of this loving order I know of is the instruction given in Doctrine and Covenants 121:34–46, including these lines:

No power or influence can or ought to be maintained, by virtue of the priesthood [or whatever Godly authority we have to bless others], only by persuasion, by long-suffering, by gentleness and meekness, and by love unfeigned;

By kindness, and pure knowledge, which shall greatly enlarge the soul without hypocrisy, and without guile. . . .

Let thy bowels also be filled with charity toward all men, and to the household of faith, and let virtue garnish thy thoughts unceasingly; then shall thy confidence wax strong in the presence of God . . .

And thy dominion shall be an everlasting dominion, and without compulsory means it shall flow unto thee forever and ever.

These principles apply as much to women who order their lives within the Order of the Son as they apply to men who also hold the priesthood, which is "after" that Order. When my internal voices are self-critical or even self-hateful, these principles teach me how to talk to myself. They are ordering principles for all loving relationships.

Just as bones order our physical body to give it strength or a carpenter's square orders the placement of bricks to build a wall that will bear weight, so God's laws provide order and structure on which to build a life that will hold up under the stresses and strains of love. Because they resist decay longer than any other body part, bones are regarded by many cultures as a symbol of the spirit, the "indestructible life force" of an individual upon which a mortal life is built.[6] This premortal identity as monarchs and gods in embryo must be named anew in mortality even though it is the most fundamental part of who we are. Our eternal identity and godly potential orders our truest understanding of ourselves, giving us confidence to love without jealousy or fear.

What are the essential orders that help you remember who you are and have promised to be? What symbols and practices commemorate your ordering of your life as a disciple of Christ? Consider how you order your scripture study, your family life, your temple attendance, your goals and pursuits, and your time for self-reflection and spiritual communion. What have you learned so far about the daily orders that help you stay on track with your priorities and stay open to the spontaneous needs of those you love? How do such orders help you gain the integrity to love well?

Order Establishes Trustworthiness

Ordering our lives through obedience to God's laws helps us be trustworthy in all our relationships. As much as we begin to trust God by observing order and consistency in the universe, we begin to trust ourselves as persons of integrity when we consistently order our lives by righteous principles. Order encourages trust.

I remember a beloved older cousin, Doug, who married while I was still in high school. As I wondered about what love is and how I might recognize it if it came along, Doug shared with me his definition of love. "Wendy," he said, "you spell love 't-r-u-s-t.'" Doug's definition is still valid and wise. I can see that trustworthiness is foundational to love, and that trustworthiness flourishes in the stability, calm, and predictability that order facilitates. As I gently order my life by obedience to God's laws, I can begin to see myself as someone who can be trusted with other human beings.

Bottom lines are a way to help order our lives in ways that help others trust us and help us trust ourselves. An important step in recovering from addictions is establishing bottom lines—behaviors we simply will not do, and those we will absolutely do. Such absolutes help us defeat addictive patterns that undermine integrity and trustworthiness. Bottom lines are not flexible or creative, but they provide strong foundations on which creativity can thrive.

A recovering bulimic needs to avoid bingeing and purging, but this big bottom line might be impossible to keep unless smaller bottom lines are kept—bottom lines such as never eating ice cream alone, or always eating breakfast. Big, universal bottom lines may be impossible to hold unless we discover and respect smaller bottom lines personal to us.

I think perhaps I am a recovering mortal, a recovering natural woman. Part of the ordering of my life is to get clearer about my bottom lines—the hungers I cannot neglect, the number of unordered days I cannot exceed, and the delusional notions I will not believe again. While not every relational decision can be decided by a bottom line, bottom lines help us develop integrity and self-discipline foundational to moral behavior. Bottom lines help others trust us, or trust us again, so love can take root. Are there areas in your life and relationships that would benefit from some bottom lines? What small bottom lines might help you keep the big bottom lines that matter most to your personal identity and mission?

When our lives are properly ordered by obedience and sacrifice, we in essence raise our hand to sustain the order by which God operates in the world. We order our lives according to his laws. When we unite our efforts with others who are also ordered in this way, we begin a process by which we gain access to the powers of heaven. Joseph Smith teaches, "By union of feeling we gain power with God."[7] Ordering our personal lives through obedience and sacrifice is the first step in preparing us for this unity and spiritual power. We join a circle of believers who are learning to pray Zion into existence with our righteous desires and acts.

Receiving

The principle of receiving characterizes the gospel as pervasively as the principle of order. After baptism initiates us into the order of God's Church, the first commandment given to us is to receive the Holy Ghost. I note the officiating elder does not give us the Holy Ghost or command the Holy Ghost to fall upon us; rather he says to us, "Receive" (John 20:22), to open the door and let the Spirit in. We are also entreated to *receive* God's commandments (Proverbs 10:8), servants (Doctrine and Covenants 84:36), words (James 1:21), blessings (Doctrine and Covenants 93:20), and grace (Romans 5:17). Perhaps the most important thing for us to *receive* is the love of God, that pure fruit that alone can truly nourish and heal the soul (1 Nephi 8:15–18). One of the most oft repeated injunctions of the Savior is to ask, that we may *receive* (Matthew 7:7–8).

I once had the privilege of traveling in the game reserves of Kenya, where a monkey taught me something about receiving. One night, we stayed in a sort of tent hotel, and in the morning, dozens of tiny spider monkeys were using one of the tent tops as a giant trampoline. They ran up into the overhanging trees, jumped onto the tent top, bounced a few times, then scampered down and ran up the trees again. I stood for some time, morning muffin in hand, enthralled by their antics. A tapping on my shoe interrupted my reverie. I looked down to see a little spider monkey touching my foot and looking up at me. As he caught my attention, he lifted a tiny, cupped monkey hand in what I guess must be the universal sign for "please?" I broke off a piece of my muffin and offered it; he grabbed it and ran. I marveled at the means by which even a little animal could communicate his desire to receive. I think it took courage for that little monkey to approach me with his needs, and he reminded me as he took the muffin and ran that even when we get what we want, it is scary to get close.

I realize I am not always as clear or as brave as that little spider monkey. I may get the courage to ask, but I am afraid to wait around for the answer. Or I may insist I need nothing, spreading my fingers wide so anything landing on them sifts right through. Someone trying to help me can pour on endless supplies of love and support, but nothing sticks if I do not make a receiving place.

Other times, my hands are clenched fists, grasping and hoarding my relationship holdings lest they get away. In such a state, what I have is never enough to make me feel safe. I cling to yesterday's manna for fear of tomorrow's famine, and by the time I take a nibble, it has lost all its nutrients.

In order to truly receive, my heart must be like the monkey's cupped hand—willing, open, accepting what I am offered and trusting it is enough.

I learned more about receiving years ago when working with a client, a dear sister in great pain. She imagined herself standing at a door with Christ on the other side, as the scripture describes (Revelation 3:20). She wanted desperately to feel closer to him, to feel his love. She felt as though she were pounding on the door to him with all the effort and obedience she could muster, pounding until her hands were bloodied and her arms were weary, but she could not push the door open. I ached for her, and I wondered with her why God did not open this door. As I silently prayed for help the Spirit seemed to whisper, "The door to the soul opens in." We must pull it open and receive the Lord. Something in this changed perspective helped her imagine new answers for old problems. She began working on receptivity instead of insistence and perfection. Peace came.

I learned much from this experience. Too often I think my pleading for change, my overt misery about the status quo, my doing and doing with more and more attention to detail, or my browbeating over my spiritual inadequacies will get him to *remove* my difficulties and weaknesses, which is the solution I want. What he offers instead is usually peace *in the midst of* difficulties and strength in the presence of weakness, if I will but open the door and receive.

Sometimes our receiving hands are filled a little at a time. Willingness to receive what God is willing to give us, even if it is not all we think we need, is more like traveling with a compass than with a road map. Most of us would rather have the map. Here in the wilderness, God more often offers the Liahona.

How do you cultivate a receiving heart? What helps you remember and believe you are a cherished child of a loving Father who knows you by all your names, and who provides and cares for you personally? Are there symbols, images, experiences, musical selections, scripture passages, stories, people, or places that help you open your hands and your heart to receive?

Receiving Leads to Humility

As if receiving the Spirit or care from others were not challenging enough, the principle of receiving also challenges us to receive ourselves, with all our dependencies and needs. Some of us aren't too keen about the idea of admitting our needs, especially if we have been humiliated for being vulnerable or needy. The world esteems the powerful. It can feel shameful to accept our status as beggars with hands outstretched to God (Mosiah 4:19). We might imagine him feeling disdainful or judgmental of our poverty, as we may feel about the beggars who reach out their hands to us.

God does not deride human neediness as we do. Instead, he chastens us for our illusions of self-sufficiency:

> Because thou sayest, I am rich, and increased with goods, and have need of nothing; and knowest not that thou art wretched, and miserable, and poor, and blind, and naked: I counsel thee to buy of me gold tried in the fire, that thou mayest be rich; and white raiment, that thou mayest be clothed, and that the shame of thy nakedness do not appear; and anoint thine eyes with eyesalve, that thou mayest see. As many as I love, I rebuke and chasten: be zealous therefore, and repent. Behold, I stand at the door, and knock: if any man hear my voice, and open the door, I will come in to him, and will sup with him, and he with me. (Revelation 3:17–20)

Christ's Sermon on the Mount shows us the spiritual progress we can make when we are willing to receive. It proclaims, "Blessed are the poor in spirit [those who acknowledge their spiritual poverty and dependence on God]: for theirs is the kingdom of heaven" (Matthew 5:3).

When we accept at soul-level our dependence on God's bounty, we begin to mourn the ways we have ignored others' needs, profited emotionally from their weakness, or basked in our imagined superiority. This humble sorrow elicits the consolation of the Spirit: "Blessed are those that mourn: for they shall be comforted" (Matthew 5:4).

As we see ourselves more honestly, genuine meekness can replace shame, false pride, and all the erroneous beliefs that uphold them. This is suggested by the third beatitude, "Blessed are the meek: for they shall inherit the earth" (Matthew 5:5). In meekness, we can afford to really listen because we don't always have to be right. We can afford to need people and let them need us because both our humility and our compassion are genuine. We see how we are alike in our struggles more than how we are better or worse than others. Such meekness nourishes emotional intimacy with others and with God.

Emotional closeness is not without its drawbacks, of course. Many of us believe, "If others knew me as I truly am they would never like me or help me, so I must build good walls and provide for all my needs alone."[8] We may give, but out of the silent hope we can "buy off" God so he won't allow us to get hurt again. We may serve, but do it to feel morally one-up on those we put up with. We may anticipate others' needs deftly and expect others to anticipate ours so we won't have to be so vulnerable as to ask. We may choose to believe we really don't need a thing and resist knowing we are wretched, and miserable, and poor, and blind, and naked. Or we may assume our needs don't deserve to be met, or are too huge to be met—so we never ask.

A good question for all of us—especially those who feel resentful of others' "failures" to meet our needs—is, "Have I made my needs explicit?" Being explicit requires us to face our fear of appearing selfish, foolish, or vulnerable. Even more, being explicit requires us to face our fear of being disappointed. To be sure, we will not always get what we want, and it is important to learn that disappointment is tolerable. Then we don't have to avoid disappointment at all costs by never needing or asking. We can see that disappointment is not an indicator of the unfairness of the universe, the self-centeredness of our friends, or our own worthlessness or stupidity. It is simply disappointment—unpleasant but survivable.

A friend of mine prays regularly for eyes to see the evidence that she is loved. Such a prayer acknowledges that we control our willingness to receive. We can open the door to God's comforting presence, even if tonight he comes without the other gifts we desire. We can ask God to help us ask for what we need, tolerate disappointment, trust that goodness is out there somewhere, and open our hands and hearts to receive. How well do you seek, see, and receive the evidence that you are loved?

Receiving the fulness of the Holy Ghost, receiving ourselves, and receiving one another is the second step toward gaining that love or "union of feeling" that accesses spiritual power and builds Zion (see above).

Blessing

The third principle of love and power is to pour out on others the gifts we've received—to teach, heal, lead, feed, strengthen, and engender spiritual life in other people. Our unique life purpose unfolds as we are drawn to bless others out of all God has given us.

How can we bless others without bankrupting ourselves? After completing his mortal ministry, Christ came without fanfare as a resurrected being to the banks of the Sea of Galilee. There the Lord asked Peter the poignant question, "Lovest thou me?" Three times the question, three times Peter's heartfelt affirmation, and three times the Lord's simple request, "Feed my sheep" (John 21:15–17). This is Christ's fervent call to every disciple seeking to love well: feed my sheep. But lest we feel overwhelmed by others' hungry mouths (or our own), consider what happens in the story before Christ sends the disciples to feed the flock.

Peter and the others have been out fishing through the night and have caught nothing. In the early morning they are invited by a stranger on the shore to cast their net again. When they cannot draw in the net for the multitude of fish, they know this stranger to be the risen Lord, for they first met him under just such circumstances. When the miracle is repeated, Peter recognizes in its abundance an identifying characteristic of the Master. Notice the tender details as the story continues:

> As soon as they were come to land, they saw a fire of coals there, and fish laid thereon, and bread. Jesus saith unto them, bring of the fish which ye have now caught. Simon Peter went up, and drew the net to land full of great fishes, an hundred and fifty and three: and for all there were so many, yet was not the net broken. Jesus saith unto them, Come and dine. . . . Jesus then cometh, and taketh bread, and giveth them, and fish likewise. (John 21:9–13)

Only after he has provided for them beyond their capacity to draw it in, built the fire, tended it to coals, kneaded the bread, cleaned the fish, cooked the food, and served the meal does the Savior send his disciples out to feed others. And feed them what? From the abundance he has also provided. What a powerful reminder of the intimacy with which he knows our needs. He does not condemn the disciples for their hunger, but provides nourishment to body and spirit. He does not ask them to give from what they do not have but to simply distribute whatever catch he has provided.

We too must first feast at the cookfire of Christ if we are to feed his sheep with pure hearts. We must draw in the abundance he offers before we set up the soup kitchen. We must feel deeply our own need for the Savior in order to have compassion for the hunger of others. Out of his fulness, Peter later writes to the church:

> Feed the flock of God which is among you, taking the oversight thereof, not by constraint, but willingly. . . . And when the chief Shepherd shall appear, ye shall receive a crown of glory that fadeth not away. . . . [Cast] all your care upon him; for he careth for you (1 Peter 5:2, 4, 7).

As we receive (let in, acknowledge, value, trust, appreciate) the love and spiritual nourishment Christ offers us directly and through others, we can then reach out our hands, filled by him, to bless others. Motivated by empathy, we feel our common plight with a hungry world. Continuing the progression outlined in the Sermon on the Mount, when hunger and thirst for righteousness replaces our illusions of self-sufficiency, God can fill us (Matthew 5:6). We extend mercy to others as we acknowledge the mercy we so desperately need (Matthew 5:7). Our hearts are pure from being cleansed by the Atonement of Christ and because we truly see ourselves for who we are: needy, weak, and inclined to sin just as ar those we serve (Matthew 5:8). Our heart's motives become more pure, and our intentions more honest. The Beatitudes affirm the pure in heart shall see God, and in this honest place we do begin to see him. We see him in the faces of our brothers and sisters. We begin to love them despite their sins and failures without holding ourselves apart, for we realize he has loved us in just this way. We can finally accept without shame all he offers us because we can give to others without pride.

As the Apostle Peter, recipient in the above story, states, "As every man hath received the gift, even so minister the same one to another, as good stewards of the manifold grace of God" (1 Peter 4:10).

Blessing Others from Our Strengths

Each of us has saving missions to perform and gifts by which to serve. A popular phrase today is "Build on your strengths." My husband adds, "strengths that strengthen others." One of my favorite films is *Chariots of Fire*, the story of Eric Liddell, an Olympic runner who later became a powerful Christian missionary in the Far East. During one scene in the film, his devout sister wonders why he wastes his time running when he could be devoting himself to missionary service. She can see no potential for good in Eric's athletic pursuits and wants him to go to China to preach the gospel. But he says to her, "I believe God made me for a purpose, for China. But he also made me fast. And when I run, I feel his pleasure." The film portrays how Eric's athletic gift, when combined with obedience to God, allows him to testify powerfully of God's grace and touch many lives for good. Liddell later also became a devoted missionary in China.

Sometimes we must search through the rubble of a thousand halting actions and interactions to find how God has made us fast, and why. We must discover and rediscover what really matters to us, what we love to do and who we love to be even when it is difficult. But by these bright beacons we chart a life course. We may raise children or orchids, build computers or legal arguments, paint pictures or fences, teach Primary or graduate students, make houses or homes. But when doing what we are called to do, a certain lightness of foot often accompanies our efforts. We find direction in what feels easy, energizing, and enjoyable.[9] In the ways God has made us fast, we find the missions to which God calls us, however improbable or common.

Once we discover how we are fast, we must still discern the times and seasons of our personal missions, endure the doldrums of training, suffer the indignities of failure, and search for direction and balance. Careers may bring money or praise, and careers often have an important place in life, but matters of mission will be connected to serving God's children. Our work, like God's work, finds its worth in the worth of a soul. When we do not have an outlet for serving others, our lives do not reflect our true nature. Even if our available channels for giving love are not the ones we would prefer, even if our talent for loving is meager, we must find ways to care and serve or we will start to shrink inside. Not loving will ultimately hurt us more than not having been loved.

How seriously do you take your capacity and duty to love within your sphere? Do you have the courage to take risks, make mistakes, and try again as you develop your gifts? Can you tolerate the messiness and confusion that are the beginning of all learning and all relationships? Do you rejoice in your capacity to engender life in others, or do you shy away from your calling as a savior on Mount Zion? God calls us to feed the world, one meal, one hungry soul at a time. Every hand is needed in its place.

Not all of our missions are easy, energizing, and enjoyable, however. Some are difficult, draining, and dreaded. Moses, Hagar, Sariah, and Enoch did not always feel enthusiastic about the tasks God gave them. I don't always like parenting, or visiting teaching, or serving. I wonder if what I do matters enough to be worth the effort. I am tired. I don't know how to be helpful. I don't want to offend. I can barely keep up with my own life without taking on part of someone else's. I wonder if miracles can occur in such small increments and would prefer a bigger bang. Fear in one form or another opposes my desire to do good.

As I consider the vastness of the world's needs, it is good to remember that during his mortal ministry Christ did only good, but even he did not do all the good there was to do. He did not heal all the lepers, feed all the hungry, and raise all the dead. Much of the time he trusted the people around him to figure out how to get by. As I try to shoulder a share of the world's challenges, I too can do good without thinking I have to do it all.

Of course, sometimes I not only don't want to do it all, I don't want to do anything! Then what? I once read an article in some running magazine by a man who said his body was over-programmed to conserve energy at all costs. That sounded pretty familiar. In order to get himself to exercise, he had to fool this energy-conserving predisposition. This was actually quite possible, however. He would get home from work and put his exercise clothes on "just to be comfortable, *not* because I'm going anywhere." He would then go look out the door "just to see what the weather is like, *not* because I'm going out in it." He would then decide to walk down the street "just to see what the neighbor is doing, *not* because I'm going running." But once dressed and outside and in motion, it was not that hard to keep going.

This technique is exactly what I need to get past my internal resistance to anything requiring energy. I talk myself into tiny, unobjectionable steps, sneaking past the internal energy-conservers who would probably eat and nap all day if they had their way. "I'll just look up the phone number to make sure I have it, not because I'm actually going to call right now." "I'll just make a visiting teaching appointment, and I can always cancel it later." "I'll just drive by her house and say hi, but I don't have to stay." I know it sounds silly, but in this most unheroic of ways I manage to calm down the internal voices that think their job is to save me from anything hard. I ease my way into the loving acts I would (mostly) really like to do.

And when this fails, I just plain ask for help: encouragement, reminders, ideas, company, listening, or inspiration. Sometimes I need to bite the bullet and get busy, but sometimes I first need someone to hold my hand or teach me how.

Reaching out our hands, individually and collectively, to bless one another out of the bounty we have received is the third step in building Zion unity. Such unity brings down power from heaven and brings us closer to the God whose face we seek.

Prayer

As we place our lives within the order of the Son, receive the Holy Ghost and all his incumbent blessings, and minister to others out of the fulness we have enjoyed, we move toward a new kind of relationship with God. His ways are our desires. His will is our will. We gain spiritual power to have our words acknowledged as if from his mouth. This principle is described in *Lectures on Faith*:

> And through the whole history of the scheme of life and salvation it is a matter of faith: every man received according to his faith . . . and nothing was withheld from him when his faith was sufficient to receive it. He could stop the mouths of lions, quench the violence of fire, escape the edge of the sword . . . women could, by their faith, receive their dead children to life again; in a word, there was nothing impossible with them who had faith. . . . By their faith they could obtain heavenly visions, the ministering of angels, have knowledge of the . . . general assembly and church of the first born . . . [and] of God the judge of all, of Jesus the Mediator of the new covenant.[10]

Some prophets and saints have acquired such faith and become so pure in heart that whatever they ask, God does. Jesus offered this power to his disciples (Luke 17:6). Enoch was granted this blessing by God, and through it built Zion (Moses 7:13–18). King David prayed, "Hear my prayer, O God: give ear to the words of my mouth" (Psalm 54:2). Alma prays for his brethren, adding, "And may God grant that it may be done according to my words, even as I have spoken" (Alma 29:17). Mountains move at the word of the brother of Jared (Ether 12:30). God hears these disciples because they have first heard him. He empowers them to enact their loving intentions and preserve their most precious relationships in time and eternity. As Peter assures us, "For the eyes of the Lord are over the righteous, and his ears are open unto their prayers" (1 Peter 3:12).

The Lord invites us to seek such power—the power to speak to God and be heard, to speak to the elements and be obeyed, to call down the powers of heaven to heal and to bless. We practice such power as we put words on our experience until we come to understand our past. We practice such power as we put words on our intentions until we see them enacted. We practice such power as we teach, bless, and serve one another in Christ's name, growing in faith and facility with the word of God. Practicing faith is not like practicing football or practicing for a play, however. We do that kind of practicing to get better at football or to become a better actor. We don't practice faith to get better at seeing angels or moving mountains or turning stones into bread. We practice faith to get better at trusting God and becoming more like him so we can find him more readily. We practice spirituality to own our sins and repent more thoroughly. We practice spiritual gifts to see other people's needs more clearly and help them more wholeheartedly. We practice faith not to get better at spiritual magic tricks but to get better at charity, the pure love of Christ. We increase in spiritual power as we increase in that charity. God's will becomes our will when we are filled with his love and his spirit.

Prayer Enacts Miracles of Charity

Charity is supreme because of its saving power in our lives and in the lives of others. When this gift is active within us we are patient and kind; unmotivated by jealousy, pride, or self-promotion; and not prone to anger or criticism. We find sin uninviting and we delight in truth. We are resilient, faithful, and optimistic. We endure in righteousness to the end (Moroni 7:45). It would be hard to imagine a more pervasively beneficial gift. The prophet Moroni teaches that this most desirable form of love is something we cannot develop completely on our own. It must be sought with our whole soul through prayer:

> Wherefore, my beloved brethren, pray to the Father with all the energy of heart, that ye may be filled with this love, which he hath bestowed upon all who are true followers of his Son, Jesus Christ; that ye may become the sons of God; that when he shall appear we shall be like him, for we shall see him as he is; that we may have this hope; that we may be purified even as he is pure. Amen. (Moroni 7:48)

Someone has said that if we prayed for charity as fervently as we pray for our children to be healed or for death to be forestalled, we might receive this gift more readily. That brought me up short. My prayers for almost anything are more fervent than my pleading for charity. I am already afraid "my heart cannot implement in action the demands of all the people to whom my heart responds."[11]

So the Lord reminds me I am not alone, but part of a charitable circle seeking to love and bless the world. Zion is characterized as a place where there are no poor (Moses 7:18). I take this to mean that in Zion there is no one with nothing to give. Each of us has some store from which to share with our fellow travelers on the journey of the soul. Each of us has a place in the circle of Zion. Whether our contribution is outwardly apparent or is veiled from the awareness of others, we are each necessary to the whole.

After his initial call, my former stake president spent several months trying to determine his errand from the Lord for his little stake of Zion. One of his counselors advised him, "Just close your eyes, and tell us what you see." The stake president decided to go to the temple to seek this vision. As he prayed in the terrestrial room, what he saw was completely unexpected—a soul-piercing image of the haunted eyes of children who had been abused. Deeply shaken, he contemplated the meaning of this mournful image. As he took up a solitary chair in the celestial room at the completion of the session, he saw a contrasting image, a vision for his stake. He saw the bright, laughing eyes of children nurtured in loving homes; the strong, confident strides of youth who know who they are and where they are going; and the able backs of adults, anointed in the temple and yoked with Jesus Christ to bear the burdens of the kingdom with joy and thanksgiving. These visions guided his administration.

I suspect this stake did not have some unusual abundance of abused children. Rather, this experience testifies that the Lord truly sees us. He sees when our eyes are darkened by lovelessness in all its forms, our confidence shattered and our backs bent beneath long-standing burdens. He sees, and he sends his healing love through the succor of others. I believe our names are always on the altars of heaven, where the Savior petitions the Father on our behalf. As we pray together in Christ's name, we are privileged to echo his petitions. When Christ descended from heaven to the Nephites and Lamanites, fresh from the devastations of terrible days of darkness and destruction, his culminating act was to bless their trauma-wounded children one at a time, encircling them with angels in celestial flames. I try to imagine the eyes of such children, full of visions of the love of God tenderly extended to them one by one. How it would change the world if every wounded child and youth and adult could be so loved.

Jesus also showed each of those assembled the scars in his hands, reminding them he too had been both wounded and healed, and that Zion is built on a vision of turning our inner wounds into testifying scars which remind us of lessons learned and engrave us with compassion, but do not devastate us anymore. He shows us his scars, he offers us his healing, and he invites us to bless and heal and love others out of the wisdom life has written in our flesh.

Curiously, this stake president came to understand the course that would lead to the happy ending he envisioned was home and visiting teaching. He is not the only inspired leader to come to that conclusion. Going as healers and messengers to one another, teachers were to bless each member's life temporally and spiritually, one person at a time. They were to become conduits of a mighty river of love that would reach into every home of the stake. That river is reminiscent of the one described in Ezekiel and John the Revelator's visions. This river of living water comes out from the altars of the temple to heal a dying world. How might the following description be fulfilled today?

> And, behold, waters issued out from under the threshold of the house . . . and the waters came down from under . . . the house, at . . . the altar. . . .
>
> And when the [angel] that had the line in his hand went forth eastward, he measured a thousand cubits, and he brought me through the waters; the waters were to the ankles.
>
> Again he measured a thousand, and brought me through the waters; the waters were to the knees. Again he measured a thousand, and brought me through; the waters were to the loins.
>
> Afterward he measured a thousand; and it was a river that I could not pass over: for the waters were risen, waters to swim in, a river that could not be passed over.

And he said unto me, Son of man, hast thou seen this? Then he brought me, and caused me to return to the brink of the river.

Now when I had returned, behold, at the bank of the river were very many trees on the one side and on the other.

Then said he unto me, These waters issue out toward the east country, and go down into the desert, and go into the [Dead Sea]: which being brought forth into the [Dead Sea], the waters shall be healed.

And it shall come to pass, that every thing that liveth, which moveth, whithersoever the rivers shall come, shall live. . . .

And by the river upon the bank thereof, on this side and on that side, shall grow all trees for meat, whose leaf shall not fade, neither shall the fruit thereof be consumed: it shall bring forth new fruit according to his months, because their waters they issued out of the sanctuary: and the fruit thereof shall be for meat, and the leaf thereof for medicine. (Ezekiel 47:1–12)

The living water forming the river of love that extends healing and nourishment to everything in its path comes out of the temple, the house of the Lord Jesus Christ. When Christ speaks of himself as the source of living water (John 4:10), he reminds us he is the source of all healing power. Then he adds: "He that believeth on me, as the scripture hath said, out of his belly shall flow rivers of living water" (John 7:38). We are to not only partake of the charity and healing power Christ offers us, but to become a source of that charity and its healing power for others. And what is the power spoken of? Nephi sees "the fountain of living waters" in vision, and is told these waters "are a representation of the love of God" (1 Nephi 11:25). God's love, his charity, is the source of healing in our lives. His love is the healing balm we bring to others.

Claiming Our Charity

Someone once told me about an ice skating group that conducts major competitions that no one may enter who started skating before age ten. This group realizes those early skaters have an advantage that late skaters can simply never recoup. Some of us feel we have a similar disadvantage at love, one we can never fully recoup—and perhaps that is true. I suspect the God of justice and mercy applauds rather than condemns those who come to loving late in life, and who fight to love appropriately despite the odds against their ever "competing" with those to whom love comes more naturally. We can still learn to skate and to love, even if we will not do it as skillfully or optimistically as others. And then we can congratulate ourselves as we would congratulate a winner in the Special Olympics, not condemn ourselves for not performing like a world-class athlete. The all-encompassing importance of love in the gospel of Christ can feel like a huge condemnation when we feel love-impaired. But perhaps this too is one of the burdens which Christ's gentle yoke can help us carry.

Or maybe it is a burden he can simply teach us to put down. As I struggle over my own handicaps with love, I expect there to be something more to love than concrete steps like ordering, receiving, blessing, and praying—something big and mysterious and just outside of my grasp. Some part of me, some child for whom love is still magical and consuming, seems to think love means things like giving everyone everywhere what they want without limits, never needing things someone I love does not feel up to giving, always being cheerful and affectionate, cooking for people and always liking it, or never being critical. Unless I can do such near-impossible things, I can think it too dangerous for me to try to love people, for I will only disappoint them when I fail. Hurting those I love is a damage I never want to inflict, which only seems possible if I feign incapacity to love and keep my distance. But I am reexamining my childish definitions of love. While I can identify some loving people who have some of these mysterious traits, I can also see that sometimes these acts are not loving at all. I am learning that no one can love so well as to never disappoint another. Not even God.

So maybe I do not belong in the Special Olympics of love. Maybe love is not some mystery I can never solve. Maybe working at trust, humility, blessing, praying, and letting people in—maybe these small moves, consistently practiced, are enough to qualify me as a disciple, worthy to ask for the spiritual gift of charity which God bestows on *"all* who are true followers of his son, Jesus Christ" (Moroni 7:48; italics mine).

Christ models charity with his entire life, but most fully in his atoning sacrifice for us all. During the Atonement, Jesus enacted fully his willingness to know us deeply and completely in all our experiences and failings and to not turn away. Trusting in Christ's charity means we are willing to know ourselves in his presence and to show him—flawless and perfect and beloved of the Father—the whole of the flawed, imperfect beings we are. He invites us to do this not to prove his superiority or shame us for our vulnerability, but to demonstrate his willingness to know us completely—by name, by wounds, by strengths, by sins, by desires, by heart—and to still stand at our side. Even more wonderful, he is willing to be known in turn. He is willing to let us "see him as he is" as we become "like him" through the receipt of the gift of his greatest attribute, charity.

That mutual willingness to know and be known, and to be fully embraced in that knowing, is the best definition of charity I can come up with. Charity is to be willing to truly know another, to allow them to know us, and to respond to that knowing from our deepest values.

God has invited us to come up to the mountain of the Lord's house to meet him personally. He has endowed us as a people with the keys, ordinances, and spiritual gifts to attain this blessing if we will claim it. We do not always respond to this invitation as did David, who said to God, "When thou saidst, Seek ye my face; my heart said unto thee, Thy face, Lord, will I seek" (Psalm 27:8). Even with God, we get nervous about getting too close. But imagine what God offers us in return:

> I will rejoice in [Zion], and joy in my people; and the voice of weeping shall be no more heard in her, nor the voice of crying. . . .
>
> They shall not labour in vain . . . for they are the seed of the blessed of the Lord, and their offspring with them. And it shall come to pass, that before they call, I will answer; and while they are yet speaking, I will hear. . . .
>
> I will extend peace to her like a river, and the glory of the Gentiles like a flowing stream. . . . As one whom his mother comforteth, so will I comfort you. . . . And when ye see this, your heart shall rejoice, and your bones shall flourish like an herb: and the hand of the Lord shall be known toward his servants. (Isaiah 65:19, 23–24; 66:12–14)

Our "bones shall flourish," like a living tree by a river of love, producing fruit in every season from which to feed and heal a hungry world. God will hear and answer us before we have finished speaking, and our labor, however difficult, will not be in vain. We will begin to become a Zion people. We will gain strength in all our bones and muscles, power through Christ to carry whatever burden he places upon us, power to save and seal those we love, power to help all he asks us to help, and power to build Zion on earth and prepare us as a people to enter the presence of God.

HEALING PRACTICE FOR CHAPTER EIGHT: LEARNING TO LOVE

Order. Write quick answers to the following questions:

- What are ten ways you consistently order your life right now—daily, weekly, monthly, yearly (a daily shower, recording checks, phone calls home when at work, making your bed, church on Sunday, Christmas traditions, paying tithing, and so on)?

- What are ten ordering principles you have liked in the past but did not do consistently this month (journaling, scripture reading, brushing your teeth, exercising, calling friends, cleaning your desk, eating fruit, and so on)?

- What are ten ordering principles you have never really tried that you think might help you (budgeting, monthly temple attendance, a system for phone messages, a chore chart, staying away from computer games, a weekly date with your spouse, prioritizing your goals each day, and so on)?

- What are ten ways you order your life right now that are excessive, rigid, or unhealthy (skipping breakfast, clothes shopping every weekend, excessive cleaning, never throwing anything away, too much television or internet, and so on)?

- On a scale of 1 (low) to 10 (high), how much structure is there in your life? In your family's life? In what areas are you too rigid? In what areas are you too loose?

- Considering all of the above, what is one change in the ordering of your life you think would be worth making for yourself for the next forty days? What is one change you would like to see in your family during that time period?

Receiving.

- Make a list of spiritual, emotional, physical, and other needs you have right now. How could your home or visiting teachers assist you with one of those needs? Practice the humility of making your need explicit to them. Be willing to take no for an answer without blaming or to bask in the sweetness of feeling helped and cared for without guilt.

- Spend thirty minutes in nature, consciously tuning in to the beauty of nature and receiving it into your soul.

- If the only things you had in life were the things you had personally thanked God for, what would you be missing? List one hundred things you are grateful for in your life right now, and let your heart receive them.

- Make a quick list of ten little things you could do to spoil yourself a little. Pick one to do. Notice the thoughts that go through your mind to stop you from doing it. Do it anyway, and notice what you can do to open your heart to receive the pleasure in it.

- What would you ask of someone close to you if you were going to ask for exactly—100 percent—what you want? How could you make this desire explicit? Could you take no for an answer without pouting or withdrawing?

Blessing. *On a scale of 1 to 5, with 1 being scarce and 5 being abundant, rate how much you have of the following:*

spare time	compassion
athletic ability	organizational skills
faith	food
listening skills	hope and happiness
computer skills	job-finding skill
money	musical or artistic talent
sense of humor	professional skill

From the above list, or other skills you have,

- What is one skill you could use to fill a need of each person in your family right now? Each person you home or visit teach? Your community or neighborhood?

- Where you have enough and to spare, who else might benefit from what you have to offer, and how?

Praying.

Prayer is a gateway to spiritual order, a vehicle for receiving, a place to learn our missions and priorities of service, and a prerequisite to the bestowal of charity, love's highest form. Prayer is the heart of spiritual growth at either a personal or a communal level. Try at least one of the following:

- Pray out loud. This is the surest cure for wandering attention.

- Pray longer. Give yourself fifteen or thirty minutes to really pour out your soul to God. In five minutes you will get past the redundant repetitions of common prayer, and you can begin to talk to God about what is real.

- Pray more consistently. I can't imagine having a guest in my home whom I did not greet each morning or say good night to each evening. Prayer is simply a polite way to acknowledge God's presence in my house. I function best if prayer is (at least) the first and last thing I do each day.

- Pray more gratefully. What would we have if we had only those things we had personally thanked God for? Sometimes offer prayers of only gratitude.

- Pray as a commitment to action. Stop after each prayerful request and ask yourself what you could do if you had to commit to take some action on what you asked God for. What action would you be committing to as you asked God to bless the food you eat? (Are you committing to eat healthier food that God could bless?) What action might you commit to as you pray for the missionaries? (Will you commit to give them referrals, rides, or meals?) What about asking God to bless someone who is sick? (Are you committing to visit or call them?)

- Pray with paper. Make a list of things you want to talk to God about. Make a list as you pray of inspiration you receive or commitments you make.

- Pray with imagination. Keep your eyes open and imagine God seated nearby. Speak to him as you would to a beloved friend, confidant, or parent. Let yourself receive his kind attention and affection.

- Pray with a listening ear. Tomorrow morning, simply ask God to help you know what you can do for him. Then stay on your knees and wait. Allow your mind to remain open to whatever comes into it. If a person or task or need comes to mind, act on it according to your best judgment. The skeptic or sage in me resists believing everything that comes into my head at such times is directly from the mouth of God; however, I believe when my motives are pure, he is drawn close. This kind of prayer helps me find my priorities. It helps me feel each day that I have done one right thing.

- Pray for charity. Pray earnestly, with all the energy you can muster, for the gift of charity. Let that prayer be a commitment to action.

- As you pray, imagine Christ nearby praying for you. What might he pray for on your behalf? What might it feel like to hear and see such a prayer? (See John 17 and 3 Nephi 19.)

CHAPTER NINE
THE PRESENCE OF AN ABSENCE

When the light rested upon me I saw two Personages, whose brightness and glory defy all description, standing above me in the air. One of them spake unto me, calling me by name and said, pointing to the other—This is My Beloved Son. Hear him!

—JOSEPH SMITH (JOSEPH SMITH—HISTORY 1:17)

Mormonism starts with a startling story. A young boy seeks the light and wisdom promised him through the scriptures, and God makes good on that promise with floodlights of revelation and hope. The temple symbolically replicates the drama of a prophet's vision-call, making it accessible to us. The temple is our dress rehearsal for a very real and personal debut. Through temple ordinances, the Lord is bringing us to Palmyra, to Sinai, and beyond. We've learned our lines, invested them with all our tender feelings, and we hope the audience is in place to receive us. As we wait for the curtains to rise, we tune our hearts to play out our convictions about what we want most and who can give it to us.

I have climbed Mount Sinai and visited Palmyra. The light that pierced the stillness of the mountains and inflamed the branches of the Sacred Grove fired my imagination of the holy, but its rays remained, for me, unpopulated. Yet of the temple God says, "all the pure in heart that shall come into it shall see God" (Doctrine and Covenants 97:16). I do not know quite how to take God's promise. Perhaps he unveils himself to us in many ways. I still believe he has invited us to seek such encounters and to learn from those who have had them.

The story of the brother of Jared's meeting with God provides a prototype for transcending the veil (Ether 1:32; 3:28).[1] This story begins at the Tower of Babel when God confounds the language of the people. One might say the brother of Jared seeks the gift of *un*-interpretation of tongues.

He prays that God spare his friends and family by preserving their language intact. God hears the brother of Jared and sends him and his clan, language unconfounded, on one of those wilderness treks referenced repeatedly in scripture. The Jaredites traverse an uninhabited wilderness, cross "many waters" (Ether 2:6), endure more wilderness, and then make a four-year encampment on the edge of the great sea dividing the lands.

Here, at the end of his long journey through a lonely, desolate world, the brother of Jared climbs a high mountain in search of the Lord. Through mountain mists veiling his holy presence, God speaks to the brother of Jared and commands him to build eight more barges by which to cross these great waters to a promised land. The brother of Jared completes this task, and then again approaches the Lord whose voice he has heard but from whose presence he is shut out.

The brother of Jared speaks: "O Lord, I have performed the work which thou hast commanded me, and I have made the barges. . . . And behold, O Lord, in them there is no light" (Ether 2:18–19). It is a good starting place for a dialogue with God: affirming we have been faithful in the things he has commanded us to do thus far, and seeking light.

The Lord answers the brother of Jared with the first of two essential questions in this exchange: "What will ye that I should do . . . ?" It has become apparent to me that when we approach the Lord at the mortal veil, he does not ask us what we have accomplished, how we have lived, or even whom we have served, but what we have wanted. Everything important about us seems to flow from the answer to that question. "What will ye . . . ?" he asks the brother of Jared, or in other words, "What do you want from me? What is your will? What do you most desire?" Nephi, Solomon, John the Beloved and others have also been asked such a question (1 Nephi 11:2; 2 Chronicles 1:7; Doctrine and Covenants 7:1). It is an appropriate question for that moment of self-review inherent in an encounter with God, for what we want may truly be the ultimate test of who we are. Our answers to this question provide us with direction for our journey, motivation to complete it, and insight to overcome its inherent obstacles.

While the brother of Jared's answer is prosaic—he simply wants a way to light his barges as he crosses the sea—it provides a fitting metaphor for what we need as well: the spiritual light by which to travel that God alone can provide. Truth, direction, and wisdom are the lights we seek, as are knowledge of who we are and understanding of the things of God. The light God invites us to seek above all others is the light of his presence, the knowledge of who he truly is, not in some abstract sense but in relationship to us and at the most personal level.

"What Will Ye . . . ?"

What do you want? Perhaps you find answers to that question in your historical identity ("I have always wanted . . ." "In my family, people want. . . ."), your body's current hungers ("I want food, sleep, excitement, warmth . . ."), your concerns for others ("I want to cure world hunger . . . help my sister . . . free political prisoners . . . comfort my grandchild . . ."), notions of what is good or bad ("I want to tell the truth . . . start exercising . . . paint better . . . get promoted . . ."), or some perceived lack you hope to remedy in the future ("I want to afford a house . . . be thin . . . get well . . . have a baby . . . earn more money . . ."). What do you *really* want? What matters most to you?

Psychologist Abraham Maslow writes, "It isn't normal to know what we want. It is a rare and difficult psychological achievement."[2] Many things get in the way of knowing and getting what we want. For example, when we have learned to pay too much attention to what others want we can lose access to the frequencies that broadcast our own desires. Some of us have been trained to distrust what we want, suspecting it will lead to self-indulgence, laziness, or immorality (and sometimes we are right to be wary). Sometimes we can only imagine our wants in terms of temporal gifts money can buy, and we have a harder time recognizing the deeper needs underneath these externalities. Or we may feel so powerless to get what we want and so fearful of disappointment that we do not even let our wants into consciousness. Sometimes our wants are as confounded as the languages of Babel because different parts of us clamor for different things. We lose our leadership capacity to hold our truest self apart from our parts so we can make decisions that reflect our truest values. Nothing seems to bring real satisfaction when one part of us clamors for things another part of us disclaims or feels ashamed of. In all these cases knowing what is wanted is vexingly difficult.

One of my clients complained repeatedly about always feeling responsible to fulfill others' desires or wants at the expense of his own. Hoping to give him the experience of articulating and receiving what he wanted, I began asking him at the start of each session what he wanted out of that hour. I tried this several times, but he either ignored me or argued with me, so being a conflict-averse soul I conveniently "forgot" to ask again. Apparently he didn't forget, however, because a few weeks later he announced to my surprise that I was driving him crazy with this what-do-you-want stuff. He blurted out, "I don't know what I want! I'm scared to death to find out! I'm even more scared to actually ask for it!" The question had haunted him even when I stopped asking it. It took him to the heart of his healing quest.

Just knowing and asking for what we want can make us feel vulnerable and needy. If this were not uncomfortable enough we must then consider the morality as well as the feasibility of our desires. We instinctively know that what we want speaks volumes about who we are, and so our entire identity, every name by which we are known, seems to be called forth with this question.

At other times we think we know what we *should* want, but we are not really convinced all these shoulds will bring us happiness worth the price. We are not convinced we can live up to such lofty wants. Or we may get so busy asking God to protect us from what we fear and telling him what we *don't* want that we don't let ourselves get around to asking what he really wants for us, or what we would want if we were not so worried.

I have learned to spend time reflecting on what I want. I think about the true wants underneath the obvious wants, the impact of my wants on others, and the forms my wants might fairly take. I consider how my current life choices reflect my wants, both those I approve of and those I don't. I generally learn through such exploration to trust my truest wants are good, but I also face the humbling reality that my most immediate wants may not be. I begin to see where my wants are in conflict with each other, and I learn to negotiate settlements that all parts of me can support. To paraphrase a familiar saying, the great tragedies of my life occur when I give up what I want most for what I want now. This is a tragedy I pray for wisdom and courage to avert.

Getting What We Want

However, knowing what we want is only the beginning. How to get what we want is just as difficult to determine. What the brother of Jared wants is light, but the plot thickens as God seems to block the most obvious paths to obtaining it. God says:

> What will ye that I should do that ye may have light in your vessels? For behold, ye cannot have windows, for they will be dashed in pieces; neither shall ye take fire with you, for ye shall not go by the light of fire. . . . Therefore what will ye that I should prepare for you that ye may have light when ye are swallowed up in the depths of the sea? (Ether 2:23, 25)

Interestingly, God does not solve the brother of Jared's problem in this case as he has in others. Nor does he minimize the problem by saying, "You should just have more faith and not be afraid." In fact, God acknowledges in rather harrowing terms that they will be "swallowed up in the depths of the sea"—hardly a comforting image. So God says no to fire and no to windows, and then God asks the brother of Jared what he wants God to do, within the legitimate boundaries of what he will not do.

Interesting to me is that it is out of God's "nos" that the brother of Jared creates a "yes." The brother of Jared does not ask, "What's the matter with fire? I'll be careful!" Or "There will be waves fierce enough to dash out windows? Maybe I should rethink this whole promised land thing!" Or "If you can't figure this out, how am I supposed to?" I'm not suggesting such thoughts never crossed his mind, but if they did, he seems to tame his doubts and curb his frustrations enough to allow the two images God has suggested but prohibited—clear glass and burning fire—to imaginatively merge within his mind to create a new possibility. He uses *fire* to "molten out of a rock sixteen small stones; and they were white and clear, even as transparent as *glass*; and he did carry them in his hands upon the top of the mount" (Ether 3:1; italics mine). There the brother of Jared again calls upon the Lord, asking him to touch the stones and make them shine.

We read, "when the brother of Jared had said these words, behold, the Lord stretched forth his hand and touched the stones one by one with his finger. And the veil was taken from off the eyes of the brother of Jared, and he saw the finger of the Lord" (Ether 3:6; see 3:4–5). The Lord reaches his finger through the veil, into the sight of his waiting disciple, offering new light to bless this man and his posterity in ways that far exceed what the brother of Jared has ever imagined. The light God offers is not just a temporal solution to a temporal problem, but the possibility of learning to see in new ways. As the brother of Jared models discipleship by holding on to what he wants—light—without insisting on how to get it, he opens up a space for creativity and vision, for the light God ultimately offers the brother of Jared is in more ways than one a light that has never been seen before (Ether 3:15).

When God both asks what we want and demonstrates how we can't have it in our current state of knowledge or vision he may be offering us the possibility of a miracle. Within his refusal to give us what we think we need lie new ways of traveling, new names and identities, new forms of light we can never imagine as long as the old forms are enough. In moltening rock, the brother of Jared strikes the creative spark of a new possibility out of old impossibilities, and then he brings his creation to the Lord, hoping it will be worthy of the Spirit's holy flame. In that process he finds more than light; he finds its ultimate source.

Like the brother of Jared, I must stop insisting on success as I define it or freedom from fear as I anticipate it before I can begin to imagine that the gift God offers is not merely a solution to my old problems but a new way of traveling in the world, a new way of understanding who I am and what I can do, and a new relationship with him. Then I can begin to consider what I might gain from my struggle, not just what I might lose.

Let me offer a more familiar example. A client working on self-esteem comes to believe God is inviting him to stop a self-indulgent sexual practice. At first, the client can only imagine outcomes of frustration and white-knuckle obedience. Giving up this old pattern feels like only loss, and he doesn't believe he can succeed without great cost. Only after much reflection on what God is like and how he operates does my client begin to imagine the possibility that God is not trying to take something valuable away from him, but is inviting him to something better—that God is not trying to shame him into submission, but to raise him up to a new understanding of himself in the world. Seeing this invitation as an opportunity to create or learn or love or heal rather than just another potential for failure allows this client to see things in a new "light." He is not sure what he will learn or whether he will always succeed, but he opens his heart to imagine new forms, new paths out of where he is to where he has never been.

Another example: The desire-impaired client I mentioned earlier finally decided at age forty-five that one thing he wanted was for his mother to stop making him responsible for fixing her life. I asked him how it happened that he became responsible for his mother's problems. "Oh, it's hard to describe," he said. "Her facial expressions, tone of voice—subtle things." I clarified, "I'm not interested so much in how she lays this responsibility at your feet, which is something you probably can't change anyway. I'm curious about why you pick it up." He just stared at me as this distinction registered. "That," he said after some thought, "is what I have never been able to figure out." After some discussion I offered, "Could your willingness to feel responsible for her be a way of trying to win her love and protection at last? Or could your anger with her be a way to insist the clock be turned back and that she parent you as you deserved but never got?"

By the next week he had obviously given these possibilities a lot of thought. He reported, "It feels like fixing my mother's life is my only chance of being approved of and loved. When I get angry, it is as if I'm trying to drag her back in time with me and try to make her do it right this time. I think I understand I cannot change the past or change her, but if I let go of that hope, what do I have left? If my own mother couldn't love me, who will?" Wanting love in his life but still insisting on getting it through the old, and in his case, ineffectual, source of maternal care, my client struggled to see he no longer needed his mother as he once did. She no longer held the key to his passage to love unless he continued to place it in her hands. He could now care for himself if he was willing. God's love was available. He could access other sources of support and care more within reach. Yet he could hardly remember the many people who liked him, respected him, and validated him. He took his mother's considerable incapacity to love anyone at all as a personal affront. Nor could he readily imagine a loving relationship that did not replicate this faulty maternal one. He built his life on the assumption that only if he could get his mother's love and approval or make her into someone different would he ever have companionship, attention, security, or happiness. He both needed and resented his mother, and every woman like her, even as he created them in her image.

When we believe the blocked paths we can currently imagine are the only ways to get what we want, the result is usually either self-pity or blame. In contrast, mature desires provide clarity, direction, and motivation even in the face of initial disappointment. I have come to see my own self-pity and blaming as reliable indicators that some part of me is holding on to misplaced hopes and has relinquished power to claim and work for what I want. I have never been too interested in positive-affirmation statements, but I have found power in the reminder, "I relinquish self-pity and blame, and I claim my power to know, trust, and seek what I truly want."

Here are some questions I find helpful as I try to identify and live truthfully from my best desires:

- What could I be doing to make my life better?

- Why am I not doing it?

- How do I fill in the blanks: "One part of me wants _____, but another part of me wants _____." What do the different parts of me want, and why?

- What do I, the true self, want? How can I make sure that each "part" of me is heard but that no subpart takes over the decision about what I want most or how to get it?

- To whom or what am I giving up my power to get what I want, and why?

- With whom do I need to be more honest about what I want?

- How can I learn what my loved ones want and help them get it, especially when it appears to conflict with what I want?

Such questions help me articulate and achieve what I want. I find them worth reflecting on again and again. They help me chart a course toward what I want most, and what God wants for me.

Of course, getting what I want most is not always easy, pleasant, or even possible. Then I get to learn again that safety, success, accomplishment, and ease are not the only indicators of God's presence in my life. My personal comfort is not the only token of the Comforter's nearness. In fact, the Comforter often discomforts us with truths we'd rather not see and losses we'd rather not know we can tolerate as he guides us toward what we want. Much creativity, vision, and learning lie on the other side of discomfort, inadequacy, hunger, failure, and fear.

So when faced with a long voyage through dark and roiling seas, it behooves us to go to the mountain and molten out our own stones, forming new ideas out of old impossibilities, new ways of seeing to replace the unenlightened lamps we have walked by in the past. Then we are to remember that even our most creative responses to the challenges of life are never, in themselves, enough to light our path. No matter how much fire we put into the process of creating them, without God's transcendent touch, our stones are only stones and they will leave us in the dark. Our works by themselves, even our best works, will never save us or never give us the light we need for our eternal journey. We can molten our white stones out of the cold, black rock of our challenging lives, but light comes only by the Savior's hand. Our task is still to bring something to God to touch. Where we can discern the light of new life through the thick opacities of failure and frustration—there, perhaps, we begin to see the face of God.

Will You Believe?

As the brother of Jared presents his stones to God, he prays:

> I know, O Lord, that thou hast all power, and can do whatsoever thou wilt for the benefit of man; therefore touch these stones, O Lord, with thy finger, and prepare them that they may shine forth in darkness . . . that we may have light while we shall cross the sea. Behold, O Lord, thou canst do this. We know that thou art able to show forth great power, which looks small unto the understanding of men. (Ether 3:4–5)

With this request, the brother of Jared acts in faith on his conviction that God's power, which looks small to humankind, is sufficient to enlighten not only the stones, but also the human mind and heart. God's power is manifest quite literally as the scripture continues:

When the brother of Jared had said these words, behold, the Lord stretched forth his hand and touched the stones one by one with his finger. And the veil was taken from off the eyes of the brother of Jared, and he saw the finger of the Lord. (Ether 3:6)

As God reaches his hand through the veil, he offers light to both the physical world of stones and barges and to the spiritual world of human understanding. His "great power, which looks small unto the understanding of men," is power he offers to share: power to enact our righteous desires in time and in eternity.

The brother of Jared falls down in fear at the sight of God's hand, convinced with most of us that one cannot see God and live. God reassures him and asks if he has seen more than his finger. The dialogue continues:

Nay; Lord, show thyself unto me.

And the Lord said unto him: Believest thou the words which I shall speak? (Ether 3:10–11)

This second question seems odd, out of place: "Believest thou the words which I shall speak?" If you had just seen the finger of God, wouldn't you be just a little impressed? Don't you think you would have no choice but to believe? But God's question reminds us again that belief is always a choice (see similar questions to Nephi in 1 Nephi 11:4–5, the people of Benjamin in Mosiah 5:1, and Lamoni and his queen in Alma 18:22–23 and 19:9). Alternative voices and visions always vie for our acceptance. Yet here in the absence of certainty we learn to trust God—here in the dark in our home-made barges facing fierce winds and waves that will drive us to destinations we have never seen.

So I wonder if it is not precisely my answer to this question that admits or denies me access to the presence of God. How often I have prayed for guidance, received it, and then, because it lacked absolute certainty or happened a month ago instead of this morning, undermined its source. How often I have insisted God's answers fit within my mental scheme of things, my graduate school training, my family culture, my deadlines, my earthly inspired and therefore suspect notions of what truth is and should be.

In contrast, the brother of Jared simply chooses to believe, not because God's words make sense for he has yet to speak them but because the brother of Jared trusts the Lord. The brother of Jared knows through long experience in the desert of prayer and discipleship God's character and attributes. He knows by his own experience God's words both describe and create truth. He learns he can stand in God's presence, not because he, the brother of Jared, is good, but because God is good—so good his love and mercy are truly boundless. So good he will not seek to punish or overpower us, but only to bless us and save us in meekness, long-suffering, gentleness, persuasion, kindness, and love unfeigned (Doctrine and Covenants 121:41–42). So good he can be trusted with the whole of the imperfect, uncertain beings we are.

So when God asks the brother of Jared if he will believe, the brother of Jared replies,

> Yea, Lord, I know that thou speakest the truth, for thou art a God of truth and canst not lie.
>
> And when he had said these words, behold, the Lord showed himself unto him, and said: Because thou knowest these things ye are redeemed from the fall; therefore ye are brought back into my presence; therefore I show myself unto you. (Ether 3:12–13)

The Lord says the brother of Jared is redeemed from the Fall and brought back into God's presence on the basis of this, his knowledge of God: "Because thou knowest these things ye are redeemed." What things does the brother of Jared know that redeem him? "I know that thou speakest the truth, for thou art a God of truth and canst not lie." Simply put, the brother of Jared knows the Lord. He knows through the long experience of the journey that God can be believed, even when his answers are unsettling, because he does not lie. Not about troubling things like the unsuitability of fire or windows or the fierceness of the raging deep. Not about hopeful things like the land of promise or his power to give eternal life to "all . . . who shall believe on my name; and they shall become my sons and my daughters" (Ether 3:14). This is the knowing that brings the brother of Jared into God's presence where he can see God's face in all its unveilings.

Faith versus Certainty

It is curious to me that even after God has noted the brother of Jared's unequaled faith (Ether 3:9), he still asks him if he believes the words God will yet speak (Ether 3:11). Having faith, having a testimony, apparently does not mean there are no choices left to make.

The concept of a testimony comes from the legal notion of testimony as a record of what someone has seen, heard, and experienced. In religious matters, it includes our experience of spiritual feelings or insights. But the meaning of our experience, the sense we make of it, and the conclusions we draw from it are always chosen from multiple possibilities. One may have experience or testimony about God's nature and love without having complete, personal certainty about every doctrine or historical event or future outcome not yet experienced.

Sometimes we become disillusioned when we are less than certain about things other people claim to "know beyond a shadow of a doubt." We may wonder how others can be so certain about anything, let alone invisible things. If we are not certain, we may doubt the validity of what we *have* felt or even our worthiness to receive spiritual knowledge. We may even wonder if there is such a thing as spiritual knowledge at all. We wonder what we can believe.

Author Anne Roiphe warns us about "that most dangerous human emotion: certainty."[3] I don't much like having the certainty I so desire characterized as dangerous. I want certainty that my discernment is accurate, my intuition inspired, and my conclusions correct, especially when the winds and waves pound at the door of my rudderless barge. I want a little time to test the durability of my sixteen glowing stones before I take off with them across the ocean. I want to understand the scientific principles behind what makes them shine and who will do the repair work if they break. Certainty seems appealing when we are afraid. But I have to agree that in mortal matters, certainty is precarious at best. Periods of questioning or disillusionment are not all bad. Illusions are the dangerous baggage I *want* God to disillusion me of. In the midst of great storms it is best to travel light.

Theologian David Tracy speaks of "good enough knowledge."[4] That is a definition of faith that rings true to me. Despite a plethora of spiritual experiences that bring much peace and power and confidence in the Lord into my life, I still live by faith—evidences I choose to accept as sufficient even though they might not feel like enough to anyone else, and even though at some stages in my journey they may barely feel like enough for me. Faith is what God asks me to make do with in this life—faith good enough for barge-building, good enough to hope in, good enough to share with enthusiasm, but seldom good enough to completely rid my life of uncertainty, questions, or the need for humility as I interact with others of different experience.

It can feel harsh to have to grow up and accept that uncertainty and risk are part of life. When unsettling events make us feel like we've lost our ticket to certainty, we hope someone's discernment or scientific training or church status or professional accomplishments are so sure we can still feel safe believing. The Savior and the Holy Ghost, our sources of spiritual truth, are not as tangible, controllable, or close at hand as certainty seems to require.

Ironically, it is Satan who would have us believe we are entitled to a world where no one will hurt us, undermine us, or make us afraid. He boasts he can deliver such certainty and safety to us. If we are foolish enough to believe him, then we may look to drugs, work, sex, money, religious excess, or a hundred other feel-good addictions to numb us from the real pain of the real world—pain he has convinced us we don't deserve and should be able to avoid. Accepting Satan's boast, we may cocoon ourselves in the safety of our defenses, trying with increasing desperation to fend off the hurt and fear that are instructive reactions to the world we have been sent to in order to learn, by our own experience, good from evil.

God makes no such promises. He, in fact, tells us quite honestly ours is a lonely, dreary world where we will have to live largely by faith. He asks us to trust that the knowledge he offers us, though less than certain in an earthly sense, suits our purposes here. And that one day we will have more sure words of prophecy and truth.

Though Christ chastises us for unbelief, he has compassion on the man with whose words I so strongly identify: "Lord, I believe; help thou mine unbelief" (Mark 9:24). Faith and doubt vie for our allegiance, and the winner is a matter of our choice as much as the convincingness of either argument. Sometimes the harder I insist on certainty the further I get from truth. Faith is a choice we make amid alternatives, not what is left after all competing worldviews have been neatly eliminated.

Whereas the veil of uncertainty and the necessity of faith are part of God's plan, let us rejoice in them and call them good. Receiving God's promise of light without guarantees, and knowledge without certainty, helps me make room for a bigger world than the one I can tie down. In fact, uncertainty is a necessary precursor to new discoveries and new creation. I remember it is *after* Alma the Younger has seen angels and the throne of God that he writes, "I have fasted and prayed many days that I might know these things of myself" (Alma 5:46). The sure knowledge he next claims is "made known to me by the Holy Spirit of God," not by miraculous visions or angelic manifestations. Nor are his experiences universally convincing to others, as real as they are to him. Paradoxically, to calmly claim our faith and belief even amid inevitable uncertainty is to claim the blessings of peace, humility, and trust. Certainty will one day be ours, or at least I presume it will. Meanwhile, faith is apparently enough to bring us closer to the God we choose to trust.

The Presence of an Absence

As the vision continues, the Lord teaches the brother of Jared who he, the Lord, is in his many names, then offers that identity to the brother of Jared and to all who will believe on the name God reveals:

> Behold, I am he who was prepared from the foundation of the world to redeem my people. Behold, I am Jesus Christ. I am the Father and the Son. In me shall all mankind have life, and that eternally, even they who shall believe on my name; and they shall become my sons and my daughters (Ether 3:14).

As dependent as we are on God for help and guidance in our earthly endeavors, we can get too preoccupied with seeking God for information, favors, safety, and relief from our fear of the dark. When we do, we may forget to seek what matters even more: knowledge of the God who provides for us. What will ultimately heal us is not the balm of this world's comforts. It is knowledge of God, including understanding of his character and attributes and a sense of how he feels about us personally and individually. Our goal is not only to gain favors but also to know God—to commune with the Lord in such a way that we enter his presence, or perhaps grasp and experience how fully we are already in it.

Psychologist Susan Deri defines a symbol as "the presence of an absence" because symbols allow us to hold onto something in symbolic form that is absent in physical form.[5] She adds, "Symbol formation always takes place in the context of longing. The symbol provides a means of connecting separated regions, of crossing over boundaries."[6] Ultimately all temple symbols are formed in "the context of longing." They hold us in a present hope as we search for our absent Lord. Temple ordinances provide the symbols that help us cross the boundary from this "separate region" that we inhabit into the region he inhabits.

The temple also reminds us he is not very far away. As Kathleen Flake has observed, the Joseph Smith Translation of Mark 14:21 infers the sacrament was not only instituted to commemorate the death or absence of the Lord, but his presence.[7] As the Savior tells his disciples, "This is for you to do in remembrance of my body; for as oft as ye do this ye will remember . . ." Remember what? His death? Well, certainly, but even more: "for as oft as ye do this ye will remember *this hour that I was with you*" (italics mine). We are to remember his presence, his closeness, the hours that he has been with us, and will be with us yet. Similar sentiments shape the institution of the sacrament among the Nephites in 3 Nephi 18:7: "And this shall ye do in remembrance of my body, *which I have shown unto you*" (italics mine). It is the living presence of the Lord in our midst, not his absence, which we commemorate when we participate in the sacrament. It is his living presence amid the blind and leprous of Jerusalem we strive to replicate with our healing efforts in Salt Lake City or Paris or Beijing. It is his living presence in the Sacred Grove we seek to replicate in sacred temples, bringing us toward holiness. It is his living presence in the most intimate spiritual experiences of our lives he asks us to keep ever before us as we partake of the living emblems at his table.

This Man

The vision continues as the Lord asks the brother of Jared not to reveal what he has received until an appointed time (Ether 3:21), a caveat that often accompanies aspects of sacred revelation or ordinances. Moroni tells us God then shows the brother of Jared the entire history and destiny of the human race from the creation to the end of human history. Throughout, Jared's brother learns even more about God's nature, character, and attributes, and about the nature of our earthly sojourn. These are temple themes, and this an endowment experience. Finally, Moroni says he cannot write all things that happened to the brother of Jared, but "it sufficeth me to say that Jesus showed himself unto *this man* in the spirit . . . and he ministered unto him even as he ministered unto the Nephites; and *all this*, that *this man* might know that he was God, because of the many great works which the Lord had showed him" (Ether 3:17–18; italics mine). My daughter has pointed out to me how intimately this is stated. "All this," not so a nation might be born or saved, although that happens too. Not so the world might change or a new land be discovered, although that happens too. But "all this, that *this man* might know that he was God." We come to know God by name, one person at a time. This is how intimately he knows us. This is how much each one of us matters to him.

There is one prayer the Lord always seems to answer for me as I seek the passage to his presence. That prayer is, "What lack I yet?" When I ask with a sincere heart, the Lord is always willing to show me my sins, my weaknesses, who I need to apologize to, and who I need to forgive. If I want to truly know him, I must become more like him: "For how knoweth a man the master whom he has not served, and who is a stranger unto him, and is far from the thoughts and intents of his heart?" (Mosiah 5:13).

What do you want? Will you believe? Who are you willing to be? These are the questions God still asks those who seek his face. So despite my longing for certainty, I choose God's plan of faith, agency, uncertainty, and opposition. I choose to believe him, even when the evidence is sometimes confusing and contradictory, because I too am learning over a lifetime of experience that God can be trusted. He is a God of truth and he does not lie. It is not enough that I chose his plan of agency once in the councils in heaven; I must continue to choose it every hour of every day by my determination to find the presence of my absent God through all of life's upheavals, and by my determination to uphold the agency of each of his children. I choose my dying bones and sinew, the sacred gift and tutor of my body, trusting in the redemptive power of God to heal and renew me within it. I choose mortality, trusting its brutal inevitabilities can call forth the truest desires of my heart. I choose relationships, trusting in God's will to empower me within them in eternity though I struggle within them now. I choose to believe that *this woman* too can afford to trust that God will reach out his hand to me—not because of my goodness or merit, but because of his.

Paul teaches that we "enter into the holiest by the blood of Jesus, by a new and living way, which he hath consecrated for us, through the veil that is to say, his flesh" (Hebrews 10:20). In other words, Christ does not just stand at the veil or behind the veil. He is the Veil, the Gate, and the Door by which we enter heaven. This veil is not just a protective barrier to keep spotted us away from the unspotted Holy One. This veil is a passageway to the Father, and so it represents the Savior, who is our Passage home in both senses of that word: he has paid our passage, our fare, and he is the strait, narrow channel between all the extremes of this world. I want to use every moment of this brief existence to learn to be like him, to put his healing presence into every empty, absent corner in my soul. Meanwhile, I wait with a bright hope for the day when God reaches through the veil to take my hand again, for I choose to believe, despite the shadows cast by life's uncertainties, that he will do so.

HEALING PRACTICE FOR CHAPTER NINE:
THE PRESENCE OF AN ABSENCE

- *Clarifying Wants.* Before approaching God in prayer with a problem, write or say your answers to the following:

  - What do I want?

  - What could I be doing to make my life better, and why am I not doing it?

- To whom or what am I giving up my power, and why?

- How can I be more honest with others about what I want?

- Is what I want within my prerogative to change, or is it within the stewardship of someone else?

- How can I learn what others want and help them get it, especially when it appears to conflict with what I want?

Clarifying Beliefs

- What are the five most fundamentals beliefs of your personal knowledge system?

- Why do you believe them?

- What characteristics of God are most important to you?

- What experiences have led you to see God that way?

- What would you have to know about God to trust him more?

Molten Stones

- What is a problem you are facing at this time that seems impossible to solve?

- What "nos" has God suggested through personal inspiration or prophetic utterance that constrain how you can solve this problem?

- What creative solution can you molten out of the mountain and then ask God to make shine?

CHAPTER TEN
In His Presence

———⚮———

The kingdom of God cometh not with observation: Neither shall they say,
Lo here! or lo there! for behold, the kingdom of God is within you.

—The Savior, Luke 17:20–21

Many questions come as I try to imagine the celestial room of the soul. To the extent the kingdom of God is within me, where and how do I find it? What is Christ offering me in the celestial realm that supersedes the heavenly-enough terrestrial kingdom, which the world's religions describe as the ultimate reward? Are celestial experiences only available here to the endowed? Or does the endowment simply help us identify, value, and seek the celestial, which can be found by others as well? What sets celestial living apart from the solid, terrestrial decency that seems difficult enough to attain without presuming to better it? Is the celestial characterized by a higher level of righteousness than the terrestrial? By a different personal identity, or a different relationship with others? By a transcendent experience with God? How can I presume to characterize the kingdom of God within?

The Nag Hammadi Library, a collection of ancient scrolls written and hidden away in the first centuries after Christ, was discovered and translated only recently.[1] Much of it reads like so much gibberish to me, but some of its books feel like lost treasure. A few of these scrolls purport to be lost gospels of Jesus or writings of his disciples. From the apocryphal Gospel of Thomas:

> Jesus said, "Blessed are the solitary and elect, for you will find the kingdom. For you are from it, and to it you will return . . ."
>
> Jesus said, "If they say to you, 'Where did you come from?' say to them, 'We came from the light, the place where the light came into being on its own accord and established itself and became manifest

through [its] image.' If they say to you, 'Is it you?' say, 'We are its children,' and we are the elect of the living father.' If they ask you, 'What is the sign of your father in you?' say to them, 'It is movement and repose."[2]

Movement: Motion in any direction. Change. Creation. Freedom. Embodiment. Connection. Strength. Work. Inhale. The spirit brooding upon the face of primal waters. Life.

Repose: Rest. Sabbath. Solitude. Relaxation. Mindfulness. Receptivity. Flexibility. Patience. Exhale. Christ speaking to the troubled sea, "Peace, be still." Entering into God's rest.

I see both movement and repose in the paradoxical injunction of Joseph Smith from Liberty Jail to the Saints he loved:

> Therefore, dearly beloved brethren, let us cheerfully *do all things that lie in our power*; and then may we *stand still*, with the utmost assurance, to see the salvation of God, and for his arm to be revealed (Doctrine and Covenants 123:17; italics mine).

I wonder what it would be like if my life balanced between movement and repose—cheerful doing and assured stillness—instead of teetering as it so often does between telestial sin and terrestrial adequacy; between frantic, chaotic battles and exhausted cease-fires; between aimless wandering and rebellious, heel-digging halts. I am in need of atonement, at-one-ment. At-one-ment with myself that leads to claiming my full identity. At-one-ment with others in charitable relating. At-one-ment with God that ever brings new life. In at-one-ment, I begin to imagine celestial glory.

At One with Self

> Jesus said, "If those who lead you say to you, 'See, the kingdom is in the sky,' then the birds of the sky will precede you. If they say to you, 'It is in the sea,' then the fish will precede you. Rather, the kingdom is inside you, and it is outside of you. When you come to know yourselves, then you will become known, and you will realize that it is you who are the sons of the living father. But if you will not know yourselves, you dwell in poverty and it is you who are that poverty."[3]

Movement. Although no ritual action takes place in the celestial room to prefigure the kingdom of God to come or what we might do there, the endowment experience is certainly not over until we experience its celestial culmination for ourselves. There are identities to contemplate here, both God's and ours. We come to the celestial room to take a trial run on the throne of our inner kingdom, the throne of our own life. We rehearse returning from our lonely testing grounds of discovery with new rights and wisdom and the skills to reign, and we try on that sovereignty to which we have been anointed, subject to the sovereignty of God. Pictures of these rooms portray brilliant lighting and pleasing decor. Beautiful seats are the fitting furnishings for this room—little thrones lovely enough to remind us of our worth, common enough to remind us we all have thrones here, and that our personal dominion is not over others but over ourselves.

It seems many parts of me live within this kingdom. When the rebellious parts of me have been subjected, when the exiled parts of me have been reclaimed, when the truth-speaking messengers have been received and the inner sick ones healed, rightful leadership can be attained in the kingdom of God within. Internal voices of distraction and anger can be enlisted instead as ambassadors, advisers, and servants in this inner kingdom. Internal exiles that have cried in vain to be heard can be restored as heirs apparent I will nurture, tutor, and assist to "grow up in God" (Doctrine and Covenants 109:15). The true self is instated as the fair and compassionate monarch, the anointed and spiritually prepared priestess. I can begin to establish my dominion over myself without hypocrisy, guile, force, or pride, but in kindness, humility, fairness, compassion, and strength. My dominion can flow to me without compulsory means (Doctrine and Covenants 121:42–46). All these inner parts sustain the leadership of the true self. I sit on the throne of that at-one-ment fully clothed in all the emblems of godly identity and power.

This work of self-awareness and personal growth is what this book attempts to explore. However, learning to recognize and fairly govern all aspects of ourselves so we may claim the throne of our inner kingdom is clearly the work of a lifetime. From the Gospel of Philip:

> As for ourselves, let each one of us dig down after the root of evil which is within one and let one pluck it out of one's heart from the root. It will be plucked out if we recognize it. But if we are ignorant of it, it takes root in us and produces its fruit in our heart. It masters us. We are its slaves. It takes us captive, to make us do what we do not want; and what we do want we do not do. It is powerful because we have not recognized it.[4]

The evil in my heart hardly feels like an appropriate contemplation in the brilliance of celestial glory. Still, I concede that evil's power is reduced when it is recognized for what it is. It is not easy to search out the dark and unkempt corners of our souls and bring them into the light. Energy and courage are needed to chase after our fears and abdications, to wake up from our trances and stupors, and to live instead embodied and whole. We are drunk with a thousand intoxications, but Jesus only can fill us if we thirst. When we become first sober, then thirsty, then sated with living water, we begin to come together where we have come apart, and to claim celestial space. These are the efforts that seem to allow for movement toward self-unity that engenders true repose.

One Sunday morning, as I was leading the music in Relief Society, I looked out on the smiling face of a sister in my ward. My heart constricted. Ours was not a comfortable relationship, and far too often my Sabbaths were slightly soured by the reminder of my struggles with her. It is hard to nurture animosity while singing the songs of Zion, however, and I longed to know the secret that would free me from the bouncing ball of judgment that alternately landed on her (for her imagined faults) and me (for my uncharitable and prideful stance). I had spent a lot of time trying to figure this one out, and knew only that I felt judged by her, and so I judged her in turn. Then as I led the music, a still, small voice spoke to my soul with startling clarity: "You do not compete." Compete? Was that the problem? Compete for what? My confusion immediately gave way to amazement at this piercing analysis. Of course that was the problem! Outside of my consciousness, I had thought we were competing for God's love, and that she was winning. I had further thought that to catch up I would have to be like her, and I couldn't imagine how to pull that off. "You do not compete" captured both my folly and its remedy in an amazing economy of words that seemed to imply, "Relax. I love you both, in all your differences."

I could move again, free to be myself, and free to be secure in God's love for us both. I stepped out of the circles of jealousy and fear in which I had made endless rounds, and I stepped onto the way of truth and life. With an amazing economy and precision of language, God's message to me that day gave me an option for movement where my own thinking had me fettered and bound.

> You were a temple, (but) you have made yourself a tomb. Cease being a tomb, and become (again) a temple, so that uprightness and divinity may remain in you. . . . Knock on yourself as upon a door, and walk upon yourself as on a straight road. For if you walk on the road, it is impossible for you to go astray.[5]

> Acquire for yourself strength of mind and soul, and intensify the struggle against every folly of the passions of love and base wickedness, and love of praise, and fondness of contentions, and tiresome jealousy

and wrath. . . . Guard your camp and weapons and spears. Arm yourself and all the soldiers which are the words, and commanders which are the counsels, and your mind as a guiding principle. . . . Bring in your guide and your teacher. The mind is a guide . . . reason is the teacher. They will bring you out of destruction and dangers. . . . May God dwell in your camp, may his Spirit protect your gates, and may the mind of divinity protect the walls.[6]

Repose. Of course, God's tutoring words about competing did not eliminate my feelings of animosity with this sister. Though they gave me direction, I still had to walk the road they implied. Ironically, insecurity is such a familiar emotion that it provides a certain security. But each time I find myself teetering on the brink of old judgments and fears, I remember the counsel of a wise mentor to "smilingly" bring myself back to my chosen course—to what I know by the Spirit to be true. Trust in God's love is still not automatic for me, but it is a choice I can make again and again, gently taking my face in my hands and turning it toward repose.

This is my solution for most of the ongoing battles of my life, the ones to which I know the answers I do not always live: Gently, smilingly, turn back to the light of Christ, choosing to trust in his love. Gently, smilingly, come back to his bright truths about who I am, so self-awareness can coexist with self-acceptance instead of leading only to self-condemnation for all my inadequacies.

June Singer writes:

A wise person once said the goal of the masculine principle is perfection and the goal of the feminine principle is completion. If you are perfect, you cannot be complete, because you must leave out all the imperfections of your nature. If you are complete, you cannot be perfect, for being complete means you contain good and evil, right and wrong, hope and despair. So perhaps it is best to be content with something less than perfection and something less than completion. Perhaps we need to be more willing to accept life as it comes.[7]

I think there is wisdom in this idea. I note that while God is perfect, the universe he creates and inhabits comes complete with good and evil, right and wrong, and hope and despair. God does not seem to need to banish sorrow or annihilate evil in the universe in order to find joy. One of the principle teachings of Christ was that the Jews could find freedom even when the Romans occupied their land. His teachings push us to hold in the same hand our changeless circumstances and our soaring freedoms, our sinful past and our repentant hopes, our weakness and his enabling power.

God may dwell in celestial glory, but he is not afraid of the dark. He does not make evil disappear. He transforms it and brings it to naught.

> Let Christ alone enter your world, and let him bring to naught all powers which have come upon you. . . . Let him dwell in the temple which is within you, and you may become for him a priest and a Levite, entering in purity. Blessed are you, O soul, if you find this One in your temple.[8]

At One in Relationships

> [The kingdom] will not come by waiting for it. It will not be a matter of saying 'here it is' or 'there it is.' Rather, the kingdom of the father is spread out up on the earth, and men do not see it.[9]

The kingdom of God is not only within us; it is also outside of us, spread out invisibly in the world in myriad peaceful, hopeful interactions. Where the spirit of God is cherished by two or three who gather in love, an outpost of his kingdom is established. We feel when we have entered its borders, for our hearts are set in motion with godly desires.

Movement. As my husband and I planned our trip to Sofia, Bulgaria, to retrieve our oldest daughter from her mission, I anticipated the scene again and again—stepping out of the customs area and catching a glimpse of her dear face, throwing my arms around her, and laughing. The vision always made me weep for joy. Images of her would appear even in my dreams, where she would come home for the day or for dinner, then have to go back to her field of labor. In my dreams I held her and did not want to let her go.

In crowded restaurants or walking down a street, I would start to cry, anticipating our reunion. Demons of my own imagination taunted me with other scenarios, however: What if she were killed in a car accident? What if she were kidnapped by terrorists? What if I got ill and could not go to pick her up, and then I died before she got home? What if . . . ? What if . . . ? What if any of the thousand unthinkable things that can happen, happened? I had never been separated from one of my offspring, these three people I love more than life, for such a long time before. I wonder: Is celestial life to always feel this kind of love for everyone and not just when they are gone?

The happy moment of reunion comes, just as I have imagined it but without any dreaded interruptions. I feel as if my heart will burst with gratitude and joy. We see the places she has been living, worshiping, working, and we feel her love for the Bulgarian people. She tells us of their sacrifices, their struggles, and their faith: A single mother with a small child whose greatest dreams in life are simply to have a little apartment to call home, a car to drop her daughter off at school, access to dental and medical care; a Relief Society president whose husband left her when she joined the Church because she would no longer participate in his hard-drinking life-style; an investigator who forfeits her job, her home, and her family to live the Church's standards so she can be baptized. I have heard the stories, but when I meet these people and their stories come to life my heart convicts me: I take so much for granted.

I'm not really sure why one family in particular touches me so. We search them out, my daughter no longer certain where they live after a rumored move. The husband is the branch president in the city where she first worked as a missionary; the wife is the seminary teacher. We walk up and down the streets looking for a tiny candy store they reportedly run, but we see nothing that seems to fit the description. We are ready to give up when I recognize in the silence among us a collective moment of prayer. Almost immediately, a woman appears from a basement walkway, and rec-ognition passes between her and my daughter. The woman's face radiates intelligence and joy as they embrace in a flutter of words I do not under-stand except with my heart. She confides that something had prompted her to come outside, that she could think of no reason to do so but had come outside anyway. My daughter tells us she is sure such things happen to this sister twenty times a day.

The sister enthusiastically welcomes us into her home. She and her hus-band are college graduates in a country with such high unemployment that they are living with two children and her mother in a ten-foot square room. They have a single twin bed for the five of them, a small sink, a hot plate to cook on, and a single bare lightbulb at the ceiling. Our daughter reminds us that this couple, living in a place much like this, also took in two of her investigator's friends when they lost their apartment. I remember how loath I am to share my spare bedroom if it means I'll have to change the sheets. All is neat and tidy and clean. I feel ashamed of my carpeted house with more rooms than people. I feel unworthy to enter the heaven she has created here. Suddenly I can vividly imagine what it would feel like to try to live in the celestial kingdom unworthily. She insists on giving us drinks and candy from her meager store. "Don't feel guilty," my daughter tells me softly, seeing my profound discomfort at taking anything from her. "Feel grateful."

The woman tells us she used to pray for a prestigious job in an office where she could dress up and feel important. Then she prayed she could just find a job that was not on the street. Then she prayed she could just find a job. She and her husband sold popcorn in the plaza for ten cents a bag through more than one hard Bulgarian winter, most of their profits going to the popcorn cart owner, until they were able to get this tiny basement room with a window through which they sell candy and other incidentals to passersby. But she reports, she learned humility from her street job, learned to tolerate the cold and enjoy the moment, even in the dead of winter, and she is grateful to God for teaching her. She radiates her gratitude for the presence of his Spirit.

I have read her story in my daughter's letters and marveled at it, but somehow being here and seeing it for myself humbles me to the depths of my soul. Several years ago, Bob Quinn, a friend and church leader in my stake, said, "In those moments when the Spirit is with us it is as if we are perfect." Something about that rings true to me. I look at this woman and see perfection. I remember those moments when I have felt that wholeness, when I have operated as if in another realm, walking by faith, prompted at every turn, full of the spirit. They are the most meaningful moments of my life. I think to myself, I would give everything I have to have the kind of godly presence and constant spiritual companionship this woman seems to enjoy. And then I acknowledge, tearfully, that she *has* given nearly everything she has, while I cling to my privacy, my possessions, and my pride. My daughter says when the missionaries have tried to give this couple food or other things, they refuse the help or pass it on to someone even needier than they.

Later my daughter says, with tears in her eyes, "It isn't fair. It isn't fair that we have so much, and these faithful people have so little. I will be so grateful to live the law of consecration. What a blessing that will be." I know, of course, even from personal experience, that there are millions and millions of people in the world with far, far less than even this humble Bulgarian family. Truly they are the rich, in part because they seem to know and feel grateful for their relative bounty, even though it looks like poverty to me. I remember the description of Zion as a place where there are "no poor among them," and remember again that in Zion there is no one with nothing to give, no one without richness to share. I feel impoverished next to their spiritual and emotional bounty, and wish they could share its secrets with me. My life is enriched by their joy. I am the beggar here.

I feel determined to follow their example—to serve more, give more, help more, and love more, but when I try to organize my life to do so I feel stymied. Just as I desire their spiritual bounty, I hope to share my temporal one, but what is within my reach? I feel my dependency on God to shape my desires and inspire my acts. I know I can do little temporally from across the world for this family in Bulgaria (though they have done much for me), but I am equally perplexed as to how to truly help those nearer at hand. What gifts within my ability to give would empower others, not simply patronize them? Where do I begin when there is so much suffering, so much need? I know it is not as simple as giving everything away, but I want to wrench myself from the insidious belief that suffering and poverty are too complicated to impact at all. While I acknowledge humbly the spiritual gifts God has brought these people despite their poverty, or perhaps because of it, I feel I cannot share in the bounty of their faith without sharing with them my temporal surplus.

He answered and said . . .

"No man is able to go on that road, except one who has forsaken everything that he has and has fasted daily from stage to stage. For many are the robbers and wild beasts on that road. The one who carries bread with him on the road, the black dogs kill because of the bread. The one who carries a costly garment of the world with him, the robbers kill because of the garment. The one who carries water with him, the wolves kill because of the water, since they were thirsty for it. The one who is anxious about meat and green vegetables, the lions eat because of the meat. If he evades the lions, the bulls devour him because of the green vegetables."

When he had said these things to me, I sighed within myself, saying, "Great hardships are on the road! If only Jesus would give us power to walk it!" he looked at me since my face was sad, and I sighed. He said to me, "Why do you sigh, if you, indeed, know this name 'Jesus' and believe him? He is a great power for giving strength. For I too believe in the Father who sent him. . . . "It is I! Recognize me, Peter. . . . Do you not understand that my name, which you teach, surpasses all riches, and the wisdom of God surpasses gold, and silver and precious stones?"[10]

Repose. Our first Sunday back at home, my daughter and I walk into Relief Society. The lesson title is written on the board: Tithing and Consecration. The haunting scenes that have not left me since I sat in my Bulgarian sister's home return with greater impact. The time has come for me to do more. I write out checks to charities and sign up to take food to the homebound. I do my work with integrity, listen to my children and friends, offer my talents, talk over with my husband how we can serve more. I wonder if I can commit something more each day to serving beyond what I am doing now. It sounds like a trivial offering, yet when I think of doing more, I realize how full my life already is. Gratefully, some of it is full with giving. I remember my old adage that if a thing is worth doing, it is worthy doing badly, rather than not doing it at all. Perhaps if I allow myself to do this thing badly, then I will at least do something. Close counts in more than horseshoes. I ask God to show me how, to put me to work, to help me remember. But I also ask him to help me know my limits, to help me not sidestep my truest and most difficult responsibilities, to help me worry less about things I cannot change, and to help me trust him not to overwhelm me. I know if I am to give as I intend I will have to live more consciously, more prayerfully, and with more self-awareness and self-care than ever.

> In this world the slaves serve the free. In the kingdom of heaven the free will minister to the slaves.[11]

> Jesus said, Love your brother like your soul, guard him like the pupil of your eye.[12]

At One with God

> The earth rolls upon her wings, and the sun giveth his light by day, and the moon giveth her light by night, and the stars also give their light, as they roll upon their wings in their glory, in the midst of the power of God.
>
> Unto what shall I liken these kingdoms, that ye may understand?
>
> Behold, all these are kingdoms, and any man who hath seen any or the least of these hath seen God moving in his majesty and power. . . .
>
> Behold, I will liken these kingdoms unto a man having a field, and he sent forth his servants into the field to dig in the field.
>
> And he said unto the first: Go ye and labor in the field, and in the first hour I will come unto you, and ye shall behold the joy of my countenance. (Doctrine and Covenants 88:45–47, 51–52)

The kingdom of God is more than an inner realm and more than outer relationships, however. A real God sits enthroned in glory, whose real kingdom we seek.

I notice I am generally quite content to imagine God high in the heavens, listening from some far away throne room to my very human prayers. If I try to imagine instead inviting God to come close, to enter my little room and be seated nearby, I can hardly tolerate the emotions inherent in the image. I stop him at the perimeter, and even then I am flooded with fears and tears. I feel an instinct to drop to my knees and protest with Isaiah, "Woe is me! for I am undone; because I am a [woman] of unclean lips, and I dwell in the midst of a people of unclean lips" (Isaiah 6:5). No wonder Moses speaks with utter amazement about the nothingness of man relative to God. No wonder the brother of Jared cringes in fear and protests unworthiness before him. Yet I want to move closer to God, even if doing so evokes potent feelings of unworthiness in all my most tender places. If I cannot now go where he is, will he yet come near to me? Even imagining such a scene proves instructive to my heart. The temple invites us in many ways to practice moving toward such celestial proximity.

Movement. When I lived in Michigan, I drove almost daily to the park-lined river near my home to walk. Something inside me leapt for joy when I entered the solitude of this river space, like the babe in Elizabeth's womb leapt at the voice of the mother of God. As I walked I reached my mind deep into the fertile earth of life to draw from its abundance. In spring, I delighted in the vision of a bright, low mist covering the face of the river like a white veil preparing her for prayer. In fall, I reverenced the sight of morning sunlight inflaming the red maple leaves with a holy fire that burned but did not consume. I wondered at geese arching across the sky like ribbons on the tail of a kite, held in a timeless order by invisible string. On heavy summer days, I felt the air charge as wind dusted my face with rain, and every nerve ending of exposed skin responded to its anointing. In winter, my mind molded my muscles to match the tender body of virgin snow entwined with the branches of the trees in embrace. I attended to the whispered silence of an evening fog that muted the landscape with stillness so profound it seemed to stop time, until a winged messenger sounded the trumpet call to start it up again.

One fresh morning, I looked up to see a brilliant red scene of river and tree and sky and bird so beautiful it went directly from my eyes to somewhere in my stomach and held there with my breath. I felt as if the dawn of first creation could not have been more glorious. Even the ducks floating in the water nearby seemed mesmerized by the sight. Poetry could never do it justice—this passing moment in an ordinary day so full of beauty it spilled over into mystery and holiness.

On the best days, for the hour I walked, I relished my proximity to divinity. My body became a vehicle for receiving the world instead of an object of others' scrutiny. My mind shifted from its focus on my own inadequacy to awareness of the world's abundance. My life energy leapt out to its source through my hands, my eyes, and all my capacities, emulating them in whose image I am made.

I used to think I could not afford to take the time to walk, to search out beauty, to sit in stillness, and to contemplate. I have learned I cannot afford not to. Creation testifies there is a God who delights in beauty and order and endless variety. In the beauty of his creation I reclaim my God-given delight in being alive. I feel. I see. I fuel my capacities to create beauty, order, and new life as I revel in what God is making in the world. Closeness to him is not an idle curiosity or a stewardship to be squirmed out of because of fear. It is an imperative.

> For the son would not become father unless he wore the name of the father. Those who have this name know it, but they do not speak it. . . .
>
> If one does not acquire [the name of the father and the son and the holy spirit], the name "Christian" will also be taken from him. . . .
>
> This power the apostles called "the right and the left." For this person is no longer a Christian but a Christ.[13]

Perhaps nature is one way the celestial calls out to the Christ within us to come home.

Repose. One is hard-pressed to really separate movement from repose when immersed in the spirit. They seem to blend across a gentle arc. However, there are appropriate times for intimacy and appropriate times for independent action, even with God. The danger in independence is that we will not remember to come home, and so God invites us back in many ways.

I once read an article written by a feminist Orthodox Jewish woman. Acknowledging that many would see that self-description as an oxymoron, she asserted her religious tradition's potential for encouraging women's self-actualization. As an example, she cited the Orthodox Jews' observance of the Sabbath day. No food is cooked, no appliance is turned on, no car is operated, no word is written, and no work of any kind is performed. She invited us to imagine what it would be like for a modern woman if, on one day out of seven, no one had a right to make any claim on her time or energy. She could spend the entire day in meditation, prayer, rest, and contemplation of her life direction. I have to admit the idea was enormously appealing—and embarrassingly foreign. It is not just the justifiable demands of a young family that impinge on my Sabbath, for those days are past for me. It is my own fear of being still. Wayne Muller writes:

> There is astounding wisdom in the traditional Jewish Sabbath, that it begins precisely at sundown, whether that comes at a wintry 4:30 or later on a summer evening. Sabbath is not dependent upon our readiness to stop. We do not stop when we are finished. We do not stop when we complete our phone calls, finish our project, get through our stack of messages, or get out this report that is due tomorrow. We stop because it is time to stop. . . . The galaxy will somehow manage without us for this hour, this day, and so we are invited—nay, commanded—to relax,

and enjoy our relative unimportance, our humble place at the table in
a very large world.[14]

I wonder what it would be like to not only permit myself but also to
require myself to order my week around moments of contemplative rest
instead of ceaseless doing. Is this what church leaders keep trying to tell us
and what we keep ignoring about keeping the Sabbath day holy? What if I
planned my Sabbath rest as carefully as my work projects? What if I carried
that contemplative approach into my everyday life, stripping it of its frantic
busyness? What would happen to my capacity to live fully and to engender
life in my work and relationships? What would happen to my feelings of
nearness to the Father?

> An ass which turns a millstone did a hundred miles walking. When it
> was loosed it found that it was still at the same place. There are men
> who make many journeys, but make no progress towards any destina-
> tion. When evening came upon them, they [see] neither city nor village,
> neither human artifact nor natural phenomenon, power nor angel. In
> vain have the wretches labored.[15]

Jesus said, "If you do not fast as regards the world, you will not find
the kingdom. If you do not observe the Sabbath as a Sabbath, you will not
see the father.[16]

Perhaps Sabbath is the celestial room of time, the celestial day that
breathes life into our temporalities while we await God's eternal rest.

Holding On to Letting Go

We can't stay in celestial space for long down here, however. How do
we learn to hold on to the hope of eternity when life covers it from our view?
Psychology hypothesizes that when a child is young, he doesn't realize his
bright red ball or his mother's face still exists when covered up. As he grows
a bit, he learns to delight in the game of peek-a-boo, presumably because
he is just grasping that mom might still be there when he cannot see her,
and he loves to see this possibility confirmed. But he still does not hold her
image for long. In a few more months, "out of sight" is no longer "out of
mind," however. He crumbles when mom leaves, distressed and bereft in
his acute awareness of her absence. This is a major developmental milestone,
even if it distresses his parents. Only after many months of a seemingly
endless cycle of Mom going away and then coming back does the child
begin to hold the image of mom inside, where it is a constant inner source
of guidance and reassurance.

Psychologists say such a child has acquired "object constancy"—the ability to tell an object remains constant in time and space even when invisible. Object constancy is acquired only as the child repeatedly experiences the object's disappearance and reappearance until the connection is made that the ball and Mom never really go away but are just not always seen. Once attained, object constancy helps the child remain emotionally stable and secure even when mom is gone, because he has replicated her calming presence within his mind and heart. He can no longer be completely alone.

I have wondered if one of the tasks of mortality is to acquire object constancy with God. As we feel the Spirit, then lose awareness of it, feel it, lose it, feel it, lose it, perhaps God is trying to help us acquire this inner assurance that does not dissipate, but that is held firmly within. We are no longer so dependent on God's immediate presence to hold on to faith, to hope, and to righteous desire. We can stand alone without crumbling. The kingdom of God is within us. We don't have to hold our breath, clinging tightly to this moment's assurances lest they slip away. We can afford to be happy then sad, connected then independent, peaceful then excited, because we can trust all of these things to come around again and again, independent of our ability to see them or hold them steady. We can move more easily between movement and repose, work and rest, connection and loss. We can let people in and let them go without giving up on love. We can receive the spirit and then still hold onto faith when doubts or trials cover it up.

Breathing Space

I do not yet know all the answers to the questions with which I began this chapter, but I believe there is to be a celestial room within my soul, a place and time of both movement and repose. In this celestial rest perhaps time and space do converge, as Einstein claimed they do, in one eternal now. In that moment of presence, of being present *here* in the present *now* with the present *I Am*, I am as if perfect.

I want to stay in this hallowed space, and never completely feel ready to leave it. But this is the truth that helps me trust: the hallowed will return. I don't need to capture it like a caged thing. If I keep moving forward into my life, then take my Sabbath rest, God will return. Whatever else the temple prepares us for hereafter, we come to it to learn here and now that God is present even in his absence, and that his kingdom is not far away. We learn principles by which we become the livers of our lives: sovereigns of our inner kingdom, willing servants to others, grateful worshipers of the living God. Then, having taken our inner throne, practiced charity and consecration, and gained object constancy with God, we are prepared to make the vows and treaties that will join us in holy alliances with others in the sealing rooms that complete our celestial experience.

Movement. Repose. Movement. Repose. This is the rhythm of celestial life, the rhythm I have so much trouble breathing. I keep trying to hold this breath—to hold beauty, to capture glory, and to stay in wonder. I want to stay in celestial space until they kick me out. Is that so bad?

But we are not here to carve a perfect life into lifeless stone. A held breath suffocates. Trust. Take life in and let it go. Enter this presence— the presence of earth and water, tree and bird, in this moment's glittering vision; the presence of soul, of spirit and body, alive in this moment's breath; the Presence that brings present space and this present time into one eternal now, one perfect note, one timeless grace of motion and light; presence, vibrating through our bones, our sinews, our loins, our breath. This presence of mind, of heart, and of body and spirit is not limited to one room or one time. We can take it out into the world and find God there on even the darkest night.

> Those who say they will die first and then rise are in error. If they do not first receive the resurrection while they live, when they die they will receive nothing.[17]

HEALING PRACTICE FOR CHAPTER TEN: IN HIS PRESENCE

- *Self-exploration.* Go back and reread your morning pages, looking for themes and insights you want to act on. Make a plan.

- *Relationships of love.* Close your eyes and imagine someone you love—a spouse, roommate, child, companion, friend, parent, and so on. Remember as clearly as you can what about them you cherish, enjoy, or respect. Imagine bringing that image into sharp focus, brightening the colors and intensifying the emotion to increase or enhance that feeling of love.

  Now imagine someone you don't particularly care for. Sincerely ask God to help you see this person as he sees him or her.

- *Relationships at large.* Close your eyes and imagine your ward, your community, and the world at large. What do you see? What problems are you immediately most aware of? It may help to list those that are most compelling to you. If you could imagine a spokesperson for each problem, what would that person say to you, and what would they ask you to do?

Where are you "not poor" right now? What things do you have enough of? What do you have to spare? (Time, money, energy, wisdom, experience with the difficulties of life, skills, talents, compassion, leadership, perspective, testimony, unique perspectives, and education are a few possibilities.)

Is there some overlap between the "problem" list and the "riches" list? What does your true self feel would be reasonable for you to do about it?

- *Days of rest.* Brainstorm:

  - What would you like the Sabbath to be more of or less of for you personally?
  - What three specific things might you do to make the Sabbath more of a day of true rest and spiritual resurgence?
  - How could you bring some of those elements into every day of your life?

- *Presence.*

  - · What would you like to do, however badly, to express your feelings about God in your life right now? Consider drawing, painting, singing, dancing, writing a poem or a song, gardening, walking in nature, or praying as ways of bringing him closer.
  - What is the one thing you are not doing regularly right now that most feeds your spiritual life when you do it?
  - Go outside and look at the world, and reach out to its Creator with all your heart.
  - Come inside to a private place and tell God your deepest feelings. Ask him what would have to happen for you to feel his presence more fully as a comforter and companion. Listen.

CHAPTER ELEVEN
To Receive and Be Received

When you attend the temple and perform the ordinances that pertain to the house of the Lord, certain blessings will come to you: You will receive the spirit of Elijah, which will turn your hearts to your spouse, to your children, and to your forebears. You will love your family with a deeper love than you have loved before. You will be endowed with power from on high as the Lord has promised. You will receive the key of the knowledge of God. . . . Even the power of godliness will be manifest to you.

—Ezra Taft Benson[1]

Once in proper relationship (at least ceremonially) with our personal histories, our bodies, our work, our demons, our communities, and our God, we are prepared to enter the sealing rooms. Here we recover, or rather gain at last, our full potential. Within mortal families, individuals experience most poignantly the purging influences whose heat can either embitter and destroy us or fit us for eternal life. Then, in eternity, relationships give form to our holiest promises. The epitome of celestial promise is that we may become joint heirs with Jesus Christ of all that the Father has, including the opportunity to engender spiritual life in others throughout eternity. That spiritual begetting can be practiced in mortality as we teach, testify, lift, serve, and comfort.

The scriptures use a variety of metaphors to describe our relationship with God. We are the clay and he is the potter, reminding us we are like inanimate objects in his shaping, all-powerful hands (Isaiah 29:16; 64:8). We are the branches and he is the vine, making us living things that draw our life from him (John 15:5). We are the sheep and he is the shepherd, reminding us he will protect and nurture us as we come to trust him and follow his voice, perhaps as a dog trusts and follows its owner (John 10:14–16). We are the servants and handmaids and he is the master, putting us in the relationship of a dutiful and grateful slave to an owner, albeit a benevolent one who has purchased us with his blood from sin, our former master (Leviticus 25:55). We are the offspring and he is the Father, becoming a part of his family—those he chastens and corrects, loves and sustains, and ultimately makes heirs to all he has (Galatians 4:6–7).

But then, perhaps most astonishing of all, we are the wife and he is the husband (Hosea 2:1–13). He mourns when we are disloyal, receives us if we will return, and joins us to him as his full and intimate partners—beloved, desired, chosen, one. This final image from the scriptures would be beyond presumptuous if it were not God himself drawing the picture. He has proposed to us, and he humbly awaits our answer. Will we vow our full fidelity, love, and trust, that we may become equally yoked with him? If so,

> I will betroth thee unto me for ever; yea, I will betroth thee unto me in righteousness, and in judgment, and in lovingkindness, and in mercies.
> I will even betroth thee unto me in faithfulness: and thou shalt know the Lord. (Hosea 2:19–20)

We enter most fully into family relationship with God through temple covenants and sealings. Throughout history, there has always been an earthly lineage with rights to the priesthood through which to bless others. As we offer sealing ordinances to our ancestors, I wonder if there is not a kind of backward causality put in place whereby they gain the opportunity to join this chosen lineage, becoming parents who can bestow a righteous heritage upon *us*, their children, even if they did not do so in mortality. *We in turn* become as if we had been born into this covenant that extends back to Abraham, Isaac, and Jacob, and can extend that covenant inheritance to *our children*.

These promises are not unconditional. Though he loves and chooses each of us, we become part of his chosen people, his heirs, only as we also choose him. Like Israel of old, we can forsake these privileges, disinherit ourselves, and cut our link out of the golden chain of promises. But those who desire can join this lineage and partake of these blessings through sealing ordinances for the living and the dead.

Ordinances sealed by the Holy Spirit of Promise make our choices legal and binding in the courts above. In the sealing rooms, God's endowed, empowered sons and daughters now become husbands and wives. We, like God, may organize our families after priesthood patterns. As partakers of the covenant blessings of priesthood, posterity, and promised land offered to Abraham, Isaac, and Jacob, we create families in which every child has legal access to these same blessings.

The sealing blessings, then, are less about something we get and more about the right to give something away. We get to give away the gospel. We get to give the right to the priesthood and access to the powers of heaven to the people we love most—our children here and in eternity.

Separate and Single

These wonderful possibilities await us all. But with the large number of people in the Church who are single, not sealed, childless, or unhappily married, I hesitate to broach the subject of sealing ordinances for fear of providing yet one more painful reminder of these earthly losses. Let me pause here to note that the endowment's purpose is to prepare each of us as single individuals to enter the presence of God—a goal sufficiently challenging to keep any of us busy for a lifetime, whether or not we are married. By temple custom, maiden names are used for women in the temple during endowment ceremonies for the living and for the dead, emphasizing that we are *all* single in the eternal perspective when we are baptized, washed, anointed, endowed, and brought to the celestial room. Single men and women often have a particular affinity for temple work, perhaps out of a special empathy for the universally single deceased persons for whom we officiate.

Let us also note that once endowed we are fully endowed. We have access to all the rooms of the temple, including the sealing rooms. In fact, sealing ordinances are the only ordinances one can perform for the dead without having personally experienced them. This policy reminds us that no blessing will be denied those who keep their temple covenants.

Into the Fire

If we *are* privileged to marry, what ideals will inform that relationship? Will marriage provide endless copies of wedding day loveliness, like mirrors in the sealing rooms—everyone smiling, tender tears of joy, makeup perfect, families gathered round? Well, no. It feels a little jarring to jump from the heights of celestial bliss into the realities of family life, but that is what we will do—in life, and in this chapter. Back in the real world, the real value of the Spirit's promises is both tested and realized. So what assumptions about gender will guide or challenge our relationships? Why sexual fidelity? How will we choose a marriage partner? Why temple marriage? What should we expect after the honeymoon fades? Let's get practical.

Men and Women, Adam and Eve

Latter-day Saints derive many assumptions about our gender roles, especially in marriage, from the Adam and Eve story. Unfortunately, we also derive a lot of our ideas about both marriage and the story of the first marriage from our secular culture. From that worldly, male-dominated cultural perspective, many scriptural statements appear to denigrate women even though the same statement, if applied to men, might feel quite different.

For example, if Adam were the last act of creation instead of Eve, then we would probably not assume that meant Adam was an afterthought or second-class citizen, as the world sometimes assumes about women. We would be more likely to claim Adam came last because everything in the creation culminates in that which matters most.

We also tend to read into Eve's designation as a "help" to Adam that women are men's assistants. Yet the word translated here as *help* is used elsewhere in the Old Testament *only* to refer to the Lord (for example, Psalm 33:18). We have a different view of woman's role as a *help* to man when her role is compared to God's role as a *help* to us.

We learn through Latter-day revelation that Eve's noble name, the *Mother of All Living*, is not just a name Adam gets to pick, but is the name by which the Lord calls her (Moses 4:26).

In our secular culture we would not be surprised to read, "a woman shall leave her father and mother and cleave unto her husband, and they twain shall be one flesh," but of course this is not what the scriptures say. We don't always notice the counter-cultural nature of Adam's prophecy and assertion that a man shall leave his father and mother and cleave unto his wife (Moses 3:24), a prophecy Adam would soon fulfill by partaking of the forbidden fruit and leaving his Edenic home to follow Eve.

I note these things not to claim Eve is better than Adam—other scriptures expound on Adam's nobility and status—but to point out that sometimes our culture biases us to see Adam's nobility more readily than Eve's.

The common features of the roles of Adam and Eve are expounded in Moses 5:1–16, which specifies that after their expulsion from Eden Adam and Eve *together* labor, have children, pray, receive revelation and commandments, prophesy, worship, sacrifice, teach their children, and bless the name of God. These reminders are important to people undertaking the challenging task of building a partnership of equals in a world dominated by confusion and excesses of many kinds when it comes to gender.

Marriage inevitably pushes us to grow by both challenging our culture-bound assumptions and by showing us our personal weaknesses and strengths. I note with amazement that both husbands and wives are quite capable of seeing their spouse as overly dominating the marriage relationship—sometimes in the same marriage. We come into marriage wanting to be accepted and cherished exactly as we are, which never fully happens. Then we get to struggle to offer that acceptance to our spouse while working on our own "unacceptabilities" the best we can. Like Adam and Eve, we help each other, we offer each other companionship, and we try to learn to keep our hearts open at close quarters where they get bumped a lot. We try to learn to receive, and to be received.

Why Sexual Fidelity?

One of God's most unrelenting commands is to be sexually and emotionally faithful to our spouse. Why this priority? Why so rigidly uncompromising? Why at all?

I was once visit teaching a young mother and her three-year-old daughter, who was happily eating pretzels. We do not need a commandment from God to tell us to eat pretzels. We can figure out all by ourselves if we like them, and the choice to eat them or not is ours. But having learned about eating pretzels from her own experience, this little girl next discovered another use for them: sticking them into her little nose. This was not a happy experiment, however, because she also discovered quite quickly that (a) pretzels don't feel very good in one's nose, and (b) pretzels are much harder to get out of one's nose than to put in. Her mother successfully rescued her, and this child will not likely put herself in this predicament again. She learned quickly not to stick pretzels in her nose because that has virtually no redeeming value and produces considerable discomfort. We don't need a commandment from God to not stick pretzels in our noses.

In contrast, most of the things God takes the trouble to instruct us about are much less clear cut and much more important to get right. The things he commands us to *avoid* usually prove painful and debilitating, but at first, they often seem to have merit and much potential for solving problems, feeling good, and being interesting. Also, much of what he commands us *to do* at first looks time-consuming, cumbersome, hard, and scary, but in the long run has the potential to provide valuable benefits to us and others.

Frankly, getting married and committing to one person for the rest of eternity can, at many stages of the process, look like a really stupid idea. Many young people wonder, rightly, how they can ever get enough information to make such a decision well, or if they are cut out for such huge responsibilities, or if they even like the idea of living with one person, *any* one person, forever. What's more, it doesn't take a lot of looking around to realize many married people don't always look all that happy, that they break up their families with alarming regularity, and that even the ones who are "happily" married don't always have an easy time of it. Were it not for the nearly irresistible appeal of believing we will be loved, understood, cared for, and desired by someone who makes us feel loving, sensitive, and generous in turn, many of us would probably not undertake marriage without inciting hormones, cultural expectations, or God's injunctions. Hormones can be satisfied outside of marriage, and cultures decreasingly expect such commitments, but God's commandment to marry remains.

And what about this commandment to abstain from sex outside of marriage? Sometimes the sexually promiscuous are filled with guilt and immediately change course, but others have a difficult time renouncing their behavior because they believe that fornication or adultery solves a lot of their problems, there is a lot to be learned from it, and it can be enormously exciting. Clients have asked me if they can truly repent when they really don't feel a lot of regret about their choices. They aren't sure if they have been duped into thinking adultery is evil, or if they are completely depraved that they do not find it more abhorrent. But if sex outside of marriage were completely and "unadulteratedly" terrible, uncomfortable, and had no apparent value, then we would not need God to warn us so strongly against it. Like stuffing pretzels up our noses, we would figure out for ourselves quite quickly it is not a good idea.

The problem with sex outside of marriage is that it can seem like a good idea at first. We might think that it can solve many problems for us, that we can learn a lot from it, and that it can be a lot of fun. But God tells us the truth: sex outside of marriage also causes huge problems and pain for other people, short-circuits our own growth and development, leads to sometimes serious or permanent disease, brings children into an unstable and unclear parental relationship, undermines our spiritual confidence, and makes us angry and irritable and sneaky with those we have covenanted to love (I could go on). These and other problematic aspects are not always apparent until long after the damage is done. And extracting oneself from these problems is a lot more difficult than extracting pretzels from one's nose.

In addition, marital fidelity brings many blessings and worthwhile challenges into our lives. Fidelity is not just an arbitrary test of our capacity for self-denial. Marriage also invites us to express and enjoy the capacity of our body and spirit for pleasure, relaxation, excitement, wonder, tenderness, self-awareness, and sensitivity to another. In fact, research indicates married people have more sex than unmarried people, despite media portrayals to the contrary. Our covenants warn us against sexual gluttony, but lest we fall into the trap of believing sexual abstinence is the highest ideal, our covenant to receive our partner and give to them reminds us sexual anorexia is as unhealthy a preoccupation as sexual addiction.[2] Just as anorexia for food will short-circuit emotional growth and eventually kill the body, sexual anorexia is problematic to both the denied and the denying partner. Sexual anorexia is a faulty solution to marital and personal difficulties and is often based on faulty assumptions about the body, power, relationships, virtue, and self.

Even within marriage, then, sexual gluttony and sexual anorexia pose challenges to both spouses. Sexual anorexia in one partner can be almost as damaging to the marriage as sexual addiction in another, and both can lead to vicious circles of frustration and guilt. When God invites us to work toward healthy sexuality, he is inviting us to fully receive the gift of our body and our spouse, and to feel and grow our capacity to love. He is inviting us to find and meet our real needs, to solve our real problems, to gain true self-love, and to know the full extent of our true power instead of bogging down in distracting preoccupations with either having or avoiding sex. He is inviting us to the sacred lessons of emotional intimacy. Though such intimacy can be frightening to those who have experienced the dangers of false intimacy, it is ultimately the path out of the lonely telestial world.

How Can I Choose?

Given the myriad difficulties involved in finding a mate and making a family work, it is amazing the majority of us choose to try it, even given that it is a commandment to do so. Even when we pray sincerely about whom to marry, spiritual assurance can turn to human doubt with minimal provocation. So many possibilities out there, so little time. How can we ever know if we have made the best possible choice and have found the one relationship most worthy of our eternal commitment? Many of us simply find a way to fall oh-so-in-love to blind ourselves a little to the ridiculousness of trying to make such a crucial choice with such minimal data. Some of us also realize being "in love" is not a particularly rational, trustworthy, or lasting emotional state, and so doubts surface anyway. The fact that we believe marriage to be an eternal covenant does not always help those wary to begin with. We can't very well tell ourselves to just try him if we aren't sure, or that we can always take her back if we don't like her. Well, we can, but if we do we are not making a covenant with God. We are substituting a worldly, conditional purchase for a covenant stewardship of another's heart and soul.

More than one prophet has counseled that there is not one perfect spouse for each person. God does not just make up a roster in heaven and wait for us to discover whose name he has listed next to ours. We are to find someone we can love and who can love us, and then we are to take our choice to the Lord for confirmation. There may be many wrong choices the Spirit will discourage, but also many good choices the Spirit can confirm. Once we make that covenant, this person becomes our chosen one and only, and we have the right to God's help and blessing to turn what may have started as a chance attraction into a relationship worth perpetuating. God promises to work all things together for our good if both partners keep their covenants with him and work together to that end. Ironically, research suggests the more accurately we see our future spouse's weaknesses before marriage the less likely we are to divorce.

Even though there is no *Consumer Reports* to check for potential spouses, most of us are looking for the best deal we can find in a marriage partner. The dark underside of choosing a partner can be the selfish hope that we have gotten a bargain: the person with the most personal assets and the fewest deficits to exchange for what we offer in return. We may subsequently feel disappointment if the bargain goes sour—if our partner embarrasses us in public or ignores us in private—and wonder if we could have done better. Often those most intent on getting an "eight-cow spouse" (to borrow from the old Mormon film classic *Johnny Lingo*) are more interested in supporting their own self-esteem than their partner's.

Others imagine marriage as a cure-all for emptiness or loneliness. They are waiting for someone else to give their life meaning by choosing them. A young friend of mine stated with conviction that she knew how to cook, clean, and care for young children, so she was ready for marriage. She looked to marriage as a cure from the loneliness of her life. That she slammed doors in a rage when she didn't get her way, had little notion of how to make herself happy, pursued no meaningful interests, and spent every dime she received didn't seem relevant to her. Most twelve-year-olds can make a meal, clean a kitchen, and babysit, but the skills and maturities to make a successful family in today's world, let alone in eternity, are somewhat more complex.

Another friend spends all his time trying to figure out how to meet women, searching for someone to bring companionship and meaning to his life. Developing his personal capacity to make and keep a few friends, define a value system, or commit to a personal mission seems superfluous. He is afraid to waste precious time on such suspect pursuits when that time could be used instead finding someone to love him, which he insists is the only way to fill his emptiness. Needless to say, despite his outward charm and good looks, the women he wants tend to run from the giant sucking sound they hear when he is around. Few of us are interested in being the oxygen to fill someone else's internal vacuum.

Still another friend wonders why marriage is necessary at all. If healthy individuation means taking care of oneself and finding one's own happiness and meaning in life, then why bother with relationships? Isn't marriage just an excuse for unhealthy dependency?

Eternal marriage is not intended as a showcase for displaying our mate-attracting potential to the world. It is not a store in which we have a right to what we can pay for. It is not meant as a shortcut to finding a meaningful and fulfilling life on the wings of someone else's esteem. Its purpose is not to provide an excuse for emotional clutching or the security within which to keep our emotional distance. It is something else.

Temple Glimpses at Marriage

God commands his children to marry where feasible, and if possible to marry within the new and everlasting covenant. Perhaps he commands us to do this because it may not look like a sensible thing, but because within marriage we can fulfill our highest potential for creativity, growth, learning, and self-actualization. To be sure, some of us will fulfill our personal earthly mission and potential without marriage, while many others fall far short of doing so within marriage. But for most of us, marriage is the best school in becoming like God, not merely glimpsing him or spending a few days in his home. Without marriage, it is simply more difficult to find both the deep security and the appropriate humility we need to grow in essential ways toward our identity as heirs of the God of love.

Like baptism, marriage is a kind of new birth. As at birth, each partner may receive from the other a new name, access to a new body, and a new set of roles, rights, and relationships. We gain access to new parts of our identity when we marry, including our identity as a spouse, a sexual being, and a parent. We also gain access to a deeper understanding of the opposite sex, and of the fulness of our own identity with a wide range of traits that include independence and dependence, strength and openness, thinking and feeling, discipline and care, and giving and receiving. We try to learn to enforce our boundaries without building barriers. We try to compromise with another without compromising ourselves. In those processes, our own identity is strengthened and solidified.

Once endowed, we don't need to make any additional covenants at the marriage altar other than to receive the other person. We don't need to promise to take care of our partner, to be faithful, to provide for or protect them, to stand true for richer or for poorer, or to consecrate all we have to the benefit of our family and spouse because we have already made these promises to God during previous gospel ordinances of baptism, confirmation, and the endowment. There, we have vowed to repent and forgive, to live the gospel: to sacrifice and consecrate our all; to offer help, comfort and testimony to others; and to refrain from sex outside of marriage. These are our covenants with God, and in that covenant relationship by which we claim him as our God and he claims us as his people, he also empowers us to claim our human relationships. Our commitment to our spouse flows out of who we are trying to become as God's anointed.

Temple marriage also differs from worldly marriage because it is not about taking ("do you take this woman to be your lawfully wedded wife . . ."), but about receiving. Receiving suggests our willingness to be open to another, whereas taking suggests controlling another regardless of their will, making an object instead of a subject out of what is taken. To receive someone of our own free will and choice is an act of respect, humility, and acceptance of another human being. Receiving is a vital and dynamic concept in our faith. We are invited to receive the Holy Ghost, to receive our endowment, to receive God's laws, and to receive other people in the household of faith. To fully receive another person, like receiving the Holy Ghost, requires our willingness, humility, effort, and ongoing repentance. It is not enough to choose once to receive each other; we must choose each other again and again. The temple further differs from the world in that in the temple no one gives the bride away except herself. She alone controls her allegiance, subject only to her obedience to God.

The Reality: Life Gets Harder Before It Gets Easier

For many young people, eternal marriage is *the* temple ordinance, promising they will always be with the one they love. When I was single I imagined temple marriage was designed to commemorate a love so profound neither partner could stand the thought of separation. Only later did I realize the temple wedding is only the beginning, not the culmination, of love, and that mature married love would have very different qualities than I first imagined. I learned a wedding does not a marriage make. Not even a temple wedding. We had a ways to go to create a marriage worth perpetuating for eternity.

Researchers have identified four stages that characterize long-term relationships.[3] First is a *honeymoon* stage of idealism and high hopes. It lasts anywhere from a few days to a few years. The honeymoon stage is followed by increasing *power struggles* when the inevitable problems don't get worked out as we'd hoped. Couples spend years and even decades in this stage, working through many problems but being unable to resolve some of their deepest conflicts. This leads to a third stage of *withdrawal* and disengagement with varying degrees of disappointment in the relationship and increased independence. A precarious truce defined by resignation and stonewalling may characterize this stage. Finally, the best long-term relationships get to a stage of *renewal* characterized by forgiveness, reinvestment, and loving, open-eyed acceptance of one another. Long-term problems are worked around or transcended, and a deeper, truer love is attained. These stages show up in all types of long-term relationships, including those with spouses, parents, children, friends, careers, the Church, and God.

Honeymoon. As Bryce and Linda left the temple for the first time as husband and wife, they firmly believed they were meant for each other. There were many sweet moments of mutual understanding, service, and connection. They experienced the exhilaration of working through difficulties and realizing they were still together. Each felt the joy of being cared for despite imperfections, and the glow of feeling loving and kind with little effort. They built a life of pleasure and satisfaction. They brought children into their family and came to delight in them (at least most of the time). They each found a life's work; they built a home; they served in the Church and supported each other in that service, valuing each other's growth. They didn't always see eye to eye, but they worked through enough disagreements to assume they would continue to do so. They would not be like other couples. Theirs would be the one and only true marriage. They would always be in love.

Power struggle. Over time, the balance began to shift. The times when Bryce and Linda felt supported and in love took on a different proportion with the times they felt irritated or abandoned. They hit periods of both marriage and life when they felt capable of solving problems, changing, or being charitable. They argued, negotiated, failed, blamed each other, and tried to get each other to change. They each tried to change as well, but often more to placate their unreasonable partner than out of real self-awareness. Sometimes they let problems go too long without resolving them, assuming they weren't worth hassling about, but this was accompanied by resentment instead of mutual acceptance. There were still many good times, but the barriers of unresolved problems began to feel insurmountable.

Withdrawal. For Bryce and Linda, over time marriage increasingly felt like a bad grade-school classroom they put up with because they had no choice. As in that classroom, the only pleasures too much of the time were organizing their desks or free reading, rather than interacting with others or learning. The Important Other in the room always seemed vaguely annoyed, irritated, or indifferent, someone to be placated if possible until the bell signaled time to escape. For each of them, that dangerous Important Other was, of course, the person each had covenanted to love, cherish, and receive as an eternal mate. They shut down when hurt or misunderstood, not realizing the shutting down was the worst, and self-imposed, injury. They wanted to be loved better, but they each felt stingy and resentful and unlikable even to themselves as they withheld love from each other. They didn't realize the Important Other was also their true teacher.

As the glowing feeling of being in love fades into ordinary living, what we start to miss is not just being loved, but seeing ourselves as loving, giving people. When we are oh-so-in-love, we don't just feel lucky to receive, but happy about how easy it feels to give. We feel generous and kind, accepting and good. Over time, we may begin to resent our partner for no longer inspiring such warmth, for no longer making it so easy to feel good about how loving we are. We blame him or her for selfishness or inconsiderateness, but we hate just as much how selfish and inconsiderate we feel around our spouse. We focus our attention on how to get our partner to love us better, and we withhold love from him or her to even the score or refuse payment for services not rendered. But withholding love just makes us feel even more unlovable. It creates miserliness in the soul. When we refuse to love, we refuse our own nature, and we start to shrivel inside.

Loving many people we don't have to live with is usually much easier than loving a few people we do have to live with. In this tiny family microcosm of the world, we create or destroy world peace, the earth's resources, and the millennial kingdom of Christ. It is easier to worry about the anonymous masses or even the compelling needs of relative strangers than to commit fully to knowing, receiving, and loving one person. Marriage tutors us in the graduate school of loving: loving one individual as fully and completely as we can. That God offers us marriage is a testimonial that each of us is worth that kind of individual, one-on-one, committed love from someone for the whole of our life. Even more, marriage is a testimonial that each of us is capable of learning to be more like our heavenly Parents and to love as they love.

Renewal. When the inevitable challenges of marriage and parenting continued, sealing ordinances reminded Bryce and Linda of their covenant with God to learn to love and cherish this spouse, these children, even when loving is difficult, painful, or boring. They began to really get that marriage would not just change the other but the self, and that the changes required would not be superficial but deep and difficult . . . and exhilarating. They worked harder at releasing each other from control and judgment, valuing each other's agency as intently as God honored theirs. They learned a much deeper humility before one another's agency. They got curious about how each other felt and came to be. They worked to continue to invest passionately in each other without prescribing each other's choices. They saw each other less and less as a reflection of their own failings, and more as a separate individual deserving of deep compassion. They learned to set each other free as God sets us all free, without giving up on each other in the process. They came to welcome each other into the human race of mistakes and foibles without rejecting each other's divinity. Each gained compassion for his or her humanity as well. And as they did so, the fires of love could be rekindled with a more enduring and warming flame.

I see many couples whose long-term relationships follow a similar course not always apparent to onlookers. My husband and I first met in France, and we often repeat the French saying *"Plus qu'hier, moins que demain"* between us—"More than yesterday, less than tomorrow." After almost four decades of living through all the stages described above, I can assert that those words once again describe the love we share. While some seemingly unsolvable challenges still test our will and skill, our love and commitment to each other are strong. I believe we have gained this better ground in large part by determined effort to practice the attributes associated with the powers of heaven, as described below.

The Spiritual Practice of Relationship

Both husbands and wives would do well to review often the rights and obligations of the heavenly powers with which we have been endowed, as described in Doctrine and Covenants 121:36–46. In addition to the priesthood holders specifically addressed in these verses, anyone who holds a stewardship of love can benefit from this instruction. These verses speak volumes to me as a parent and spouse. That I have quoted from them repeatedly already suggests how deeply I value them as a guide for life:

> The powers of heaven cannot be controlled nor handled only upon the principles of righteousness.
>
> That they may be conferred upon us, it is true; but when we

undertake to cover our sins or to gratify our pride, our vain ambition, or to exercise control or dominion or compulsion upon the souls of the children of men, in any degree of unrighteousness, behold, the heavens withdraw themselves; the Spirit of the Lord is grieved; and when it is withdrawn, Amen to the priesthood or the authority of that [individual].

Behold, ere he [or she] is aware, he [or she] is left unto himself [or herself], to kick against the pricks, to persecute the saints, and to fight against God. (Doctrine and Covenants 121:37–38)

Even though we have been endowed and sealed in the temple, heavenly power to do good can only be claimed through righteousness. If our pride in our children's accomplishments, our ambition for another's validation, or our desires for control dominate our familial relationships, then we will hurt ourselves against the pricks of that pride. Others will feel that we persecute them. We will be at odds with the God of agency on whom we depend to obtain our desires.

I think I learned these lessons most powerfully when my children hit the terrible twos and the traumatic teens, and when my marriage hit the limits of our ability to solve its problems. What made these times terrible and traumatic had little to do with my children or my spouse, however. My own tendencies to shame and control them became more apparent at such times, and caused me the painful awareness that it was I who was terrible and traumatizing. I wasn't trying to be traumatizing, of course. I was trying to get my children to make right choices, to get good grades, to become good people. I was trying to get my husband to be home more, to listen better, and to help out. My goals may have been okay; my methods were not. In fact, I fit quite neatly into the description given as these verses continue:

We have learned by sad experience that it is the nature and disposition of almost all men [and women], as soon as they get a little authority, as they suppose, they will immediately begin to exercise unrighteous dominion. (Doctrine and Covenants 121:39)

As I sought from others answers on how to *control* my children and *get them to behave*, how to *handle* my husband and *manage* our relationship (all words I used and thoughts I had), I was brought up short against the following:

No power or influence can or ought to be maintained by virtue of the priesthood, only by persuasion, by long-suffering, by gentleness and meekness, and by love unfeigned;

By kindness, and pure knowledge, which shall greatly enlarge the soul without hypocrisy, and without guile—

Reproving betimes with sharpness, when moved upon by the Holy Ghost; and then showing forth afterwards an increase of love toward him whom thou hast reproved, lest he esteem thee to be his enemy;

That he may know that thy faithfulness is stronger than the cords of death. (Doctrine and Covenants 121:41–44)

I realized God was asking me to let go of control without letting go of my passionate and full-hearted investment in my loved ones, my intense involvement in helping them, hearing them, teaching them, and enjoying them. My first task was to love each family member fully, kindly, purely, and meekly, and without hypocrisy or guile. This meant working harder at controlling my own procrastination, selfishness, messiness, and rebelliousness and worrying much less about such tendencies in others. It meant loving them with my whole heart, trusting their intentions, believing in their goodness. It meant getting more calm, curious, and compassionate, rather than more insistent, demanding, and judgmental. And sometimes it meant stating more clearly and calmly my limits, needs, desires, perspectives, and bottom lines. My second task within that context of great love was to accept, however, that I could not control them. Period. I could ask nicely, explain my position and feelings, listen to understand, praise and encourage compliance, and try again, but I could not, and should not try to, control.

I remember once when a colleague told me that a parent's job is to help children get what *they need*. I am embarrassed at how forcefully that line struck me. I realized in an instant how often I operated as if my children or spouse's job was to give me what *I needed*: to feel proud of them so I could feel like a good mother, to make me feel in control and anxiety-free, to help me accomplish my goal to have an exemplary family, and to reinforce my lagging self-esteem. Things began to change as I began to accept that my family members had their own agendas quite separate from mine. Relating to them well involved helping them clarify and accomplish their goals, not getting them to accept and accomplish my goals for them. The same applied to my spouse. I could then rightfully expect my family's support of my goals, and a synergy of cooperative effort could ensue.

For me this scripture also means I have to build a relationship with each family member wherein they know without a doubt that my love for them is "stronger than the cords of death." Unless they truly believe this, they will esteem me as an enemy, and I will be bereft of influence upon their souls. We say of the Savior, "We love him, because he first loved us"

(1 John 4:19). He has influence on our souls when we trust he loves us, will sacrifice for us, feels deeply our sorrows, understands us to the core, and wants above all to help us get what we need. Then we are drawn by his love to love and desire him in return. Doctrine and Covenants 121 continues with a description of this Christlike love to which I can aspire:

> Let thy bowels also be full of charity towards all men, and to the household of faith, and let virtue garnish thy thoughts unceasingly; then shall thy confidence wax strong in the presence of God; and the doctrine of the priesthood shall distil upon thy soul as the dews from heaven. The Holy Ghost shall be thy constant companion, and thy scepter an unchanging scepter of righteousness and truth; and thy dominion shall be an everlasting dominion, and without compulsory means it shall flow unto thee forever and ever. (v. 45)

As we draw others to us through love, not compulsory means, our dominion within our family has hope of becoming an everlasting dominion, worth perpetuation, that distills upon us all, not out of force or obligation, but out of desire. We cannot force another to love us through duty. We cannot demand love through anger or guilt. We cannot manipulate for another's love as a substitute for responsible self-care. When we try to love others without compulsion or control, we remember how little God interferes, punishes, threatens, or coerces, and how often he comforts, provides, advises, encourages, releases, forgives, and simply waits. Nowhere are these principles more important than in our families, where our enemies, those for whom we are to pray, are sometimes those of our own household.

The Refining

Moments of personal clarity come interspersed with self-pitying scenarios when we marvel at our spouse's or child's capacities for selfishness. We realize the problem is not just with them. We start to see ourselves. Of course, problems are almost always both theirs *and* mine. Theirs are the easiest to see, but mine are most within my stewardship to change. Family, where I get the closest to others and they to me, shows me most clearly the self that I don't want to be and that I am. Even when I know my spouse or child is dancing with me, maybe even leading, I am dancing too. Sometimes we dance so long to the same tune that I forget this dance is something we have learned or made up and could change. I learn once more how family life provides the refining influences that either embitter and destroy us, or show us most clearly to ourselves so we can change. Families can help us become humble and decent enough to be fit for eternal life.

Marriage is a school, but it doesn't have to be a cold, ugly, unwelcoming one. Marriage is a mirror, but it doesn't have to be one out of an old *Twilight Zone* episode, showing us only our most grotesque qualities until we go mad with the ugliness of our image. Marriage is a dance, but it doesn't have to be a marathon where the partners are bound together in an unwilling embrace, repeating the same frantic, meaningless steps until they drop from exhaustion.

Researchers Clifford Notarius and Howard Markman study what makes a marriage work. They have concluded that the biggest factor in successful marriages is not how much people have in common, how much in love they believe they are, how committed they are to marriage or to each other, what personalities they have, or how little they fight. What makes a marriage work is the ability to resolve (not escalate or avoid) conflict.[4] This is a skill we can learn if we put our minds to it. It requires us to lay down our defensive, battle-based language and learn the skills of peace. It requires us to pick up the challenge of differences and learn the skills of negotiation and problem solving. Most of all, it requires that we listen. That we become curious instead of certain. Sometimes it also requires that we speak, clearly, even forcefully—but with love. Marriage allows us to contribute at a personal level to making the world a place that turns a deaf ear to its own difficulties or harbors war to resolve them . . . or a place that prepares for the Prince of Peace.

Marital researcher John Gottman adds an important caveat to the importance of problem solving. He concludes there are two kinds of problems in marriages. One type of problem is grounded in circumstances and can be addressed with a little creativity and good will. The other type of problem is deeply embedded in our personality and rooted in past pain. The latter are less likely to be solved, and in every marriage these are the problems that bring people to the brink of disaster. Gottman estimates that 67 percent of marital problems fall into this second category of unsolvable problems. That is a lot of unsolvable problems! Yet Gottman concludes that unsolvable problems do not inevitably lead to unworkable marriages. People can learn to negotiate around the edges of such issues, accept that they will never disappear completely, and still find peace and delight in each other. Paradoxically, accepting that some problems will not be fully resolved can be a kind of resolution.[5]

How do we find the courage and clarity to change? How do we keep investing in someone else's happiness without enabling their weaknesses or abdicating our responsibility for ourselves? How do we learn to accept unacceptable things without shutting down love or self-regard?

We trust in the Atonement of Jesus Christ. The message of that Atonement—that we are of infinite worth despite our foibles—helps us believe no one else can give us our worth or take it from us since God has already declared it. We can stop trying to manipulate others into feeding our hunger for esteem. We can trust our capacity to love well with his help even when loving is not our inclination or training. We can take the risk of commitment. Believing God alone is our refuge and defense, we can let down our guard and allow our hearts to expand to their true, godly nature.

Receiving

I think one purpose of marriage is to give us the most compelling possible forum for receiving another person. This is the path to receiving God and becoming like him. The sealing ordinances ask of us that we willingly, freely covenant to receive this one person, our spouse, and to continue to do so forever.

I know instinctively, in the marrow of my bones, what it feels like to receive my spouse. It involves acknowledging his viewpoint as being as valid as my own. It presumes his good intentions. It invites his honesty and cares for his needs. It remains open, trusting, forgiving, and kind.

God does not ask that we submit to abuse from those who are truly ill-intentioned or just ill. But as both partners willingly receive each other, each can become free. Marriage becomes a channel for God's blessings. In the honeymoon stage of marriage, we receive the other's potential, dreams, hopes, and worth, and in turn, our own. In the power struggle stage, we can receive differences, separateness, and problems as a necessary part of growth. We face that we will not fully understand each other, that someone else cannot fulfill our dreams for us, and that we will always be, in some respects, alone. In the withdrawal stage, we are challenged to receive our partner's and our own deep brokenness, insecurity, failings, and even propensities to sin, and to forgive ourselves and our spouse (whether or not we stay together). And finally, in the renewal stage, we receive our respective humanity, resilience, and deep, underlying goodness.

Other than this one invitation to receive, God's words about marriage speak only of blessings, not obligations. These blessings are suggested in section 132 of the Doctrine and Covenants:

> If a man marry a wife by my word, which is my law, and by the new and everlasting covenant, and it is sealed unto them by the Holy Spirit of promise, by him who is anointed, unto whom I have appointed this power and the keys of this priesthood . . . it shall be said unto them—Ye

shall come forth in the first resurrection . . . and shall inherit thrones, kingdoms, principalities, and powers, dominions, all heights and depths . . . in time, and through all eternity . . . which glory shall be a fulness and a continuation of the seeds forever and ever.

Then shall they be gods, because they have no end. (vv. 19–20)

We become gods by becoming like God, whose essence is encompassed in words like agency, humility, mercy, justice, and love. These blessings are attainable through our willingness to enter the marriage covenant, not because we have found the perfect partner, but because as we willingly receive another person, we also receive the Lord.

Except ye abide my law ye cannot attain to this glory . . . because ye *receive* me not in the world neither do ye know me.

But if ye *receive* me in the world, then shall ye know me, and shall *receive* your exaltation; that where I am ye shall be also. (vv. 21–23; italics mine)

HEALING PRACTICE FOR CHAPTER ELEVEN: TO RECEIVE AND BE RECEIVED

Nourishing relationship, resolving conflict.

- What are three things you could do today to positively nurture the most important relationships in your life?
- What is one problem you don't really want to address right now in your primary relationship?
- What are two reasons you have decided not to address it?
- What are two ways you could approach it if you decided to?
- What blessings might come from doing so?

Building problem-solving skill.

- Read one of the books recommended on page 247 and design your own program for increasing your skill at problem solving, nondefensive communication, or sexual well-being.

Boundaries.

- If possible, prepare a place in your home that is yours, appropriately set up for your work, creative endeavors, or meditative solitude.

Women seem particularly likely to neglect their need for a functional workspace, and men seem particularly inclined to neglect their need for beauty and variety. Whether it is a room, a closet, a bed, a desk, or a corner, make this space comfortable and reflective of your identity, regardless of whether you adorn the walls with candles and flowers or old bowling trophies. Find a way to acknowledge your individuality and mission in this private retreat.

Learning from the bottom up.

- Ask your children for their insights into how your family works. If you are nondefensive and open, they may be willing to share their perceptions of how they see their grandparents, how they see your current family, and how both affect them. Be careful not to argue, shame, or distance from your children as you do this. If you look too hurt or shamed by their observations, they will not want to share again. Especially if your relationships are strained, proceed with prayer and caution. While just bringing these issues into the open is an important step, using your discussions to discover a specific pattern that is problematic and talking together about how to change it can be most helpful.

Misplaced hopes.

- If you find yourself feeling stuck in anger with someone, consider the question, "What false hope am I holding onto that I need to acknowledge and release?" Excessive anger with ourselves or with others is often a way to keep things the same, not a way to change them. Often these are sneaky ways of holding on to the hope that some authority figure will take care of us after all, that someone else will solve something we need to fix ourselves, or that we can change the unchangeable.

Temple worship.

- Go to the temple and participate in the sealing ordinances. Listen carefully to the wording and contemplate its meaning to your current relationship. Participate in other ordinances with careful attention to the covenants and teachings that prepare you or instruct you in relationship.

CHAPTER TWELVE

HOLINESS TO THE LORD

———⊸⊶⊷⊶———

Earth's crammed with heaven,
And every common bush afire with God;
But only he who sees, takes off his shoes.

— ELIZABETH BARRETT BROWNING

Centermost in the ancient tabernacle and temple was the Holy of Holies. It housed the ark of the covenant, a large chest containing the physical tokens of God's presence among the Israelites. Inside was a pot of the manna by which he miraculously fed them on their long sojourn, the stone tablets on which God had written the Ten Commandments, and the staff of Aaron God had caused to bud and blossom as a living thing. The top of the ark formed an altar and a seat—the mercy seat, the throne of God on earth.[1]

The sacred confines of the Holy of Holies were approached only once a year on the Day of Atonement when, amid a cloud of incense, the high priest sprinkled the blood of the sin offering on the altar of the ark. This was the most holy of all holy days, commemorated at the most holy of all holy places. So sacred is the Holy of Holies to Jewish sensibilities, many devout Jews today will not go up on the temple mount in Jerusalem for fear of personally defiling the now unknown spot where the Holy of Holies once stood.

Although the celestial room is the modern equivalent of the Holy of Holies, there is also a small separate room adjacent to the celestial room in the Salt Lake temple that is specifically referred to as the Holy of Holies. Its purposes are only hinted at elsewhere in the temple. The prophet Lorenzo Snow retreated to this room upon the death of his predecessor as President of the Church, assuming he would meet with the Savior there and receive his direction. To the new leader's disappointment, no manifestation came.

Only upon leaving the temple through a common hallway available to all patrons did the Savior appear, standing in the air on a platform of gold, to instruct his newly appointed prophet.[2] The temple is the house of God, and his presence is not restricted as it apparently was in ancient times to a single room or a single day. Nevertheless, the Holy of Holies still represents a legacy of living revelation to God's prophets, and to the prophetic and holy in each of us.

While today's temples may not contain an ark of the covenant, in the ancient relics the ark once contained we see the tokens of what we still need in order to be centered in holiness. We need to firmly trust God will provide manna to our souls and care for us according to our deepest needs as we wander through this wilderness. We need to gratefully order our lives after his commandments and laws. We need hope that he can and will empower the rigid, sterile parts of us to blossom with new life as we entrust them to his care and use them for his purposes. He still offers to take his seat at the core of our being—a mercy seat. Anciently, the mercy seat was covered both inside and out with fine gold workmanship, suggesting both the blazing glory of God and the supreme inner worth of every human soul. This is not a derivative worth based merely on our usefulness or even our goodness. It is our inherent worth, to which Christ testifies when he claims us as his seed and promises us his mercy (Mosiah 5:7; 15:10–12). For us, every day can be a *day of atonement*—a day to enter God's presence with reverence and awe at Jesus's sacrifice for us. He is a God of loving mercy, as the seat of his power proclaims.

During the years of Israelite pilgrimage, the Holy of Holies was not established by the dedication of a piece of ground. It was not limited to a particular location. Its holiness was portable. Within the tabernacle, the gold-encased carrying poles were never to be removed from the rings by which the ark was hoisted. The Holy of Holies of the soul cannot be dependent on external circumstances either. It must move with us wherever we go, at the heart of our being, our temple of the soul.

Holey at the Center

As already described in this book, many of us have little hope in our own holiness and are far more aware of our "holey-ness." We may feel as if, as eventually happened with Israel, invaders have robbed us of the precious golden ark that belongs in our heart of hearts. Lacking this crucial inner grounding, one feels a deep emptiness or confusion within. In the words of a poet, "Things fall apart; the centre cannot hold; mere anarchy is loosed upon the [inner] world, the blood-dimmed tide is loosed."[3] Like ancient Israel, eventually enslaved in Babylon, we may hardly be able to imagine what it would feel like to be a covenant people, to have a homeland of our own, to worship the good and holy God instead of demanding or silent idols of our own making. We don't know how to have a holy place at our center. We have been too little comforted, protected, or helped and too often shamed, injured, or used. The swirling reservoir of primitive fear, anger, confusion, and resentment that centers our identity can convince us we are inherently and irredeemably *bad*—the exact opposite, in fact, of *holy*. Despite outward displays of obedience, we have little sense of our worth. Critical enemy voices, now internalized, rob us of the mercy seat that belongs within.

Like ancient Israel, sometimes our fiercest battles are fought in civil wars. Without a reliable inner sense of our worth, we mistake self-denigration for humility or self-aggrandizement for confidence. We fail to see that both are merely compensations for our lack of inner wholeness, compensations that both hurt us and cause us to hurt others. When our hearts are empty and chaotic, we instinctively depend on other people to love and care for us to help us heal, but once we are no longer children, no one owes us this level of unconditional service and love any more. It is humiliating to need so desperately what no one really owes us. It is hard to feel whole, let alone holy, with a hole at the heart of our being. We long for something solid to ground our sense of reality and self, lest we collapse around this emptiness at our core.

We need an ark of the covenant within us, a fitting container that will hold the evidences of God's personal love for us, and of our infinite worth. A container is something different from a hole. A hole is an absence; a container is a presence. Part of the temple's task is to help us go from holey to whole. Recovering a true understanding of our history (baptistry) and recovering our full embodiment (initiatory) are steps in this process. Recovering our creativity reminds us that even when we still have holes, we are more than our weaknesses (creation room). In fact, our weaknesses often come into proper perspective only as we focus on living from our creative gifts to strengthen and bless the world.

Wholly Centered

In the dedication of the Kirtland temple, Joseph Smith asked God that the Saints "may grow up in thee, and receive a fulness of the Holy Ghost, and be organized according to thy laws, and be prepared to obtain every needful thing" (Doctrine and Covenants 109:15). A crucial function of the Atonement of Jesus Christ is to help us find the humility and the loving care we need to find a measure of wholeness so we may truly "grow up in God," obtain all we need, order our lives on true principles, and fill the receiving container we fashion within us with the Holy Ghost. The humility Christ's Atonement inspires us to look squarely at our neediness and at the addictive, sinful patterns we use to try to feel better, without recoiling in shame and despair at the ugliness of our condition.

To gain this humility, we must acknowledge our desperate need for redemption. We must realize we are full of holes we cannot fix, our lives made unmanageable by our sinful patterns of addiction, falsity, and using and abusing ourselves and others in precisely the ways we have been used and abused and should know better than to repeat. We must acknowledge our enormous need for something no one owes us, which is the atoning life and death of our sinless Savior, to repair our brokenness and expiate our sinful responses to it. Second, and at the same time, we must acknowledge our infinite worth to God, to which the Atonement of Christ also testifies.

We absolutely don't deserve, and are absolutely worth, the full price of our Savior's blood, and we must hold these seemingly contradictory facts together in our hands and hearts. We are not, and cannot make ourselves, *worthy* of the redeeming love we need to bind our wounds and fill our inner emptiness. And we are inherently of such worth that God has organized the universe to save us, one person at a time.

He has the will and the power to save us. My unwillingness to believe and respond when God calls me by name and tells me who I am is the only thing in the universe that can override his will and power. My sins will not stop him if I will repent. My brokenness will not stop him if I will trust in his healing power. *My unwillingness to believe and respond is the only thing that can override God's will and power to save me.* As challenging as it can be to open our hearts to trust God's mercy and love, this is the ark of testimony and covenant that belongs at the center of the temple of the soul.

When we can hold in one heart these two paradoxical facts—that we are of infinite worth and that we can never do enough to be worthy of all God offers us—we can begin to find a spiritual center. When we choose to deeply trust God's love for us, even when the evidence sometimes appears contrary, we can have the humility to learn without feeling humiliated by our ignorance. We can stop demanding unconditional acceptance from other people, wearing them out with our need for validation or care. We can stop demanding perfection of ourselves, wearing ourselves out with our shaming obsessions. We can stop pouting to God about our trials, because we can trust they do not mean he has abandoned us. We can stop drowning in our own inertia and can risk trying to improve, because we won't be overwhelmed by disappointment and shame if we fail again.

It takes more courage and more stamina to trust in love when we have been heart-injured than when we have a surer inner core. But as Truman Madsen has observed, "None of us receives enough love in this world, none of us. We're all in a measure love-starved and love-anxious."[4] And yet we can choose to trust his love as an act of will, even when we do not feel trusting. We can acknowledge our need for repentance without our inner world being threatened by collapse in humiliation at our sins. We can live in a land of promise even when storms rage around our little tent, for the land of promise will be within. Then life does not have to hurt so much, even though life has not changed at all. We are less dependent on others' recognition or approval, dependencies that leave us resentful and afraid. Instead, we choose to depend on God, and we choose to let his unseen love be enough.

Often when I pray, I find myself speaking to some unseen being that resides in the distant heavens, for that is how I most comfortably imagine God. One day I felt the Spirit whisper, "Why do you keep me so far away?" The question caught me off guard. I had thought my sins, inadequacies, and imperfections were keeping him away. Is it really *my choice* to hold him at arm's length? Apparently it is. But why?

Perhaps my favorite novel of all time is C. S. Lewis's *Till We Have Faces*. It is the story of two princesses, the only children of a cruel king. The oldest is plain but intelligent and courageous. The second is her beloved and beautiful younger sister. The beautiful sister is chosen by the gods and endowed with healing gifts. At first, she is acclaimed by the people as a savior and a healer, but later she is rejected, appears to have been killed, but in actuality takes a difficult journey toward heaven.

When the sisters meet again, the plain sister, despite her love for her beautiful sister, does not believe her tale of heavenly visitations, and she unsuccessfully tries to bring her to her senses. This plain sister becomes a powerful queen who battles for her people and reigns with wisdom, but she appears in public only behind a veil to mask her lack of beauty. She longs for her sister, wonders if perhaps she could have been telling the truth, and suffers with deep feelings of loss and inadequacy. Yet we also see her courage, strength, and basic goodness.

Near the end of the book, the plain sister realizes the beautiful sister might have been telling the truth, and she is infuriated that the gods did not make their ways plainer to her eyes so she could have more easily believed.

She too takes off on a long journey, intent on taking this complaint to the gods. She eventually makes her way to their vast hall of judgment, naked and alone. She begins to read her complaint. In fact, reads it over and over and over without stopping, but in the reading, she comes to see it was not the gods who blocked her from seeing. She'd *had* a glimpse of her sister's vision. Her desire to hold on to her sister's adoration and not share her with the gods had kept her from believing. She hears at last the ugly truth of who she has been.

She writes:

> I saw well why the gods do not speak to us openly, nor let us answer. Till that word can be dug out of us, why should they hear the babble that we think we mean? How can they meet us face to face till we have faces?

This brave sister, however, does not shrink from this knowledge. She is willing to see. She continues to learn, her self-understanding deepening. As the story ends, she realizes she and her sister have each been on a journey, have carried each other's anguish, and have both become noble, wise, and beautiful in the process. They have come together to a place of truth, and of glory.[5]

It can take a lifetime for us to see ourselves for who we are, and the first truths we must face are not the happy ones. We must courageously see the ways we have yielded to the tempter's power, betrayed ourselves and others, and clung to our sins and our weaknesses. We must repent of pettiness and pride, jealousy and fear, replacing them with true humility and faith. But as we do, we can begin to recover our hope (garden room), spiritual discernment (world room), and place in the community of Zion (terrestrial room). These are powers we came to earth to develop. Now God can show us the rest of the truth: our light.

It is not an easy thing to build a gold-adorned mercy seat and place it in an imposing spot in an expensive temple shrouded in mystery and kept at a distance. But it is harder by far to bring the mercy seat into one's humble, messy, private chambers, near to one's broken heart. I believe God wants to provide us with that more sure word of prophesy, that intimate election that the Holy of Holies represents. When we choose with passionate persistence his gentle but fierce love, his paths of wholeness, and his day of rest, he will not stay far away. We will truly find joy in our posterity, joy in our redemption, and just *joy* in serving in the house of the Lord.

Holy Centers

Some ancient Israelites were blessed to live in a time when the ark of the covenant was housed in Israel. A lucky few had the opportunity to contribute personally to its construction, to rejoice in reverent gratitude at its dedication. Others mourned and longed for its return to its lost place of honor in their midst. Yet they were all his covenant people. Likewise, some of us are blessed with a solid inner core that grounds our personality. Others may always mourn and long for an inner solidity they cannot seem to hold on to in this life. A lucky few may find a way to build an inner container where one had been missing, embellished with the finest artwork of their souls and the finest golden efforts of their lives. How blessed we will be if we can find a way to so build. But God's power to save us cannot be constrained by our mortal imperfections and inadequacies. He will save his children if they will let him, tabernacle or no tabernacle, ark or no ark, cure or no cure. His throne is in the heavens whether or not there is a mercy seat anywhere on earth except within us. He can save me. He can save you. When we have made this place for him within the temple of our soul, we have finally come home—to God, and to ourselves.

Some theologians believe religious rites replicate in symbolic ways the spiritual experience of a religion's founder. We can certainly see temple ordinances in that way as symbolic ways of replicating the experiences of Joseph Smith: communicating with heavenly messengers, detecting and overcoming the adversary, seeing in vision the Creation, plan of salvation, and building of Zion, and even seeing God himself.

But I don't think the temple was designed in some deliberate way by Joseph Smith to merely commemorate his experiences and give us something symbolic to remind us of them. I think it was designed by God to teach us and prepare us to have those experiences for ourselves. Ordinances use stories and symbols not only to give us home movies of someone else's trip to godliness but also to entice us to take the trip. The temple gives us a sort of virtual experience with deep spiritual realities of healing and sanctification, then reminds us these things are intended to bring us to the passage into the presence of God. The itinerary for the trip includes being born again as new creatures in Christ, who are not the people we once were. It includes nourishing ourselves with the light of Christ through the ordinance of the sacrament, then being filled with the gift of the Holy Ghost—the Testifier, Sanctifier, and Miracle Worker. It includes obtaining a remission of our sins, receiving a renewal of our bodies, and being ordained kings, queens, priests and priestesses by God. It includes a vision of "all things" from the creation of the world to the building of Zion and the Second Coming of the

Savior. It includes detecting and casting out Satan and communing with heavenly messengers using keys given to us in the Doctrine and Covenants. It includes becoming absolutely obedient, sacrificing, and consecrating all we have to build God's kingdom, and obtaining in the process the perfect faith such acts bestow. It includes becoming unified with other Saints so our prayers gain power with God to bless those we love, perform miracles in their lives, and sustain the prophets, missionaries, and youth with our faith in such a way that lives are spared, mountains moved, and prophecies uttered and fulfilled. It includes being endowed with the right to ask and to receive whatever is right, and to know by the Spirit what those right things are. It includes standing in the presence of the Lord and welcoming his return. It includes the power to claim our calling and election before we leave this scene of action so we can also claim our children in time as well as in eternity.

Taking the Journey

Some years ago, as I boarded a flight home from a city I visited often, an unusual thing happened. I was settling my eighteen-inch lap into my sixteen-inch seat and stuffing my travel bag through the half-inch space between my knees and the back of the seat in front of me when the gate agent boarded the plane, approached me, and asked if I would mind changing seats. My flash of annoyance faded quickly as I realized the new boarding pass he was presenting to me was for a nice, big, "Would-you-like-your-dinner-now-or-later-Mrs.-Ulrich?" first-class seat. Suddenly I became quite gracious about honoring his request.

How did this miracle occur? No, I did not hold a frequent-flyer card entitling me to such an upgrade, nor had I paid the additional fare. The gate agent and I had previously discovered we share a common family name, and when space was needed in the back of the plane he was kind enough to pick me to move up to the front. Needless to say, I was grateful for this kindness, which of course no one owed me and which I had done nothing to deserve.

In like manner, Christ stands at the gate for our spiritual journey. He offers to move us up to first class, not because anyone owes it to us, for we cannot pay this fare. He offers it simply because we have taken upon ourselves his name. Out of this shared identity, if we will seek and choose it, he offers us this mercy seat. We don't have to worry that some other gate agent will not recognize us and keep us in coach or off the flight, for the Savior is always the keeper of this gate, and he employs no servant there (2 Nephi 9:41). We don't have to worry that there will be no first-class space left, for there are enough seats and to spare for all. The Savior asks only that we share the food and the luggage space, that we don't imagine ourselves better than those in the back of the plane or on the ground where we belong, and that we bring all who will come to him for a similar upgrade. How I love him for his goodness to me, a sinner. These are the perspectives and potentials we begin to recover in the temple's celestial spaces.

In Moroni's culminating testimony of the Book of Mormon, we read:

> I would exhort you that when ye shall receive these things, if it be wisdom in God that ye should read them, that ye would *remember how merciful* the Lord hath been unto the children of men, from the creation of Adam even down until the time that ye shall receive these things, and *ponder it in your hearts*. (Moroni 10:3, italics mine)

God's mercy can establish us in goodness and holiness when we believe we contain only emptiness or darkness or worse inside. If Christ told his disciples they should not call him good for there is none good but God, then surely it is not *our* goodness that makes us good either, not ever. Yet, in his mercy, he speaks to us of our worth, even when we are broken and empty.

Our task then is to place our testimony of God's love and mercy at the core of our being and hold it there in sacred space as best we can, as a testimonial, a living remembrance we can come back to again and again, even when our earthly experience insists love and mercy are lies. How else could the Saints leave their incomplete temple in Nauvoo to head across the plains? They held its promise in their hearts. Ordinances and journals, scriptures and prayers are vehicles of this remembering. They help us hold on to our hard-won lessons in trust, even though we may have to learn them over and over again.

The temple prepares us to be among those faithful servants who, upon Christ's return, are found "giving meat to his household in due season," out of the fulness he has provided us (Matthew 24:45), recognizing both our holes and our holiness. It teaches us to prepare his due seat, his mercy seat, at the center of our souls and to organize our lives around that mercy, trusting its witness to our infinite worth. If we are not fortunate enough to possess or to find a way to build an ark of the covenant within our hearts and to fill it with reminders of God's power, then we can allow the remembrance that such a thing once existed in Israel to comfort us in Babylon, and we can live to the best of our ability in hope that God's life-giving power will one day so grace us again.

"Know ye not that ye are the temple of God, and that the Spirit of God dwelleth in you? . . . The temple of God is holy, which temple ye are" (1 Corinthians 3:16–17). We are God's true temple, his living, breathing house. Even when we have been desecrated and ravished, even when that desecration has done its evil work upon our heart, these things have never touched our worth. Gold and fine workmanship did not create the true value of the ark; they only commemorated it. Its true value was in the evidences it contained of God's love and power to save, in the fact that he reaches down to feed and order and quicken us when we are but former slaves wandering in the desert. What God has claimed we have no right to disclaim, even if it is our woefully inadequate selves we want to reject. He has claimed us, endowed us, and given us work to do and love with which to do it, if we will receive.

In our innermost chambers, we are holiness to the Lord.

HEALING PRACTICE FOR CHAPTER TWELVE: HOLINESS TO THE LORD

- *Emblems for the Ark.* Each of us needs an ark of the covenant within our soul, filled with the evidences of God's love and mercy. Make a list or draw or create a symbol of each item you list below:

  - *Manna.* What are the ways God provides for you, cares for you, and gives you what you truly need?

  - *Tablets.* Which of God's laws are most meaningful to you, or do you have a firm testimony of? How have they blessed you?

  - *Aaron's rod.* What miracles has God done for you, including areas where he has been merciful, directive, or healing, allowing you to bring forth new life?

  If you are missing any of the above, list what you yet want in your ark.

- *Building an ark.* Draw, create, or allow yourself to imagine a container to hold the evidences of God's love in your life. What does that container now look like? Where do you visualize it within you? How big is it? What shape, color, and details do you see? What is it made of? Would you like to change it? How? How would you consecrate it for a holy purpose? Allow yourself all the time you need to imagine and capture these details.

- *Internalizing.* Allow yourself to imagine creating this ark and placing it within you. Imagine how you would prepare, cleanse yourself, and dress to carry the manna, tablets, and rod, however you have created them, and place them in the ark. How would you invite God's presence to sanctify and preserve it? Give yourself time to let this picture come into focus.

- *Communing.* Allow yourself to feel centered around this holy of holies. What does it feel like? What message does God have for you? What message do you have for him?

- *Veiling.* Imagine creating a protective veil around your holy of holies to shield it from the world. Imagine the preparations you would undertake to enter this holy place within. Then imagine what it would feel like to leave it knowing that, even as you travel in the wilderness, God's presence is at the heart of all your encampments. What impact might this have on your sense of who you are, and how you relate to others?

APPENDIX

HEALING FROM ABUSE

———

Anything with a great potential for positive impact also contains the potential for negative impact, including religion, ritual, sexuality, power, friendships, and family relationships. Damage is done and deep offenses can occur when agency is misused in these powerful contexts. The temple is not exempt from such challenges. Even a thoughtless comment in a place so laden with many expectations for holiness can disappoint or unsettle us. The temple can be more than unsettling for victims of serious abuse, leaving them confused or upset. But the temple, like the traveler's inn in the tale of the good Samaritan, can also help us experience healing from even our deepest wounds as it connects more fully with Christ's healing power.

A Hospital for the Soul

In the most heinous misuses of agency, one person takes physical, sexual, or emotional control over another in egregious ways. Some offenders of this kind apparently lack the capacity for empathy with their victims, which is why they can perpetrate their misdeeds without guilt. Others may enter a trance-like state with a predictable script and role that may dull both perpetrator and victim to reality and place them in a negative and oppressive ritual space. Sometimes contexts such as the temple—although it is a completely different kind of ritual space—may trigger old feelings and roles, leaving victims of abuse fearful, angry, or numb in the temple without knowing why.

The temple can be an important instrument of healing for such individuals because it can provide a corrective experience, a different ending to old stories. Temple ordinances invite us back into our body, where we can reclaim our agency and personal power. In the soothing, dream-hymn cadence of the temple we find principles and patterns of cleansing from the "blood of this wicked generation" (Doctrine and Covenants 88:75).

Trauma is not universally devastating in the long run.[1] When people in stressful or abusive situations find ways to successfully cope with their struggle and receive social support, they generally heal and even grow and improve. The person who finds a way out survives, tells others, is believed and supported, and successfully integrates what happened into the story of his or her life will come to different outcomes than someone who does not.[2] When people are trapped in unspeakable situations, they often freeze or become numb emotionally as a way to escape. Some research suggests staying emotionally present in a trying situation or exercising agency and power thereafter can help us move from post-traumatic stress to post-traumatic growth.

A wounded child naturally runs home for help to the caring hands of those who love him or her. God, who loves us, has provided many hands and houses, including his house, where his healing work can go forth. The initiatory ordinances in particular suggest principles of healing from abuse of all kinds. When someone is wounded, we wash his or her abrasion, apply a healing ointment, and dress it in a clean, white bandage to protect it from further injury while it heals. Olive oil, the medicinal agent used in ancient times as a healing balm, was also used for nourishment, as a source of light, as a sign of hospitality, and for soothing and grooming. Sacred olive oil was also used to convey the identity of king or priest to God.[3] All of these uses contribute to its powerful symbolism.

Initiatory ordinances offer the traumatized (1) healing rituals, (2) protected time and space, (3) reconnection with the body, (4) help in making peace with God and self, (5) models of good boundaries, (6) help with forgiving, and (7) instruction in finding ourselves again. Let us explore these possibilities in turn.

1. Our Need for Healing Rituals

Many scholars proclaim the need for rituals in modern society.[4] Still, those who participate in any ritual for the first time may feel disoriented, even fearful as they are pulled away from familiar supports and rules. This is not all bad: sometimes outward disorientation pushes us to reorient ourselves to the unseen mysteries and joys of an inner spiritual realm. With experience, we learn the rules of abuse do not apply in God's house, where submission does not injure, vulnerability does not debase, touch does not humiliate, secrets do not isolate, and uncertainty does not signal danger. By learning these new lessons, we can hopefully find new meanings in painful past experiences and embrace rather than avoid the risks necessary to create a new worldview.

In the proper setting, ritual can be a way to control abuses of power and protect participants.[5] Because rituals empower the office and not the person, they remind us to not unduly venerate individuals just because they fulfill priestly roles. Rituals constrain how individuals may use power and to what ends, controlling excesses. In LDS temple rituals, few explanations are given by anyone, permitting the participant to assign the meaning he or she sees in the ordinance rather than empowering the ordinance worker (or anyone else) to create its meaning. Emphasis is constantly given in our rituals to agency and individual choice about participation. Remembering these elements can help us feel safer within the ritual space of the temple.

2. Protected Time and Space

Learning to face and feel old pain is a gradual process, and the goal is not to swamp ourselves with it as quickly as possible. We cannot think clearly when flooded with painful emotions or when numb to all feelings. The goal is to restore calm, compassionate, curious thought and to regain feelings of safety and control before we face pain, so we can bear what was previously unbearable and reason clearly about what it means. We then can find new rules about how and when to trust, protect ourselves rightfully, and love well.

Safety is paramount as we make this journey. A good therapist will help us stay connected with our feelings without letting us get overwhelmed by anxiety or pain.[6] This emphasis on safety is crucial in the temple as well. If we have had an uncomfortable experience in the temple, it may be enough for a while to sit in the parking lot and ponder the experience while noticing the beauty of the flowers and the peacefulness of the setting. We can give ourselves permission to do only those ordinances we feel comfortable with until we feel ready to do others. We may need to consciously remind ourselves we are feeling _____ (fill in the blank), which registers in our body as _____ (shakiness, increased heart rate, nervous stomach, tension in the neck, dry mouth, numbness, and so on) because we are remembering _____ (name the trauma without details). At the same time, we can notice

_____ (describe things we see and hear now) and know it is really _____ (today's date) and the old trauma is not happening any more.[7] It is helpful to share our feelings with someone we trust so we do not try to bear the unbearable alone.

As we overlook similarities that trigger old pain and focus on ways the temple is different, we recognize we are safe, have new options, and the past is over. When we do this, the temple can become a safe haven and a place of refuge, peace, and learning. The gentle pace of the temple reminds us the temple sits outside of time, and everything there comes back again as many times as we might need so we can understand and make our peace.

It is not uncommon for victims of trauma or abuse to believe their own unworthiness is responsible for discomfort in the temple. If we wonder if we struggle with the temple because of unworthiness on our part, we can remember that if we have answered the temple recommend questions honestly, then we are worthy to be in the temple. Neither perfection nor personal comfort is requisite to such worthiness.

Blaming oneself for having been abused is a common way of gaining a false sense of control. If we can believe we deserved the abuse or abandonment in some way, then by improving ourselves we can avoid it. Self-blame also may keep us from facing that we live in a world where adults cannot always be trusted and where terrible things can happen to us without provocation. Yet in fact we do live in just such a world, and spiritual maturity and healing require us to make peace with that fact and let go of the illusion of having been in control of the abuse or having been responsible for it when we were not.

A true healer listens until he or she truly understands us, neither condemns nor rejects, helps us place what happened in a truthful context, and allows us to experience being seen and accepted for who we are. The initiatory ordinances likewise remind us of our need to be seen and accepted in all our vulnerabilities and while we are yet imperfect, to be instructed in our true identity as children of God with the potential to become kings and queens in his kingdom.

Of course, if there are ways we contributed to our own victimization, then these can be acknowledged and corrected, secure in the promise that God is patient with our inexperience, naïveté, and weaknesses and is not looking for ways to punish us for them at the hands of the unrighteous. We did not deserve to be traumatized or abused, *and* we can still learn from the experience. We do not have to choose one or the other.

3. Reconnecting with the Body

Like innocents fresh out of Eden, victims of abuse may find themselves in a lonely, dark world, separated from their truest sense of self and split off from their body and its sensations and feelings. Without clear access to our feelings we have extra difficulty discerning the Spirit. While yet alive, we are as dead, our spirit cut off from our body's knowledge and feelings. Addictions of various kinds perpetuate the separation of mind and body, numbing the body and distracting the mind. Yet only a spirit and body inseparably connected allows a fulness of joy (Doctrine and Covenants 93:33).

When we are in a dissociated state, body, affect, and cognition seem to operate independently. The mind says nothing is wrong, but the body feels terror; the spirit perceives danger, but the body becomes numb; the body responds sexually, but the mind is a blank. As we tune into our feelings again, negative feelings of terror, rage, shame, and grief may recur and must generally be worked through to some conclusion before positive feelings can surface. Healing involves creating a new understanding, a new and more accurate story of what happened to us and why. It involves a consecration of each part of the body for its rightful purpose and to its rightful owner. A healthy adult has eyes that see clearly and accurately, a mouth that speaks the truth, a head solidly connected to the input and actions of the torso, a nose that brings pleasurable and finely tuned sensations. Healing rites legitimize and enact our need for healing touch that is not erotic or exploitive, and that invites us back into our body. The laying on of healing hands in gentle, nonsexual blessing legitimizes our need for appropriately bounded expressions of quiet care.

Touch serves many purposes. Loving parental touch helps a child orient to its body and make of it a home for the child's spirit. Reparative touch provides comfort to the physically or psychologically injured. But the sexually abused may experience eroticization of the nonsexual human need for comfort. The sexually exploited may overidentify with the aggressor even while they hate him or her, contributing to gender confusion. They may avoid identifying with adults who have failed to safeguard them, often those of their own gender. They may prefer to be "safely" passive or "safely" aggressive, depending on their experience. These complex identifications and longings may become eroticized in adulthood as same-sex attractions or promiscuous tendencies. Astoundingly, I know adults who do not remember ever being held or touched in a nonsexual way. Not surprisingly, they associate all touch with sexuality. As we identify and meet our legitimate needs for comfort and care, erotic elements can be reduced and real needs addressed within the boundaries the Lord has established.

4. Making Peace with God

It is difficult to reconcile tragedy with the idea of a God who is omnipotent and omni-benevolent. While sophisticated philosophical and doctrinal discourse can help us with such reconciliation, ultimately we choose to believe in God out of desire and faith, not convincing arguments. We choose to believe despite our doubts, not by eliminating them. Ultimately we choose to submit to God not because his ways are easy or fully comprehensible, but because we recognize with Peter that there is no place else to go, for here are the words of eternal life (John 6:66–68). As we find healing, we learn we can survive, and that while God does not promise to keep us safe in this world of agency and accident, he does promise that his power to heal, restore, and bring us home again is limitless. When his confidence in our resiliency seems to exceed our real capacity, we can know he mourns with us in our grief and will make up all our losses.

In the council in heaven, we raised our hands to support the Father's plan of agency. The creation of a new life after abuse also requires supporting that plan of agency, even when agency can be grossly misused. Submitting to God in this way is not easy, but perpetual anger and resentment are even more difficult in the long run. We have survived, and as we heal and grow, emotional chaos can be replaced by new order, variety, beauty, and life.

As healing continues, we must learn, through careful tuning of our mind and body, to distinguish right from wrong, truth from error, good from evil, the loving voice of God from the voice of the destroyer masquerading as a friendly messenger. As we reconnect with our body, we are less likely to misunderstand, attribute wrong motives, overgeneralize, underestimate, exaggerate, and minimize. We more readily embrace the ambiguity inherent in all things, perhaps because we no longer have to work so hard to see the black and white.

The silent conclusions we come to after a traumatic experience are often extreme, magical, or one-sided, but they are powerful influences on our future behavior. As we face old traumas in safer contexts, we can revisit these conclusions and fine-tune them. It takes artistry and skill to retain loving feelings for an abusive family member while still rejecting violation, to retain our capacity for pleasure while rejecting inappropriate touch, or to maintain a trusting posture in the world while protecting ourselves against real dangers. We may have particular difficulty perceiving the Spirit of the

Lord when our systems are reeling with internal cries. When we hurt, we need loving mentors to nurture, speak truth, and confirm the witness of the Holy Ghost, inaudible to us for now. Eventually, we will get calm and safe enough to feel the Spirit for ourselves.

A lingering question for many people is how to know if abuse really happened if it was temporarily forgotten. Sometimes people unwittingly invent "memories," and sometimes people "forget" real tragedies (I have personally witnessed both). As Latter-day Saints, we have deep roots in the quest for truth amid discordant opinions and uncertainty. We acquire a testimony of either spiritual or psychological truth through a similar process of accumulating evidence from many sources. Impressions, dreams, physical sensations, powerful emotions, memories, and fragments of familiarity may all contribute. Like an accumulation of spiritual experiences that lead one to conclude which church is true, a sufficient accumulation of evidence leads us to conclusions about our past. More compelling evidence leads to more accurate and dependable conclusions. However, whether in a court of law, a scientific experiment, a search for a testimony of God, or a repressed childhood memory, we rarely reach absolute certainty, and acknowledging this fact need not immobilize us in self-doubt. Learning to tolerate ambiguity and make responsible choices in the midst of uncertainty is vital to emotional and spiritual maturity.

5. Regaining Boundaries

The abused need appropriate boundaries to shield and protect them from those who would destroy or injure. Fully operational spiritual boundaries shield us from the soul-destructive power of evil. When we have been abused, we have difficulty maintaining boundaries that are flexible and permeable without being too rigid. We may too readily lay our protective shields aside and seek refuge in fantasized invincibility. Or we may have boundaries that keep everyone out and leave us lonely and isolated.

Skin and clothing are both useful metaphors for appropriate boundaries because they are protective but flexible, and both have been used symbolically in ritual throughout time.[8] For example, in ancient Egypt, a skin worn over one shoulder by the Egyptian priest symbolized authority and heavenly power. In ancient myth, Heracles wore a special leather garment for protection in the risky world of humans. In fairy tales, the hero or heroine often receives sacred clothing with magical powers to ward off evil. and in the beginning, God provided coats of skin to clothe his vulnerable children (Moses 4:27).

In important ways, sacred clothing becomes like a second skin, representative of a new, covenant-bound body consecrated to God and hallowed by his care. This body is marked with the scars of our mortal experience, suggesting that we are now fully initiated adults who have fought the enemy, have been subject to wounding, and have overcome. Sacred scars attest that, as the scriptures require, we have engraven the image of God upon our countenance (Alma 5:14), written the word of God in our flesh (Deuteronomy 11:18), and acquired spiritual understanding that transcends the intellect and infuses our very being, like the sacred marks in the hands and feet of the resurrected Christ. Such marks symbolize our covenants with God, which become our ultimate protection, accessing for us his power to preserve, defend, and restore.

6. Forgiving

Good boundaries and discernment are particularly important in the process of forgiveness. Many Latter-day Saints anxiously strive to forgive. We often feel deeply guilty if we cannot. But righteous indignation appropriately follows injustice, and it must be distinguished from anger that becomes a problem in its own right. The scriptures assert God too is angry about the ways we hurt each other, yet he forgives. When we struggle with forgiving, it may be because we think forgiving means saying what happened to us was not that bad, did not really hurt, or was really our fault. At the other extreme, we may insist a current injustice is fatal rather than merely devastating, or that there are absolutely no mitigating circumstances for the perpetrator's action. Such positions under-acknowledge our power to heal through Christ's Atonement, making a perpetrator bigger than life instead of just another wounded human being. "Either/or" thinking almost never represents reality accurately. When we have an accurate understanding of what we have lost and to whom, we are in the best position to truly turn the debt over to Christ and look to the Savior, not the debtor, for its repayment. We can leave the debtor in Christ's keeping because a fair and appropriate judgment, for now the debt is owed to him, not to us. We can begin to forgive.

7. New Identities

The healing process comes to some resolution as we incorporate into our identity a new understanding of ourselves that allows us to more fully enter God's promised state of celestial rest. This identity takes us past the role of victim and into the role of a survivor, one who has been saved.

Changing a person's name has been used in the Old Testament and elsewhere to signify such a change of identity. For example, Abram, whose name God changed to Abraham, was a victim of abuse—we might call it ritual abuse—at the hands of his father and his father's religion. But Abraham's new name, which means "father of a multitude," extends his identity beyond that of a child of his unrighteous father and into that of a mature and faithful father of the covenant righteous.

We too can claim the identities of mature spirituality as we acknowledge the pain we have experienced without allowing it to define us. Even more important, we can take upon ourselves the identity of God himself, who shares with us his power to rise above evil and transcend sin and death through the sacred plan of atonement. God says to Abraham and to all victims of domestic and other violence:

> Abraham, Abraham, behold, my name is Jehovah, and I have heard thee, and have come down to deliver thee . . . from thy father's house, and from all thy kinsfolk . . . and this because they have turned their hearts away from me. . . . Therefore I have come down . . . to destroy him who hath lifted up his hand against thee, Abraham, my son, to take away thy life. Behold, I will lead thee by my hand, and I will take thee, to put upon thee my name, even the Priesthood of thy father, and my power shall be over thee. (Abraham 1:16–18)

As I have kept vigil with others through long days of struggle and confusion, I sometimes wonder why someone cannot lay holy hands on their heads and restore health and faith as quickly as both were taken away by a perpetrator's unholy hands. The spirit has gently witnessed that a different vehicle of healing is also needed here. Christ could cure a wounded body in seconds, but to heal clouded thinking, a bruised heart, a wounded agency required months and years, even among his most willing disciples. Healing requires practice, patience, and endurance. Most of us underestimate the time required to incorporate healing into our identity and come out of old stories into new understanding. A trained therapist is generally in the best position to assist us through these psychological processes, while ordained ecclesiastical leaders can best help us with the spiritual aspects of healing.

The identity God offers *us* in the temple is the identity *of* a temple: we are the holy temples God is trying to build. All the rooms of the temple symbolically reside within the temple of our soul. Within that inner temple we each need a private, sterile room for healing, cleansing, and renewing hope in God's promised blessings, a place for receiving without having to say a word. In this sanitized, protected space, we may dress in the whole, white cloth of our covenant body, remembering as if through a veil the distant moment when we received that holy gift upon leaving the premortal existence. In the holy temple, we can begin to reclaim our precious body and wholeness. These sacred rites portend the day when all God's children will fully reclaim their physical and spiritual inheritance: the day of resurrection when Christ will come personally to us with redemption in his hands and healing in his wings.

HEALING PRACTICE FOR APPENDIX: HEALING FROM ABUSE

Knowing how to restore calm and soothe anxious feelings is essential if we are going to undertake the strenuous work of self-discovery. As we explore old traumas, certain images or feelings may distress us. We should not undertake such a process unless we have acquired and practiced the ability to relax, restore calm, and get assistance if needed. If any of the exercises below evoke a strong negative reaction, especially of fear, stop. Turn your attention to people or places that feel soothing, comforting, or supportive until you feel calm and comfortable again. Let yourself know what old experiences or feelings are being triggered, and then remind yourself you are safe and in control in the present. Let someone help you as a witness and supporter, and let yourself know and feel that you are now safe.

- **Temple meditations.** If possible, go to the temple nearest you and sit in the parking lot or on the grounds. Quiet your mind and body, and let yourself relax and take in your surroundings. If you wish, write or talk to a trusted friend about the following:

  - Write down what you think and feel as you first look at the temple. Label this description with a title or age that it might represent in your thinking (like "Reverent Me," "Lonely Child," or "Age 14").

  - Notice if there is another internal voice with a different set of opinions about the temple, either positive or negative. Write down the feelings and thoughts associated with that part of you and give it a title or an age (like "Cynic," "Hopeful Parent," or "Age 5").

  - Notice if there is yet another perspective that needs a voice. Write down the feelings and thoughts associated with that part and give it a title or an age. Continue until all the different aspects of your feelings about the temple have been expressed.

  - Which, if any, of these descriptions represents the truest, most spiritually in tune part of you? If none of them seems to fit this description, write down the thoughts and feelings that seem to represent the most calm, compassionate, curious, and objective part of you.

- What aspects of the temple do you most value and appreciate, or do you imagine you would most value and appreciate if you were able to go inside?

- What aspects of the temple evoke negative feelings? Which of the voices described above is most aware of each of these aspects or feelings?

- What would help you feel safer, calmer, more loved, or more welcome in the temple even when you are aware of that negative aspect?

- **Boundaries.** People who have been abused often have problems with boundaries. Sometimes they are too trusting with situations or people they idealize until they realize too late that they feel overwhelmed or invaded. Sometimes they are afraid to let anyone close or afraid of any situation that makes them feel vulnerable. There is not an easy "trick" to knowing whether we are being too loose or too rigid with our boundaries. Sometimes it helps to remember everyone has to learn by experience how to manage personal boundaries; we can give ourselves permission to fine-tune this process as we go without expecting ourselves to always get it right. We will survive mistakes. To help with this,

  - Visualize a sacred boundary around you that nothing evil can penetrate. What is the nature of this boundary? What does it look an feel like? What does it let in? What does it keep out?

  - Remember a time recently when you kept your boundaries firm. What felt threatening? Do you now think the threat was as serious as it felt at the time? How did you hold your boundaries firm? What did that look or sound like to others? Were there any problems with this approach? If you were in the same situation again, how might you fine-tune your boundaries?

  - Remember a time recently when your boundaries became too loose. What made you feel you had to let others in too far, or what were you hoping might happen if you let others in? Do you now think you were really as safe as you felt at the time? How did you relax your boundaries and communicate openness—what does that look or sound like to others? Were there any problems with this approach? If you were in the same situation again, how might you fine-tune your boundaries?

- Who do you know who seems to have appropriately open boundaries when the situation calls for it? How do they communicate this? How might they think about the situation differently from how you think?

- Who do you know who seems to have appropriately firm boundaries when the situation calls for it? How do they communicate this? How might they think about the situation differently from how you think? If you are not sure, ask them.

- *Holiness within.* As you begin to find the healing you seek, read Abraham 1:16–18 aloud, changing the name of Abraham to your own name and changing the circumstances from which you need deliverance to match your own. When you read the words, "I will lead thee by my hand, and I will take thee, to put upon thee my name," think of places in the temple when someone takes your hand, leads you, or conveys identities to you. Consider the ways God is reaching out to you as he did to Abraham through these sacred ordinances.

Notes

ONE: THE SEARCH

1. See for example Robert W. Firestone and Joyce Catlett, *Fear of Intimacy* (Washington, DC: American Psychological Association, 1999).

2. Boyd K. Packer, Regional Representatives seminar, 3 April 1987.

3. Ether 12:27, 37. See also Wendy Ulrich, *Weakness Is Not Sin: The Liberating Distinction That Awakens Our Strengths* (Salt Lake City: Deseret Book, 2009).

4. Malidoma Patrice Somé, *Of Water and the Spirit: Ritual, Magic, and Initiation in the Life of an African Shaman* (New York: G. P. Putnam's Sons, 1994), 258.

5. John A. Widtsoe, *Power from on High: Fourth Year Junior Genealogical Classes* (Salt Lake City: Genealogical Society of Utah, 1937).

6. Maureen Murdock, *The Heroine's Journey: Woman's Quest for Wholeness* (Boston: Shambhala, 1990), 89.

7. See verses 26–27 for a fuller context of this scripture.

TWO: LEARNING THE LANGUAGE

1. Alonzo L. Gaskill, *The Lost Language of Symbolism: An Essential Guide for Recognizing and Interpreting Symbols of the Gospel* (Salt Lake City: Deseret Book, 2003), 1.

2. Tom F. Driver, *The Magic of Ritual: Our Need for Liberating Rites That Transform Our Lives and Communities* (San Francisco, CA: Harper Collins, 1991), 93.

3. John A. Widtsoe, *Power from on High: Fourth Year Junior Genealogical Classes* (Salt Lake City: Genealogical Society of Utah, 1937).

4. C. S. Lewis, *Weight of Glory* (San Francisco: Harper Collins, 2001), 34.

5. Daniel J. Siegel and Mary Hartzell, *Parenting from the Inside Out: How a Deeper Self-Understanding Can Help You Raise Children Who Thrive.* (New York, NY: Tarcher-Penguin, 2003).

THREE: NEW BIRTHS

1. Anne Ancelin Schutzenberger, *The Ancestor Syndrome: Transgenerational Psychotherapy and the Hidden Links in the Family Tree* (New York: Routledge, 2007), 3.

2. See for example Mosiah 1:5; Doctrine and Covenants 123:7; Carlson Broderick, *The Uses of Adversity.* In M. E. Stovall and C. C. Madsen, eds., *As Women of Faith* (Salt Lake City: Deseret Book, 1989).

3. Daniel J. Siegel and Mary Hartzell, *Parenting from the Inside Out: How a Deeper Self-Understanding Can Help You Raise Children Who Thrive.* (New York, NY: Tarcher-Penguin, 2003)

4. See Wendy Ulrich, *Forgiving Ouselves: Getting Back Up When We Let Ourselves Down* (Salt Lake City: Deseret Book, 2008).

5. See Elder Richard Scott's "Obtaining help from the Lord," *Ensign*, November 1991, 84–86; "Healing the Scars of Abuse," *Ensign*, May 1992, 31–33; and "To Be healed," *Ensign*, May 1994, 7–9.

6. See, for example, Monica McGoldrick and Randy Gerson, *Genograms in Family Assessment* (New York: W. W. Norton and Co., 1985).

FOUR: CLAIMING THIS BODY

1. See for example Christine Caldwell, *Getting our Bodies Back: Recovery, Healing, and Transformation through Body-Centered Psychotherapy* (Boston: Shambahala, 1996).

2. Clarissa Pinkola Estés, *Women Who Run with the Wolves* (New York: Ballantine, 1992), 389–94.

3. Hugh Nibley, *Temple and Cosmos* (Salt Lake City: Deseret Book, 1992), 60.

4. Tony Crisp, *Dream Dictionary* (New York: Dell, 1990), 75.

5. Malidoma Patrice Somé, *Of Water and the Spirit: Ritual, Magic, and Initiation in the Life of an African Shaman* (New York: Putnam, 1994), 209.

6. Ibid., 225.

7. Crisp, *Dream Dictionary*, 74.

8. Moses 1:33. See also Joseph Smith, "Lectures on faith," reprinted in N. B. Lundwall, compiler, *Discourses on the Holy Ghost, Also Lectures on Faith* (Salt Lake City: Bookcraft, 1959).

9. Nibley, *Temple and Cosmos*, 273.

10 Estés, *Women Who Run with the Wolves*, 27–28.

11. See Joseph Campbell with Bill Moyers, *The Power of Myth* (New York, NY: Doubleday, 1988).

12. See John E. Sarno, *The Mindbody Prescription: Healing the Body, Healing the Pain* (New York: Warner Books, 1998).

13. Crisp, *Dream Dictionary*, 74.

14. Nibley, *Temple and Cosmos*, 316–17.

15. Adapted from Julia Cameron *The Artist's Way: A Spiritual Path to Higher Creativity* (New York: G. P. Putnam's Sons, 1992), 87–89.

FIVE: THE CREATOR'S CHILD

1. In Julia Cameron, *The Artist's Way* (New York: G. P. Putnam's Sons, 1992), 199.

2. Bruce R. McConkie, *Mormon Doctrine* (Salt Lake City, UT: Bookcraft, 1966), 170. See also Abraham 3:22–24.

3. Private communication, used with permission.

4. Gregory Bateson, *Mind and Nature: A Necessary Unity* (New York: Dutton Bateson, 1979), 163.

5. Hugh Nibley, *Temple and Cosmos*, 283.

6. Tony Crisp, *Dream Dictionary*, 1990), 30.

7. Ibid., 32–7, 62, 175, 226–7, 321.

8. Playing for Change, "Stand By Me | Playing For Change | Song Around the World." YouTube video, 5:27. Posted November 2008. http://www.youtube.com/watch?v=Us-TVg40ExM. See also Playingforchange.com

SIX: NOT ASHAMED

1. Viktor E. Frankl, *Man's Search for Meaning* (Boston: Beacon Press, 2006), 109.

2. Eugene England, *The Quality of Mercy* (Salt Lake City: Bookcraft, 1992).

3. Sharon Ellison, *Don't Be So Defensive!: Taking the War Out of Our Words with Powerful, Non-Defensive Communication* (Kansas City: Andrews McMeel, 1998).

4. LDS Bible Dictionary, 672.

5. Burton C. Kelly, "Hiding, Health, and Love: Some Interrelationships" in *AMCAP Journal* 18, no. 1 (1992), 42–43.

6. Ibid., 43.

7. Brené Brown, *The Gifts of Imperfection* (Center City, MN: Hazelden, 2010), ix.

8. J. K. Rowling, *Harry Potter and the Sorcerer's Stone* (New York: Scholastic Press, 1999), 299.

SEVEN: THE DESERT OF DISCERNMENT

1. LDS Bible Dictionary, 731.

2. See William J. Hamblin, (1992), "Temple Motifs in Jewish Mysticism," in Donald W. Parry, ed., *Temples of the Ancient World: Ritual and Symbolism*, 440–476; and Hugh Nibley, *Temple and Cosmos*.

3. *Documentary History of the Church of Jesus Christ of Latter-day Saints, Vol. III*, 295.

4. Thomas, M. Catherine, "Hebrews: To Ascend the Holy Mount," in Donald W. Parry ed., Temples of the Ancient World: Ritual and symbolism, 489 (italics mine).

5 See *The NIV Study Bible: New International Version* (Grand Rapids, MI: Zondervan Bible Publishers, 1985), 29, footnote to 16:2.

6. Ibid.

EIGHT: LEARNING TO LOVE

1. "Naming the Sin of Sexism," *Catholic Agitator*, April 1989, 2. In Maureen Murdock, *The Heroine's Journey* (Boston: Shambhala, 1990), 173.

2. See Camille Fronk, "The Cost of True Discipleship," BYU Women's Conference, 1999, http://ce.byu.edu/cw/womensconference/archive/1999/fronk_camille.htm.

3. Ibid.

4. See, for example, Psalms 37:23; 119:133; Isaiah 9:7; Colossians 2:5; 2 Nephi 6:2; Alma 13:1; Doctrine and Covenants 88:119; 107:41; and JST Genesis 14:27–28.

5. Ezra Taft Benson, "What I Hope You Will Teach Your Children about the Temple." In *Temples of the Church of Jesus Christ of Latter-day Saints* (Salt Lake City: Ensign, 1988), 42–3; italics mine.

6. Clarissa Pinkola Estés, *Women Who Run with the Wolves* (New York: Ballantine, 1992), 28. See Genesis 2:23; John 19:36; Ezekiel 37:1–14; Proverbs 3:8).

7. *History of the Church, Vol. 5, 23.*

8. See Patrick Carnes, *Sexual Anorexia: Overcoming Sexual Self-Hatred* (Center City, MN: Hazelden, 1997).

9. Richard Nelson Bolles, *The 1981 What Color Is Your Parachute?: A Practical Manual for Job-Hunters and Career Changers* (Berkeley, CA: Ten Speed Press, 1981).

10. Joseph Smith, "Lectures on Faith," reprinted in N. B. Lundwall, compiler, *Discourses on the Holy Ghost, Also Lectures on Faith*, 152.

11. Anne Morrow Lindbergh, *Gift from the Sea* (New York, NY: Pantheon, 1983), 124.

NINE: THE PRESENCE OF AN ABSENCE

1. See M. Catherine Thomas, "The Brother of Jared at the Veil." In Donald W. Parry, ed., *Temples of the Ancient World: Ritual and Symbolism*, 388–398.

2. Abraham Maslow. Quoted in *The Pleasures and Sorrows of Work*. Alain DeBotton (New York: Pantheon, 2009), 113.

3. Anne Roiphe, *Fruitful* (Boston, MA: Houghton Mifflin, 1996), 133.

4. See David Tracy, *Plurality and Ambiguity: Hermeneutics, Religion, Hope* (Chicago: Chicago Press, 1987).

5. Susan K. Deri, *Symbolization and Creativity* (Madison, CT: International Universities Press, 1984), 45.

6. Ibid, 47.

7. Kathleen Flake, "Supping with the Lord: A Liturgical Theology of the LDS Sacrament," *Sunstone* 16, no. 5 (July, 1993), 18–27.

TEN: IN HIS PRESENCE

1. James M. Robinson, ed., *The Nag Hammadi Library*, revised edition (San Francisco, CA: Harper Collins, 1988).

2. Thomas O. Lambdin, "The Gospel of Thomas." In James M. Robinson, ed., *The Nag Hammadi Library*, revised edition, 132.

3. Ibid., 126.

4. Wesley W. Isenberg, "The Gospel of Philip." In James M. Robinson, ed., *The Nag Hammadi Library*, revised edition, 158.

5. Malcolm L. Peel and Jan Zandee, "The Teachings of Silvanus." In James M. Robinson, ed., *The Nag Hammadi Library*, revised edition, 390.

6. Ibid., 381–2.

7. June Singer, "A Silence of the Soul," quoted in Maureen Murdock, *The Heroine's Journey: Woman's Quest for Wholeness* (Boston: Shambhala, 1990), 160.

8. Douglas M. Parrott and R. M. Wilson, "The Acts of Peter and the Twelve Apostles." In James M. Robinson, ed., *The Nag Hammadi Library*, revised edition, 391.

9. Thomas O. Lambdin, "The Gospel of Thomas." In James M. Robinson, ed., *The Nag Hammadi Library*, revised edition, 138.

10. Parrott and Wilson, 291, 293.

11. Wesley W. Isenberg, "The Gospel of Philip." In James M. Robinson, ed., *The Nag Hammadi Library*, revised edition, 152–3.

12. Ibid.,152–3.

13. Ibid., 143, 150.

14. Wayne Muller, *Sabbath: Restoring the Sacred Rhythm of Rest* (New York: Bantam, 1999), 82–3.

15. Ibid., 147–8.

16. Thomas O. Lambdin, "The Gospel of Thomas." In James M. Robinson, ed., *The Nag Hammadi Library*, revised edition, 129.

17. Wesley W. Isenberg, "The Gospel of Philip." In James M. Robinson, ed., *The Nag Hammadi Library*, revised edition, 153.

ELEVEN: TO RECEIVE AND BE RECEIVED

1. The Teachings of Ezra Taft Benson, 254, cited in Matthew B. Brown, *The Gate of Heaven: Insights on the Doctrines and Symbols of the Temple*, (American Fork, UT: Covenant Communications, 1999), 284.

2. See Patrick Carnes, *Sexual Anorexia: Overcoming Sexual Self-Hatred* (Center City, MN: Hazelden, 1997).

3. See S. Miller, D. Wackman, E. Nunnally, and P. Miller, *Connecting with Self and Others* (Littleton, CO: Interpersonal Communicatons Programs, 1988).

4. See Clifford Notarius and Howard Markman, *We Can Work It Out: Making Sense of Marital conflict* (New York: G. P. Putnam's Sons, 1993).

5. See John Gottman, *Why Marriages Succeed or Fail* (New York: Simon and Schuster, 1994) and *The Relationship Cure* (New York, NY: Three Rivers Press, 2001).

Twelve: Holiness to the Lord

1. LDS Bible Dictionary, 613–614.

2. N. B. Lundwall, *Temples of the Most High* (Salt Lake City, UT: Bookcraft, 1968), 140–142.

3. W. B. Yeats, "The Second Coming," *Michael Robartes and the Dancer* (New York: Macmillan, 1921).

4. Truman Madsen, *The Temple and the Atonement* (Provo, UT: Foundation for Ancient Research and Mormon Studies, 1994).

5. C. S. Lewis, *Till We Have Faces*, (Orlando: Harcourt Books, 1984), 294

Appendix: Healing from Abuse

1. See Judith Lewis Herman, *Trauma and Recovery* (New York: HarperCollins, 1992).

2. See Stephen Joseph, *What Doesn't Kill Us: The New Psychology of Posttraumatic Growth* (New York: Basic Books, 2011).

3. LDS Bible Dictionary, 609 ("anoint").

4. See Joseph Campbell with Bill Moyers, *The Power of Myth* (New York: Doubleday, 1988); Clarissa Pinkola Estés, *Women who Run with the Wolves* (New York: Ballantine,1992); Carl Gustav Jung, *Collected Works of C. G. Jung*, R. F. C. Hull, trans. (Princeton: Princeton University Press, 1972).

5. See Catherine Bell, *Ritual Theory, Ritual Practice* (New York: Oxford University Press, 1992).

6. See Babette Rothschild, *The Body Remembers: The Psychophysiology of Trauma and Trauma Treatment* (New York: W. W. Norton and Co., 2000).

7. Ibid., 133.

8. Hugh Nibley, *Temple and Cosmos*, 91–138.

SUGGESTED READING

TWO: LEARNING THE LANGUAGE

Parry, Donald W. 1994. *Temples of the Ancient World: Ritual and Symbolism*. Salt Lake City: Deseret Book. A collection of essays exploring the temple from many historical, cultural, and religious perspectives.

Gaskill, Alonzo L. 2003. *The Lost Language of Symbolism*. Springville, UT: Cedar Fort, Inc.

————. 2011. *Sacred Symbols: Finding Meaning in Rites, Rituals, and Ordinances* Springville, UT: Cedar Fort, Inc. Both books by Gaskill are excellent references for understanding symbols in the temple and elsewhere.

THREE: NEW BIRTHS

Cameron, Julia. 1996. *The Vein of Gold*. New York: G. P. Putnam's Sons. Good exercises in self-discovery based on personal history writing and journaling.

Lerner, Harriet Goldhor. 1989. *The Dance of Intimacy*. New York: Harper & Row.

————. 1997. *The Dance of Anger*. New York: Harper & Row. Both this book and *The Dance of Intimacy* help us see family patterns and offer practical ideas on dealing with conflict constructively, not aggressively.

Lewis, C. S. *Till We Have Faces*. 1984. Orlando: Harcourt. A fascinating novel about blindness, sight, self-awareness, and the mercy of God.

FOUR: CLAIMING THIS BODY

Byrd, Dean, and Jonathan Chamberlain. 1994. *Willpower Is Not Enough*. Salt Lake City: Deseret Book. An LDS perspective on overcoming addiction, stressing the importance of meeting our needs, not just rigid self-discipline.

Caldwell, Christine. 1996. *Getting Our Bodies Back: Recovery, Healing, and Transformation through Body-Centered Psychotherapy*. Boston: Shambahala. Some interesting exercises in learning from the body.

Sarno, John E. 1998. *The Mindbody Prescription: Healing the Body, Healing the Pain*. New York: Warner Books. A rehabilitation doctor's approach to pain elimination through emotional self-awareness.

FIVE: THE CREATOR'S CHILD

Cameron, Julia. 1992. *The Artist's Way: A Spiritual Path to Higher Creativity.* New York: G. P. Putnam's Sons. A delightful book on recovering our creative instincts, and moving through the blocks to our creativity in any domain.

Csikszentmihalyi, Mihaly. 1990. *Flow: The Psychology of Optimal Experience.* New York: Harper Collins. Describes processes by which we can order our lives so as to spend more of them in satisfying, meaningful states.

SIX: NOT ASHAMED

Brown, Brené. 2008. *I Thought It Was Me (But It Isn't): Telling the Truth about Perfectionism, Inadequacy and Power.* New York: Gotham Books.

———. 2010. *The Gifts of Imperfection.* Center City, MN: Hazelden.

Ulrich, Wendy. 2009. *Weakness Is Not Sin: The Liberating Distinction That Awakens Our Strengths.* Salt Lake City: Deseret Book.

SEVEN: THE DESERT OF DISCERNMENT

Lund, Gerald N. 2007. *Hearing the Voice of the Lord: Principles and Patterns of Personal Revelation,* Salt Lake City: Deseret Book. A thorough, practical primer on discerning God's voice.

Scott, Richard G. "To Acquire Spiritual Guidance," *Ensign,* Nov. 2009, 6–9. A powerful explanation of the process of cultivating personal revelation.

EIGHT: LEARNING TO LOVE

Ellison, Sharon. 1998. *Don't Be So Defensive!* Kansas City, MO: Andrews McMeel. An assumption-shattering book about the conflict-ridden nature of most of our communication, and how to speak the language of humility and peace.

Pontius, John M. 2010. *The Triumph of Zion.* Springville, UT: Cedar Fort, Inc. A soul-stretching exploration of the blessings and challenges of preparing for the Second Coming.

NINE: THE PRESENCE OF AN ABSENCE

Scriptures relevant to this topic include the books of Genesis, Moses, Abraham, Joseph Smith—History, and the Book of Mormon stories of the brother of Jared, Nephi, Lehi, Alma the Younger, and Christ's visit to the Nephites. The stories of Eve, Haggar, Rebekah, the wife of Manoah, Mary (the mother of Christ), Lamoni's queen in the Book of Mormon, and the many women who associated with Jesus during his earthly ministry also contribute to our understanding of what it means to encounter God.

TEN: IN HIS PRESENCE

Lindbergh, Anne Morrow. 1983. *Gift from the Sea.* New York: Pantheon. A classic on the pleasures of solitude, peace, and contentment.

Muller, Wayne. 1999. *Sabbath: Restoring the Sacred Rhythm of Rest*. New York: Bantam. A lovely text on the joys of Sabbath peace, and how to bring them into daily life.

ELEVEN: TO RECEIVE AND BE RECEIVED

Carnes, Robert C. 1997. *Sexual Anorexia: Overcoming Sexual Self-Hatred*. Center City, MN: Hazelden. A valuable book on the underlying self-assumptions that prompt both sexual addiction and sexual anorexia, with approaches for correcting those assumptions based on the twelve-step model of Alcoholics Anonymous.

Gottman, John M. 1999. *The Seven Principles for Making Marriage Work*. 1999. Practical, easy to read, research-based suggestions for helping real people do better with the real challenges of marriage and family.

———. 2001. *The Relationship Cure: A 5-Step Guide to Strengthening Your Marriage, Family, and Relationships*. New York: Three Rivers Press.

Latham, Glenn. 1994. *The Power of Positive Parenting*. Logan, UT: P & T Ink. A practical, skill-based book on raising children by focusing on the positive. Valuable for working with children of all ages and in all settings.

Lerner, Harriet Goldhor. 1989. *The Dance of Intimacy*. New York: Harper & Row. A practical book on how to deepen emotional connections without losing our sense of self.

McGraw, Phillip. 2000. *Relationship Rescue*. New York: Hyperion. A no-holds-barred look at how we can make marriage work even when we don't have our partner's cooperation if we will take rock-bottom responsibility for our own choices. Delineates several marital myths that seem to encourage blame and self-pity, and includes exercises and self-rating scales to assess how we are doing and where we need to go.

Notarius, Clifford, and Howard Markman. 1993. *We Can Work it Out: Making Sense of Marital Conflict*. A research-based book on increasing problem-solving skills in marriage. A little dry, but worthwhile.

Siegel, Daniel J., and Mary Hartzell. 2003. *Parenting from the Inside Out*. New York: Tarcher-Penguin. Attachment research is put in a practical context as the authors help parents explore how their own upbringing and background are affecting their parenting.

TWELVE: HOLINESS TO THE LORD (SUGGESTED LISTENING)

Jessop, Craig, conductor. 2001. Mormon Tabernacle Choir and Orchestra at Temple Square. "Come, Thou Fount of Every Blessing." *The Sound of Glory*. Salt Lake City: Deseret Book. A glorious rendition of this moving hymn, the final verses of which proclaim: Jesus sought me, though a stranger,/ Wandering from the throne of God./ He, to rescue me from danger,/ Interposed his precious blood./ O, to grace, how great a debtor/ Daily I'm constrained to be./ Let thy goodness, like a fetter,/ Bind my wandering heart to thee./ Prone to wander, Lord, I feel it,/ Prone to leave the God I love!/ Here's my heart! O, take and seal it,/ Seal it for thy courts above (Robert Robinson).

About the Author

Wendy Ulrich is a practicing psychologist and the founder of Sixteen Stones Center for Growth, LLC, a group of mental health professionals committed to building the emotional and spiritual resilience of LDS women and their loved ones (see sixteenstones.net).

Wendy received her PhD from the University of Michigan and an MBA from UCLA, then for many years she was part of a private practice in Ann Arbor, where she and her husband, Dave, raised their three children.

Wendy loves power tools and really enjoys woodworking projects. She hopes some of the things she writes about can be "power tools" for others in finding meaning, self-acceptance, and a deeper sense of purpose in life.